TO CHRIST I LOOK

Homilies at Twilight

WALTER J. BURGHARDT, S.J.
Theologian in Residence
Georgetown University

PAULIST PRESS
New York/Mahwah

Illustrations by Mary K. Burt.
Cover by Tim McKeen.

Library of Congress Cataloging-in-Publication Data

Burghardt, Walter J.
    To Christ I look : homilies at twilight / Walter J. Burghardt.
        p.   cm.
    Includes bibliographical references.
    ISBN 0-8091-3105-6 : $11.95 (est.)
    1. Catholic Church—Sermons. 2. Sermons, American. I. Title.
BX1756.B828T6   1990
252'.02—dc20   89-35815
                                                                   CIP

Published by Paulist Press
997 Macarthur Boulevard
Mahwah, NJ 07430

Printed and bound in the
United States of America

TABLE OF CONTENTS

ORDINARY TIME

MEDLEY

Myself unholy, from myself unholy
To the sweet living of my friends I look. . . .
This fault in one I found, that in another:
And so, though each have one while I have all,
No *better* serves me now, save *best;* no other
Save Christ; to Christ I look, on Christ I call.

Gerard Manley Hopkins, S.J.

PREFACE

This, my sixth collection of homilies since 1980, does not demand a long preface. It continues the style of a homilist who (1) was inspired by Vatican II to struggle with Scripture, (2) was led by developments within the Society of Jesus to stress the faith that does justice, and (3) was moved by a lifelong love for language to handle each word with reverence, to value imagination above abstract clarity, and to shape each sermon as a minor work of art.

The title and subtitle of this collection, *To Christ I Look: Homilies at Twilight*, reflect my stage on earth. Each day it is easier for me to resonate to Psalm 90:9–11: ". . . our days come to an end like a sigh. The years of our life are threescore and ten, or even by reason of strength fourscore; . . . they are soon gone, and we fly away." Each day it is increasingly imperative to "look to Christ"—in my life, of course, but also in homilies that should reflect my life, or at least address it urgently.

The introductory essay, "Preaching in American Words and in American Symbols," is an effort to reveal, more by concrete examples than by abstract principles, how preaching built upon popular language can delight, excite, thrill, even convert a congregation and restore a preacher's youth. It restored mine!

Walter J. Burghardt, S.J.

1

PROLOGUE

PREACHING IN AMERICAN WORDS
AND IN AMERICAN SYMBOLS

A recent book by the president of the University of Rochester has an engaging title: *God and the New Haven Railway and Why Neither One Is Doing Very Well.*[1] At one point George Dennis O'Brien is disturbed about the split between proclamation and ongoing life. He notes that most people on the train station are not likely to see church service as "one of the livelier, more salvational times of week." Their appraisal is more likely to be "Saturday Night Live, Sunday Morning Deadly."[2] And not long ago, a university professor of literature suggested that the time had come to speak truthfully to the Church about the quality of its rhetoric. "Discourse in the church," the lady lamented, "is so dull. In sermons, in social-action statements, in all the communication we hear within the church, the guiding principle seems to be blandness."[3]

'Twas not always thus in America. In the middle of the 19th century, not only novelists and poets but preachers as well were often exciting and creative.[4] Why? Because "Discourse in the antebellum period" was "rooted in a religious tradition and built upon popular language." Nor are American sermons always dull in these our decades. Black preachers from Martin Luther King Jr. to Jesse Jackson stir spontaneous amens from the sophisticated and the simple, from college teachers and the untutored. Why? Because their sermons are not only "rooted in a religious tradition" but "built upon popular language."

I shall not ask whether American Catholic preaching is "rooted in a religious tradition," despite my apprehension that our homilists are increasingly ignorant of our doctrinal and spiritual resources, to the impoverishment of our people. My focus is rather on "built upon popular language," for that phrase is synonymous with the title of this prologue, "Preaching in American Words and in American Symbols."

In harmony with my trinitarian bias, my song and dance has three movements. First, a work of *recognition,* analogous to the anagnorisis in Greek drama: I want you to perceive the precise problem at issue here, isolate it from other, related issues. Second, a work of *reconstruction,* analogous to a drama's denouement: I want to suggest how our homiletic doldrums might be lifted. Third, a work of *rejuvenation,* analogous to the comic in drama: I want to lighten the heavy weight of theory, illustrate my ideology, by revealing how preaching "built upon popular language" can delight, excite, thrill, even convert a congregation and restore a preacher's youth. Recognition, reconstruction, rejuvenation.

RECOGNITION

My initial movement is a work of recognition. What is the precise issue here? What am I not talking about, what am I talking about, and why am I talking about it?

First, my theme is how, not what. What I preach, the content of my homily, is always and everywhere the gospel, god-spell, the good news of Jesus Christ, as understood within the Church. I assume, therefore, that what issues from the pulpit is an effort to express what God has said and is saying to us, from the burning bush at Midian and the gas ovens of Auschwitz, from the cross that imprisoned Christ and the cross erected over history, through the travail of theologians and the rapture of mystics, through Roman encyclicals and Christian experience. I assume that the homilist is passionately in love with Scripture, does not shun Scripture because (to misappropriate Magdalene's grievance at the grave) the exegetes "have taken away my Lord and I know not where they have laid him" (Jn 20:13). I assume that the parish priest did not close his last theology tome when a bishop oiled his hands, because theology is the ceaseless struggle of God's people to touch the hem of God's garment, to penetrate Paul's "mystery hidden for ages in God" (Eph 3:9), to "know . . . the only true God, and Jesus Christ whom [God has] sent" (Jn 17:3). This I assume—perhaps naively, because so much evidence contradicts it. But I must assume it, else my prologue is purposeless. There is no point to a homiletic how without a wisdom-seasoned what.

Second, my how is not the husk of homiletics, the skeleton, the bare bones. Oh yes, with enough time, I can correct your composition, propel you to project, perhaps even lessen your lisp. What concerns me, what agonizes me, is the how that is part and parcel of the gospel—where the medium is the message. I am talking about style, what the Earl of Chesterfield called "the dress of thoughts." Webster's Second Edition Unabridged put it into an elegant definition 30 years ago: style is "The quality which gives distinctive excellence in artistic expression, consisting especially in the appropriateness and choiceness of relation between subject, medium, and form, and individualized by the temperamental characteristics of the artist." More simply, I am speaking of a fine art.

Third, why am I talking about style? Because if any word demands to be proclaimed "with style," it is God's word. Because without style in the sense described the gospel threatens to fall on deaf ears, risks disaster. Because the view from the pew is dismaying: We are dull as dishwater, our words are woven of timeless abstractions, our language does not excite, thrill, inflame. When I was a boy in St. John the Evangelist parish in New York City, each Sunday Mass had its quota of what we called "sharpshooters": men on one knee in the back, just waiting for the sermon—the signal to sneak out for a smoke. The tradition has been lost, but I often wonder how many of the faithful would remain if the homily followed the final blessing, how many would choose rather to "go in peace."

RECONSTRUCTION

So much for the problem. But the problem calls for a solution. How do you develop a style—a style of speech that catches the hearer, "grabs" an audience, keeps people pleading for more, makes them sorry it's over? Basically, my response, my "reconstruction," is discoverable in my title: "American words and American symbols." (Here note that I shall not be speaking sheerly of symbols in a strict sense—signs pregnant with a depth of meaning evoked rather than explicitly stated. Under the broad umbrella of symbols I am presuming to include images and metaphors as well; they are indispensable if I am to deal realistically with popular language.)

But how do you put homiletic meat on those bare bones, "American words and American symbols"?

First, a radical realization. I mean Karl Rahner's insistence 20 years ago that to preach is to translate:

> The form of preaching in a particular age must be "translated" into another form of preaching to make the message understood, particularly if the meaning of the message must remain the same. This preservation of identity cannot be achieved by the mere repetition of old expressions if the mentality and concepts change in secular society through an historical development which is not under the Church's control.[5]

The point is, the Judeo-Christian revelation, for all its divine authorship, comes to us through "human words that were already current and loaded with overtones from the surrounding world."[6] "Lamb of God" made a strong impression on the earliest Christians not only because the paschal lamb was a venerable religious symbol, but because that symbol hit them where they lived. Jesus was born and bred among people for whom the lamb was a primary source of food and clothing, a fundamental factor in their economy. Transfer that symbol to Papua, where the sacred animal is the pig, where women may nurse piglets at their breast if no sow is around, and the preacher has a problem. And, I suspect, lamb is a more likely symbol in New Zealand than in the District of Columbia, where the lamb is simply a political wimp who had best not lie with either the elephant or the mule.

Nor is it only that sacred symbols—lamb, shepherd, Son of Man, suffering servant, bread of life, kingdom, yeast, vine and branches, fountain of living water, the fish and the plow and the star, the bark of Peter—can lose significance as the Church moves from age to age, from culture to culture. Ordinary words call for translation. Can you be content with Matthew's "eternal fire prepared for the devil and his angels" (Mt 25:41) when your congregation "thinks of fire as a combustion process with oxygen"?[7]

Well then, move from Scripture to theology. After all, isn't theology itself an effort at translation, a ceaseless struggle to make contemporary sense of God's word? It is indeed. But good as it is, crucial for Christianity, indispensable for preaching the word, theology is not yet homiletics. When revelation is translated into dogma or interpreted by theology, it is not yet the preacher's word. It has its own jargon, its technical vocabulary, its classical lingo from

Nicaea through Chalcedon to Vatican II, from Augustine and Aquinas to Lonergan and Rahner. Dogma and theology must themselves undergo translation, build upon popular language, tell God's story in today's idiom. Neither the rhetoric of Roman encyclicals nor the dry bones of eschatology, apocalyptic, or the supernatural existential are calculated to turn our people on.

All well and good: Effective preaching demands translation—a concerted movement from an alien culture, from a dogmatic dress, from a scholarly abstractness to words and symbols that speak to the heart of our age, to the experience of our people. A second stage: How do you do this in the concrete? I do not suggest that we empty our rhetoric of all the classical Hebrew and early Christian symbols, that today's symbol for Christ be not the lamb but the pit bull, that the divinity undergo a sex change, that God the Father be replaced by George Burns with a cigar. Deep within many ancient images and symbols are powerful forces that need only be intelligently grasped by the preacher and imaginatively presented to set hearts aflame.

Mull over just two examples. First, a key theme in the New Testament: the kingdom of God. Do you avoid kingdom language because king brings to mind a butcher named Herod, mad King Ludwig with his crazy castles, Old King Cole calling for his pipe, his bowl, his fiddlers three—perhaps the Burger King? Because kings are anachronisms or dictators or figureheads? I say no. A delightful, insightful French film titled *The King of Hearts* (about World War II, a Scot soldier searching out a giant booby trap, and charming lunatics who crown him "king of hearts" in a mad coronation) had no trouble fascinating millions of film fans here and abroad, teen-agers, yuppies, senior citizens. It simply took imagination.

Ah, there's the magic word: imagination. The imagination that turned a turn-of-the-century French Cyrano de Bergerac into today's totally American Steve Martin, without betraying Rostand's romantic intuition.[8] The fresh, childlike approach to fantasy that Steven Spielberg brought to an utterly believable *E.T.*[9] The sheer spectacularism of Andrew Lloyd Webber's musical *The Phantom of the Opera*—like bringing the elephants into *Aïda*. I mean *The Yellow Christ* of Gauguin, the pure color that induces a particular feeling. I mean the stark symbolism of the Vietnam Memorial—58,156 names[10] etched into black granite.

Take a second scriptural symbol, at superficial glance the contrary of king: suffering servant. A wedding of words not particularly appealing to the American psyche. Servant? Why, that con-

jures up low income and menial labor, Topsy in *Uncle Tom's Cabin* or
the old-time maid in apron and minicap, the indentured servant in
the colonies. Suffering? Try redemptive suffering, as I did, in a
Jewish synagogue still harrowed by the Holocaust. Try it on blacks
struggling to live a decent human existence, to simply live. Try it on
Christians who've got it made, for whom living is the survival of the
fittest, and the devil take the hindmost.

So, do you sacrifice the symbol? I say no. It's too deeply identified with Christ, with Christianity, with the Christian. You wrestle
with it. Not, by some semantic alchemy, to transmute the base metal
of servant into the gold of master. Not, by some spiritual sedative,
to deaden the pain of suffering. Quite the contrary. By wedding
theology and imagination you contemporize two inescapable Christian realities: Belief shorn of service is lifeless, and the cross is for
ever erected over history.[11]

And still it remains true, symbols come and symbols go. The
Sacred Heart was a symbol of love that pervaded my youth and my
early priesthood; now it is scarcely alive in the consciousness of
Catholics. The Beatles are far from dead, but Beatlemania is not
the idolatry it once was. Even "The Star-Spangled Banner" is reserved for sports events and sung by pros; American hearts are
rarely clutched by "bombs bursting in air," even in the Persian Gulf.

What, then, are our contemporary symbols? Quite obvious are
a few patriotic symbols. The Statue of Liberty still beckons compas-
sionately from New York Harbor. The American flag still spangles
over public monuments and private homes. "America the Beautiful" tugs at untold hearts. And doves as well as hawks weep silent
tears before the Vietnam Memorial.

But it is cultural symbols that are riding an unprecedented
wave. Where do you start and where do you end? Some fit well
together, others are contradictory. Most are secular, some are explicitly or potentially religious. You have heavy metal and MTV; the
computer, car phones, and crack; stretch limos or a Volvo with a
baby seat; country, pop, and rock; Michael Jackson and Jesse Jackson; freedom and human rights; Madonna or Mother Teresa;
Rambo and Dirty Harry's "Make my day"; a comic-strip Peanuts
and a President's jelly beans; yuppie or Alzheimer; Walkman and
the boob tube; Sandra Day O'Connor or *Playgirl;* Sushi and Mexican beer; Super Bowl and Big Mac; prochoice or prolife; Mike
Tyson and Steffi Graf; a wasted *Challenger* or a Mars-bound *Discovery;* Wall Street and Häagen-Dazs; the "Army: Be All You Can Be"
or the Community for Creative Non-Violence; the recreational

hobo or the homeless on D.C.'s winter grates; black power and ERA; Star Wars and strawberry daiquiris; Marcel Lefebvre or John Paul II; Bill Cosby or "The Young and the Restless"; God as mother, God as lover, God as friend of the earth; AIDS and the compassionate Christ. . . . Fifty-five and counting. There is more, ever so much more—symbols my shortsightedness stops me from seeing, symbols the younger and still more restless than I can surely spy.

Precisely how any given preacher shapes a sermon within this welter of symbols I dare not tackle here. But this I do submit: Unless your preaching is molded in large measure by this context, you will be whistling down the wind—Shakespeare's "sound and fury" perhaps, but "signifying nothing." Preach as part and parcel of this concrete world, aware of its paradoxes and contradictions, attuned to its limitless potential for good, saddened or enraged by so much folly and insensitivity, alive to the grace of God with whom nothing on earth is impossible, and the "American words" will come—I promise you. Don't start with the words; start with the reality, the real-life symbols that surround you, the symbols within which, sense it or not, your own life is shaping.

REJUVENATION

But enough of theory. Now, finally, a work of rejuvenation, an effort to illustrate my ideology by revealing how preaching "built upon popular language," upon America's words and symbols, can delight, excite, thrill, even convert a congregation and restore a preacher's youth. Examples from real life.

First, August 28, 1963. Almost a quarter million Americans have marched on Washington to demand that Congress pass effective civil-rights legislation. In the shadow of Abraham Lincoln a black minister is begging his brothers and sisters not to "wallow in the valley of despair." At that moment the gospel singer Mahalia Jackson calls out: "Martin, tell them about your dream." Departing from his text, Martin Luther King Jr. hurls to the world one of history's most stirring visions.

> I have a dream that one day this nation will rise up, live out the true meaning of its creed: We hold these truths to be self-evident, that all men are created equal.
> I have a dream that one day on the red hills of Georgia the

sons of former slaves and the sons of former slaveowners will be able to sit down together at the table of brotherhood.

I have a dream that one day even the state of Mississippi, a state sweltering with the heat of injustice, sweltering with the heat of oppression, will be transformed into an oasis of freedom and justice.

I have a dream that my four little children will one day live in a nation where they will not be judged by the color of their skin but by the content of their character. . . .

I have a dream that one day down in Alabama—with its vicious racists, with its governor having his lips dripping with the words of interposition and nullification—one day right there in Alabama little black boys and black girls will be able to join hands with little white boys and white girls as sisters and brothers. . . .

I have a dream that one day every valley shall be exalted, every hill and mountain shall be made low, the rough places will be made plain and the crooked places will be made straight, and the glory of the Lord shall be revealed and all flesh shall see it together. . . .

When we allow freedom to ring, when we let it ring from every village and every hamlet, from every state and every city, we will be able to speed up that day when all of God's children, black men and white men, Jews and Gentiles, Protestants and Catholics, will be able to join hands and sing in the words of the old Negro spiritual: "Free at last! Free at last! Thank God Almighty, we are free at last!"[12]

Not a sermon, you say? Then, say I, show me a better sermon on racial justice, a more powerful American symbol in popular language. A symbol that did not die, but rose again like Christ, when Martin Luther King was killed five years later by a hidden rifleman as he stood on the balcony of a motel in Memphis.

A second example, a Presbyterian clergyman and convert from agnosticism. Frederick Buechner weds two arts: first-rate preacher and seasoned novelist. Rarely do you find combined "such fresh language, such poetic vision, such unexpected twists and such a deeply personal witness to Christ."[13] Listen to him retelling an Old Testament story in imaginative popular language.

The place to start [the gospel as comedy] is with a woman laughing. She is an old woman, and, after a lifetime in the desert, her face is cracked and rutted like a six-month drought. She hunches her shoulders around her ears and starts to shake. She squinnies her eyes shut, and her laughter is all China teeth and wheeze and tears running down as she rocks back and forth in her kitchen chair. She is laughing because she is pushing ninety-one hard and has just been told she is going to have a baby. Even though it was an angel who told her, she can't control herself, and her husband can't control himself either. He keeps a straight face a few seconds longer than she does, but he ends by cracking up, too. Even the angel is not unaffected. He hides his mouth behind his golden scapular, but you can still see his eyes. They are larkspur blue and brimming with something of which the laughter of the old woman and her husband is at best only a rough translation.

The old woman's name is Sarah, of course, and the old man's name is Abraham, and they are laughing at the idea of a baby's being born in the geriatric ward and Medicare's picking up the tab. They are laughing because the angel not only seems to believe it but seems to expect them to believe it too. They are laughing because with part of themselves they do believe it. They are laughing because with another part of themselves they know it would take a fool to believe it. They are laughing because laughing is better than crying and maybe not even all that different. They are laughing because if by some crazy chance it should just happen to come true, then they would really have something to laugh about. They are laughing at God and with God, and they are laughing at themselves too because laughter has that in common with weeping. No matter what the immediate occasion is of either your laughter or your tears, the object of both ends up being yourself and your own life.[14]

Third, take unexpectedly a systematic theologian. Karl Rahner is hardly bedtime reading, but his sermons may surprise you. One Ash Wednesday he took for topic a graphic symbol Scripture uses to declare our essence: dust. In part he preached:

Dust—truly a splendid symbol. Dust, this is the image of the commonplace. There is always more than enough of it. One fleck is as good as the next. Dust is the image of anonymity: one fleck is like the next, and all are nameless.

It is the symbol of indifference: what does it matter whether it is this dust or that dust? It is all the same. Dust is the symbol of nothingness: because it lies around so loosely, it is easily stirred up, it blows around blindly, is stepped upon and crushed—and nobody notices. It is a nothing that is just enough to be—a nothing. Dust is the symbol of coming to nothing: it has no content, no form, no shape; it blows away, the empty, indifferent, colorless, aimless, unstable booty of senseless change, to be found everywhere, and nowhere at home.[15]

Rahner goes on: I am *all* dust, never cease to be all dust, only become more than dust when I admit it, accept it, endure through it. The new thing is that the Son of God became dust. In an outrageous reversal we can say to God's Son what God told us in Paradise: "You are dust, and to dust you shall return" (Gen 3:19). Ever since then, "flesh designates . . . also the pivot and hinge of a movement that passes through dust's nothingness into life, into eternity, into God."[16]

Rahner and Buechner and King—all well and good, you say, but why not move from Germany to the U.S., from the Presbyterian scene to the Catholic, from the 60s to the 80s? How does Burghardt himself operate in the concrete—he whom the London *Tablet* recently dubbed (a dubious compliment) "the grand old man of American homilists"?[17] A legitimate question.

First, for American symbols I am profoundly indebted to film. Twenty-one years ago, on a March evening, at the Lotos Club in Manhattan, I was privileged to address the Second Annual Joint Award Reception of the Broadcasting and Film Commission of the National Council of Churches and the National Catholic Office for Motion Pictures. In the audience were such neon-light figures as Warren Beatty and Maureen O'Sullivan. My address, "To Films, with Love,"[18] said in part:

> I am here as one who lives with symbols (word, sacrament, Church), who plays with mystery (spirit and matter, divine and human, God and man). And, as a theologian, I am here to thank you for tackling more powerfully and profoundly than I the common task that is ours: human experience and its meaning: "What's it all about?". . . . What makes you so unparalleled an expression of experience is that you are now consciously all the arts in one art: you alone are sculpture and architecture, painting and poetry, music and the dance, dramatic art. . . .
>
> This evening I am happy, because I can unofficially welcome you to the fraternity of theologians, those who live with symbols and play with mystery. . . .

Some of my most effective homilies have film for springboard. I have crafted a sermon from *Chariots of Fire*—three succinct sentences of Eric Liddell, 1924 Olympic runner: (1) "God made me fast." (2) "The power is within." (3) "When I run, I feel His pleasure."[19] I have shaped a sermon from *Amadeus*—two men with diverse fatal flaws: the genius Mozart, "obscene child" who never grows up, self-centered adolescent aware of naught save his music and his pleasure; the moderately talented Salieri, eaten by envy, unable to understand how God can make him mute and gift with genius "this foul-mouthed, bottom-pinching boor," this boy "vulgar and vain, with the social graces of Caligula."[20] I have honed a homily from *The Gods Must Be Crazy*—the empty Coke bottle that falls from a plane among Bushmen in South Africa's Kalahari desert, the Coke that changes their lives, the single bottle through which Eden becomes Babel, primitive innocence discovers the ways of civilization.[21] Allow me one longer example—from a homily during a Mass of the Holy Spirit opening the academic year at Georgetown University:

> Woody Allen is loose again! This time he is *Zelig*. Leonard Zelig is a Jewish nobody, a 1920's nothing. He has no personality of his own, so he assumes whatever strong personalities he meets up with. With Chinese, he is straight out of China. With rabbis, he miraculously grows a beard and side curls. With psychiatrists, he apes their jargon, strokes his chin with solemn wisdom. At the Vatican, he is part of Pius XI's clerical retinue. In spring training, he wears a Yankee uniform and stands in the on-deck circle to bat after Babe Ruth. He takes on the black skin of a jazz trumpeter, the blubber of a fatty, the profile of a Mohawk Indian. He is a chameleon: He changes color, accent, shape as the world about him changes. He has no ideas or opinions of his own; he simply conforms. He wants only to be safe, to fit in, to be accepted, to be liked.
>
> For a while Zelig's freakish transformations make him the rage. New York welcomes him with confetti and ticker tape. He is famous for being nobody, a nonperson. His psychiatrist, Mia Farrow, is of no help to him: In her presence he cannot help playing psychiatrist. Only when she pretends to be, like him, a patient with no personality, only then does he begin to see himself for what he is: a disturbed person looking for identity, looking for himself. He identifies with her. And ultimately, after he's been a guinea pig and a side-show freak, through all manner of bitter anguish, love liberates Leonard Zelig's true self. Through comedy and tragedy, nobody becomes somebody.[22]

How use Zelig to open the academic year? The Mass of the Holy Spirit inaugurates or continues the student's search for self—a search that is not merely academic, not simply psychologic. At a Catholic college the quest is undertaken under the wings of a divine Person. In college you can easily end up a nobody: no personality of your own, a chameleon changing color with each new contact. To

become somebody, you need three gifts: light, life, and love. And
the Holy Spirit is the Spirit of all three: of light, of life, of love.

Second, for American symbols I search through songs. The
decibels indeed drive me to distraction, but I must remember that
even the decibels are a contemporary symbol. And there is a message, a powerful message—heavy or haunting, loving or lustful,
tender or raw—in American words and American symbols. Listen
as Amy Grant sings "Love of Another Kind":

> They say love is cruel
> They say love is rather fragile
> But I've found in You
> A love of another kind
>
> They say love brings hurt
> I say love brings healing
> Understanding first
> It's a love of another kind
>
> The love I know
> Is a love so few discover
> They need to know
> Jesus' love is like no other
>
> They say love won't last
> I say love is never ending
> Cause in You I have
> A love of another kind
>
> They would change their tune
> They would add another measure
> If they only knew
> This love of another kind
>
> Love of Another Kind[23]

And if Amy is dated, try Grammy winner Randy Travis. *Time* calls
him "the soft-spoken, tall-sitting, sweet-singing eye of a most conge-
nial storm." What is his music all about? "People," he reflects, "think
country music is related to a bunch of rednecks drinking beer and
fighting. They think it's all songs about drinking and cheating. But it
covers a lot bigger area than that, you know. [Pause] Covers everything."[24] And if that fails to tug at your homiletic heartstrings, per-

haps purse strings will. Do you know how many musical dollars were plunked down in the U.S. in 1987? 5.6 billion.[25]

Third, I find American words, American symbols, in everyday experience. Earlier, without heroic effort, I listed 55 American symbols, images, metaphors. They surround me, invade my privacy, circulate in my bloodstream. Today's enigma: How is it that homilists manage to ban them from the pulpit? All around me—on D.C. streets and in Atlanta's Omni,[26] in *Newsweek* and *Rolling Stone,* in "M*A*S*H" and the 40 top tunes, in Steven Spielberg's films and Whoopi Goldberg's sizzling social commentary, from AIDS and Arafat, in the scores of men and women I touch each day—all around me, every hour, I hear language that burns or soothes, wounds or heals, frightens or amuses, delights or challenges, murmurs in rapture or cries out in pain. By what sleight of hand do they disappear from our podiums? The American priesthood is an incomparable storehouse of stories. Not all can be repeated in the pulpit; but by what unwritten canon have all of them become classified information, top secret, or sacred to sacerdotal socials? I am reminded of Ralph Waldo Emerson's famous iconoclastic address at the Harvard Divinity School 150 years ago, when he railed at the junior pastor of his grandfather Ripley's church in Concord:

> I once heard a preacher who sorely tempted me to say I would go to church no more. . . . He had lived in vain. He had no word intimating that he had laughed or wept, was married or in love, had been commended, or cheated, or chagrined. If he had ever lived or acted, we were none the wiser for it. The capital secret of his profession, namely, to convert life into truth, he had not learned. Not one fact in all his experience, had he yet imported into his doctrine. . . . Not a line did he draw out of real history. The true preacher can always be known by this, that he deals out to the people his life,—life passed through the fire of thought.[27]

I admit, there is a peril in the first person singular. There is a delicate line between the "I" that stirs others to think and tell their own story, and the "I" that embarrasses, that makes others mumble uncomfortably "I'm sorry for your troubles, Father." But the risk must be dared, for in the last analysis my homily is . . . I.

Good friends: The wine of the gospel never grows old; it is always and everywhere new. Don't put this "new wine into old wineskins. . . . New wine must be put into fresh wineskins" (Lk 5:37–38). Here, for a preacher, for me, is the risk and the joy. The risk? The Italian maxim *traduttore traditore*—to translate is always, in some sense, to traduce, to misrepresent, to play traitor, especially where human frailty tries to decipher what is divine. At least the danger is ever there. The joy? Why, the exciting effort to do for God's people in my time what preachers like Jeremiah and Joel, Peter and Paul, did for God's people in their time: to express God's inexpressible word in syllables that wed fidelity to felicity, syllables that flare and flame, syllables that capture minds and rapture hearts, syllables charged with the power of God.

Such preaching, my sisters and brothers, is not an option within Catholicism; not a "nice" thing if you have the time for it, a gift for it, if you can hack it; not unimportant because supposedly *the* saving event is the Eucharist, the consecratory word, "This is my body. . . . This is my blood." Surrender the homiletic word and you must confront the sobering affirmation of that remarkable theologian-in-a-wheelchair Yves Congar: "I could quote a whole series of ancient texts, all saying more or less that if in one country Mass was celebrated for 30 years without preaching and in another there was preaching for 30 years without the Mass, people would be more Christian in the country where there was preaching."[28]

If this be homiletic heresy, here I stand and I can do no other.

ADVENT

1
NEW AGE WITH MARY
Second Sunday of Advent (B)

- Isaiah 40:1–5, 9–11
- 2 Peter 3:8–14
- Mark 1:1–8

Each year Advent poses a perplexing problem. On the one hand, the official Church makes a great to-do over Advent. Her New Year begins not on the first day of January but on the First Sunday of Advent—has so begun since the ninth century. And Advent is a season all its own, very much like Lent. Each day of Advent has its own proper Mass, pertinent readings, antiphons, responses. Symbols abound—like the wreath and the four candles before you. It is four weeks of celebration and preparation—weeks that focus on the past, the present, the future: Christ has come, Christ is here, Christ will come again. It is a glorious crescendo, increasing in power and intensity until it climaxes on a midnight outshone only by an Easter morn.

On the other hand, for most Christians Advent is "no big deal." And how could it be otherwise? How can you make much ado about Advent when you have a full-time job, a family to feed, Redskins to watch stalking a Super Bowl? How can you prepare for Christ when you must prepare for five diabolical exams? How can you concentrate on Christ when every commercial seduces you with gifts far more necessary for human living—from Cabbage Patch dolls, through Lorimar Home Videos and Amaretto di Noel, to a souped-up Saab? Time enough to celebrate Christ when Midnight Mass rolls round.

So then, how will a hopped-up homilist break through the impasse? And in a practical way, a lay way, not a monastic way or even a jesuitical way. By borrowing a page this Marian Year from Mary's book, from the first Christmas mother. Not slavishly, not

21

reproducing her daily routine in Bethlehem or Nazareth. Rather, taking to heart three sentences from Scripture, from St. Luke's Gospel—sentences that just might activate your Advent existence without permanent pain or paranoia.

I

First, a sentence in Luke after the shepherds have scurried to the stable to salute their Savior: "Mary preserved all these things, tossing them together in her heart" (Lk 2:19).[1] As before the angel in Nazareth (cf. Lk 1:29), so here before the shepherds in Bethlehem, Mary was puzzled. Have done with the picture of a simple-minded, artless teen-ager, a Pollyanna, a Dorothy in *The Wonderful Wizard of Oz*, a fairyland princess simply enraptured by choirs of angels, wide-eyed before wise men on camels bearing gifts. Have done, too, with a mother who held in her hands a complete God-given scenario from Nazareth to Calvary and beyond. For all that she believed so profoundly, Mary was puzzled. She had to ask herself what all this, what each incident, might mean: conceiving a child without benefit of man, giving birth to "the Son of the Most High" (Lk 1:32) in a feeding trough, later fleeing like a refugee to Egypt, watching helplessly as her Son moved unalterably toward the death he predicted. She had to wrestle with it all. If you don't believe *me*, listen to Mary scolding her 12-year-old runaway in the temple: "Son, why have you treated us like this? Look, your father and I have been terribly worried and have been searching for you" (Lk 2:48).[2] Hardly the words of a woman who had grasped with clarity who Jesus was. Luke puts it beyond doubt: "[Mary and Joseph] did not understand what he was saying to them" (Lk 2:50).[3]

And so for you. My first Advent advice: Take 15 minutes out of each day to "toss together," to puzzle over, to wrestle with what the Lord has told you about His Son-in-flesh. Not a course in Scripture, though I'm all for that too. Rather a reverent mulling each day of Advent over the miracle not on 34th Street[4] but in a hidden corner of the world; over the mind-blowing biblical affirmation "God so loved the world that He gave His only Son, that whoever believes in him should . . . have eternal life" (Jn 3:16); over a Son of God who could have redeemed us by whispering a word or coming on clouds of glory, but chose to take our flesh, become what we are, experience our fragile human existence, die our death.

What does it mean to you? Who *is* this child? In your day-today living, is J.C. as real to you as J.R.,[5] as Reagan or Gorbachev, as Michael Jackson or Martina Navratilova, as the man or woman you love? Let the image of Jesus, Son of God in swaddling bands, trigger your thinking—about him, about yourself, about the others who people your days.

And at some time, stop thinking! Recall Carmelite William McNamara's concept of contemplation: "a long loving look at the real." Let the stark beauty and terrible wonder of it all sweep over you. Don't analyze it; feel it! In imagination crouch at Bethlehem's crib, become a child again, touch little toes as real as any infant's, let naked reason disappear, let Christ simply be! Just look . . . and love.

Fifteen minutes a day—on the episode that changed history for ever, the puzzle of puzzles. Let your Walkman wait, your stereo sit in silence. For a quarter hour let the rest of the world go by; let the rest of the world make sense—in Christ.

II

Second, a sentence in Luke after the angel took wing: "In those days Mary arose and went with haste into the hill country, to a city of Judah, and she entered the house of Zechariah and greeted Elizabeth" (Lk 1:39–40). The point is: What did this teen-age Jewish girl do when the angel left her—left her with God's Son in her body? We can speculate, imagine. Surely she was excited, enraptured by the experience. Possibly she rocked back and forth, newly aware of her womb, touching her flesh with fresh reverence. Perhaps she mused on what her life would be like, once the long-expected of Israel grew to manhood.

This is conjecture—intelligent, of course, since the conjecture is mine, but still conjecture; there is no evidence to back it up. However, one thing Mary did has God's word for evidence. She had heard from Gabriel that her kinswoman Elizabeth was pregnant, with child for six months. And Elizabeth was old, "advanced in years" (Lk 1:18). How old, we know not; but old enough to be reproached by her neighbors for being "barren" (v. 36).

What did Mary do? She went "with haste" to see Elizabeth, walked briskly to a town in the hill country of Judea,[6] walked perhaps 67 miles. Not to spread her own good news, not to compare children with Elizabeth, not to rave over "my son the Messiah." She went, very simply, to help—for three full months, till Elizabeth's child would be born. And as soon as Mary greeted her kinswoman, the Gospel reveals, little John the Baptist "leaped in [Elizabeth's] womb . . . leaped for joy" (Lk 1:41, 44), leaped at the coming of Christ, sensed miraculously the presence of God's Son locked in Mary's flesh.

And so for you. Contemplation is good—focusing mind and heart on a Christ who walks our dust no longer. But Advent with Mary calls contemplation to action—focusing mind and heart on a Christ who is still moving from Bethlehem to Calvary. Not far from you is a kinsman, a kinswoman, akin to you in the bone of humanity and the blood of Christ; someone who needs you; someone who hurts; someone who finds it difficult or impossible to joy in life because life, as a despairing friend said angrily, "life is a bitch." If— which God forbid—you are anything like me, you need not look far for a Christ in pain. He or she is everyone from whom I turn my eyes away.

That remarkable Southern short-story writer Flannery O'Connor, who died of lupus at 39, once penned these words from her own incurable cross: "You will have found Christ when you are concerned with other people's sufferings and not your own."[7] Do that, be that, come with your Christ, with your cross, to someone too poor, too naked, too sad, too crippled to joy in Christmas, and the miracle of Mary's visitation will be repeated as it has been through the ages: The person you touch in love will leap for joy from the barren womb of sorrow.

III

A quarter hour of contemplation . . . haste to some hill of calvary . . . what is left? Only the rest of your life. The third Advent text about Mary stems from the public life of Jesus. "A woman in the crowd raised her voice and said to him: 'Blessed is the womb that bore you, and the breasts that you fed on!' But he said: 'Blessed rather are those who listen to the word of God and keep it!' " (Lk 11:27–28).

Not a rebuke from Jesus to his mother; quite the opposite. Jesus was not denying that Mary was blessed in her bearing of him; of course she was. What the woman cried from the crowd was true—but it was only part of the picture.[8] St. Augustine expressed it powerfully 16 centuries ago: "Mary was more blessed because she laid hold of faith in Christ than because she conceived the flesh of Christ. . . . Her motherly relationship to him would have been of no use to Mary, had she not carried Christ in her heart more happily even than she bore him in her body." She "conceived Christ in her mind before she conceived him in her womb." "It was by faith she gave him birth, it was by faith she conceived him."[9] In Luke's story, Mary is indeed to be praised—not simply because she gave birth to Jesus, but because she too listened to God's word, believed it, acted on it—from the glad tidings brought by Gabriel in Nazareth to the days in Jerusalem after Jesus' ascension, when the apostles "with one accord devoted themselves to prayer, together with the women and Mary the mother of Jesus . . ." (Acts 1:14). That is why we see Mary most profoundly when we see her as the first Christian disciple, the model and pattern of Christian discipleship. She listened to what God was asking, and she said yes—not only to the bliss of Bethlehem but to the sword that holed her heart on Calvary.

And so for you. Advent, the "coming" of Christ, is not simply a season, four weeks out of your year—just as Christmas, the birthday of Christ, is not confined to a single day. From contemplation to action—this is Christian living, 365 days a year. You must face up to a fact at once harrowing and heartening: God is ceaselessly speaking to you. Not too often through an angel; more often through human events. Not only through ten commandments etched in stone, but in a law of justice and love written into your flesh and spirit. Not only through a Roman document, but in the sad, starved eyes of Ethiopian children staring at you from a TV screen. Not only through "the Word of the Lord" from a pulpit, but in the grim silence of the homeless huddled over Georgetown's grates. Not only through an episcopal pastoral on peace, but in the undeclared wars that sever rich and poor, black and white, Jew and Gentile, male and female, ordained and lay, the powerful and the powerless. Tune in to the God within you and the world around you; "toss together," puzzle over, what you hear; at some point say yes, even if what you hear is not all clear; then, with the profound faith of a perplexed Mary, act . . . do something . . . carry your Christ somewhere.

Good friends in Christ: This week's issue of *Time* has for cover story "New Age Harmonies,"[10] what the subhead calls "A strange mix of spirituality and superstition . . . sweeping across the country."[11] "Nobody knows just when it all started or what it all means, but millions of Americans now find themselves trying to learn about their former lives, cure illness without medicine, meet travelers from other galaxies, know the unknowable."[12] Stockbrokers consult astrological charts; a yuppie investment banker recalls her previous life as a monk; millionaires have private gurus who pay house calls; a major petrochemical company hires a faith healer to "read auras"; and 1200 of the faithful plunk down $300 apiece at the New York Hilton "to get the word from the New Age's reigning whirling dervish, Shirley MacLaine."[13]

Not mine to ridicule all this. It is in some measure, I believe, a contemporary cry, the age-old cry, deep within the human heart for something more than the material, beyond what our eyes see, our ears hear, our fingers touch. It may well be MacLaine's "I'm just a human being trying to find some answers about what we're doing here, where we came from and where we're going."[14]

Not mine to ridicule. But this I do say: Advent declares that the New Age arrived almost 2000 years ago, was born in the "little town of Bethlehem," came to birth in a God-man who actually told us, through tears and sweat and blood, "what we're doing here, where we came from and where we're going." Advent challenges you: Are you interested enough, do you dare, to listen to the answer graven in the flesh of God's only Son, wrestle with it, say yes to it even in darkness, live it even at great risk, and carry it to those who cry for it from untold calvaries? Or are you content to sit cross-legged and keep chanting "Om"[15]?

Dahlgren Chapel
Georgetown University
and
Holy Trinity Church
Washington, D.C.
December 6, 1987

2

DO NOT OPEN BEFORE CHRISTMAS?
Second Sunday of Advent (C)

- Baruch 5:1–9
- Philippians 1:4–6, 8–11
- Luke 3:1–6

Two weeks ago my imagination ran wild. I was thinking of Advent. Suddenly I was seized by a sort of Woody Allen vision of John the Baptizer. Half-clothed in camel's hair not designed by Dior, with a leather girdle from Sunny's Surplus, munching locusts from Little Tavern, John crashes New York's Stock Exchange. Amid a furious battle between the dollar and the yen, he shouts like a madman: "Repent!" (Mt 3:2). Most of the buyers and sellers don't hear him; the trading is deafening. Most don't see him; their eyes are glued to the quote board. The few who notice him ignore him or shrug their shoulders or summon security or tell him to "get lost." He screams: "You brood of vipers! Who warned you to flee from the wrath to come?" (Lk 3:7). Now they're sure he's a jerk from Jonestown. He pleads: "Prepare the way of the Lord" (Mk 1:3). They respond: "The way of who? Get the hell out of here! Back to the jungle!"

Bizarre, off the wall? I say no. Call it anachronistic—a big word for someone out of sync with his surroundings. Twenty centuries sever John from Wall Street. But not bizarre, as if it had no relation to reality. Through John, the Church is proclaiming something to you and me. Probably not "You brood of vipers!" Not necessarily "Repent!" But, as sure as you're alive, "Prepare the way of the Lord."

But what does that mean? It meant one thing when Yahweh spoke it through the prophet Isaiah to the Israelites exiled in Babylon. It meant something else when John proclaimed it in the wilderness of Judea. It means something else again when the Church announces it to us here and now. So then, (1) a word on

27

Isaiah and John, (2) a word on the Church in Advent, (3) a word
on you and me.

I

"Prepare the way of the Lord" goes back to Second Isaiah,
what is called the "Book of Consolation."[1] Yahweh announces to
the Israelites enslaved in Babylon that their exile is ended, they
have paid double for their sins. Indeed their kingdom has been
shattered, their temple destroyed, Jerusalem and the cities of Judah
all but abandoned, at best wretched village settlements; but against
all the odds Israel has survived. The trouble is, the exiles have lost
hope; they despair of ever seeing Jerusalem again. And suddenly,
out of the blue, utterly unexpected, a promise of freedom. A heavenly voice cries out: "In the wilderness prepare the way of the
Lord, make straight in the desert a highway for our God" (Isa
40:3). And Isaiah trumpets:

> Behold, the Lord God comes with might,
>   and His arm rules for Him;
> behold, His reward is with Him,
>   and His recompense before Him.
> He will feed His flock like a shepherd,
>   He will gather the lambs in His arms,
> He will carry them in His bosom,
>   and gently lead those that are with young.
> (Isa 40:10–11)

Where are the exiles to prepare the way of Yahweh? In the
wilderness that leads from Babylon to Jerusalem. As the Redeemer
God dried up the waters of the Red Sea, made the depths of the sea
a way, a way from Egypt to freedom, so now Yahweh will make a
way in the wilderness, lead His people home free to the holy mountain Zion.[2] So then, disheartened exiles, lift up your hearts, raise
your sights, your hopes! Don't repeat the Egypt experience, when
God had to drag you kicking and screaming through the desert
into the Promised Land. As all through your history, God's road is
your road. God will lead you back from Babylon, restore Jerusalem,
rebuild your treasured temple. Just get your butts out of the mud!

Centuries later John the Baptizer strides onto center stage
echoing the words of Isaiah. Once again the Lord is coming, but

this time the Jews are not to look for a hidden God. This time God is coming in the person of Jesus of Nazareth. "I baptize you with water; but he who is mightier than I is coming, the thong of whose sandals I am not worthy to untie; he will baptize you with the Holy Spirit and with fire" (Lk 3:16). This is the one John "looked at," and looking said: "Behold, the Lamb of God" (Jn 1:36).

How at that time were the Jews to prepare for Jesus? John is not the poet we found in Isaiah; he shoots from the hip. To the Jews in general: "Repent!" To some Pharisees and Sadducees: "You brood of vipers! . . . Bear fruit that befits repentance, and do not presume to say to yourselves, 'We have Abraham as our father'; for I tell you, God is able from these stones to raise up children to Abraham" (Mt 3:7–9). John would make it big as a televangelist—except, no air-conditioned doghouse.[3]

II

Isaiah and John move me to the Church—the Church right now, here in Advent. The liturgy leaves no room for argument: The Lord is coming, and we are to prepare his way. But it doesn't seem to make sense—nowhere near the sense it made for the Old Testament prophet and the forerunner of the Lord. After all, the Lord has already come. He came in swaddling clothes 20 centuries ago—omnipotence in bonds. He comes each day all over the world under seeming bread and wine—our "Godhead here in hiding."[4] He comes to your inmost being as long as you love—love God more than God's creation. He comes in your sisters and brothers, his living images; for, as poet Gerard Manley Hopkins sang,

> . . . Christ plays in ten thousand places,
> Lovely in limbs, and lovely in eyes not his
> To the Father through the features of men's faces.[5]

The Lord is here—in you, in front of you, all around you. Why all the shenanigans about preparing the way of the Lord?

Yes, the Lord has come—thank God! He comes constantly to you: comes to you through the grace that is God within you, comes to you through the Eucharist that moves from the tabernacle on an altar to the tabernacle of your body, comes to you in the hundreds of humans who meet your eyes each day. The crucial question for each and every Christian is: How aware am I of Christ's presence?

Let's suppose a Gallup poll asked Christian America "Do the four weeks before Christmas make a difference in your life, change your practical living?" Surely most would say yes. But just what difference? End-of-year inventory? Pre-Christmas part-time job? Christmas cards? Frantic search for what gifts to whom? Semester exams one on top of another? Plane tickets home or to a sun-kissed beach?

With such changes I cannot argue; life must go on. But what of the one person who gives ultimate meaning to your life? Has America subconsciously changed Christmas into a secular event, substituted "Rudolph the Red-Nosed Reindeer" for "Silent Night, Holy Night," forgotten that the word "Christmas" is fashioned from two of the most meaningful monosyllables in history—Christ and Mass? What Christians need in Advent is not a second or third coming of Christ; he is here. We need a fresh awareness of his presence, an awareness that works a ceaseless change in our lives. Christians must recapture the rapturous feeling our Lady had as she felt the Word made flesh of her grow within her, the emotions that swept over John the Baptizer when he recognized the Savior he had been selected to run before.

III

Lovely rhetoric, reverend sir! But how do you put flesh and blood on the skeleton? Several suggestions, to trigger your own thoughts. I said that the magic word is "aware." So I begin with a question, an examination of conscience, a year-end inventory: Where does Christ rank in the Top Ten of your thinking? Not abstractly; very concretely. In shared time, in real interest, in reflection, contemplation, discussion. Above or below the Redskins or the Hoyas, Bill Cosby or Tina Turner, Rambo or "The Young and the Restless"[6]?

Second, time is indeed your enemy. I am not asking time off from your job, slacking off from study. But why not something as corny as a coffee break for Christ? There's an apocryphal story about a Dominican who is supposed to have asked the pope if he might smoke while making his meditation; His Holiness, of course, said no. Then a Jesuit asked the same pope if he might meditate while smoking. "God bless you, son!" said the pontiff. Does industry or academe today make it impossible to sip coffee for ten minutes *and* ponder on the God-man who ought to be the center of your existence?

Third, there is the second syllable of Christmas: the Christ-Mass. My dear friend the lawyer Edward Bennett Williams fought cancer for a decade. When not in the hospital, Ed started each Washington workday with 7 o'clock Mass here at Holy Trinity. Can it be difficult? Of course. But if the liturgy is the center of Catholic existence, if the Mass is the single most significant source of strength for human living, if the Eucharist is the heart and soul of Catholic spirituality, dare you limit the Mass to days of sheer obligation? Is there a better way to welcome Christ within you? Each Eucharist is an advent: a fresh coming of Christ to your inmost being.

Fourth, be aware that Christ comes to you in others. If God made woman and man to the image and likeness of their Creator; if it is true, as Hopkins sang, that "Christ plays to the Father" through the features of our brothers and sisters, is "lovely in eyes not his"; if Bruce Ritter of Covenant House can discover day after day that "sometimes God has a kid's face,"[7] specifically kids pimped and prostituted, used-up and angel-dusted; if it is true, as Christ proclaimed, that when we feed the hungry we feed him—then Advent is no longer a season, no longer four weeks. For Christ can come to you wherever and whenever your eyes meet another's eyes; for your eyes are meeting Christ's eyes, if only you have eyes to see.

Fifth, let Christ come to you on your crosses. I doubt that any of you beyond the age of two has not encountered some kind of crucifixion. The nails have countless forms, from the acne on an adolescent's cheek, through the schizophrenia that severs the human spirit, to the terminal cancer. I beg you, don't try to carry your cross alone. I'm not saying you cannot; I do say it's not a good idea. A cross makes Christian sense only if you meet Christ on it, only if on your cross you are transformed into Christ. I am reminded that a currently popular musician-singer, Bobby McFerrin, called "the beat box of all time," has a dream we can borrow. He recalls: "There's a wonderful [Hermann] Hesse story about a violinist who wishes to be the best in the world. His wish is granted, and as he's playing, he slowly disappears into the music. That's the hope of every artist. It's certainly mine."[8] The wondrous thing about "disappearing" into Christ is that you become more and more you, the unique person Christ died to shape.

Good friends: Christmas has for ages been synonymous with giving. I have no problem with that, as long as whatever you give, large or small, is symbolic of yourself—as long as the gift stands for you. But even more important, I submit that the supreme Christmas gift is the one gift that should not surprise you. Christmas will simply celebrate what you have: the gift that was first given to you from a stable in the Middle East, the gift that has been given to the world through 20 centuries, the gift that rests within you: God's own Son, God's love in flesh. This is the one gift you will enjoy most fully if you are aware that you already have it. This is the only gift you should never mark "Not to be opened before Christmas." Christmas is every day—if you prepare the way.

Dahlgren Chapel
Georgetown University
and
Holy Trinity Church
Washington, D.C.
December 4, 1988

LENT

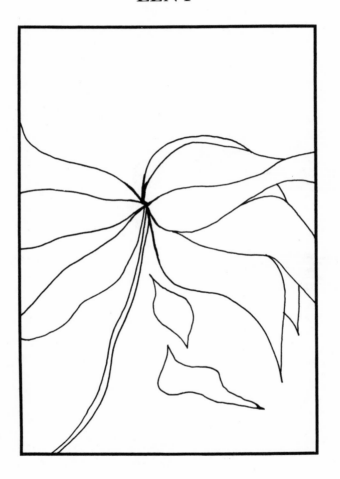

3
LENT IS FOR LISTENING
First Sunday of Lent (B)

- Genesis 9:8–15
- 1 Peter 3:18–22
- Mark 1:12–15 (Luke 4:1–13)

Some years ago, I read a delightful filler in a newspaper. A rugged old gentleman had reached the age of one hundred, and a reporter was intrigued. "To what," he asked, "do you attribute your longevity?" Responded the still spry centenarian: "I never wasted any energy resisting temptation."

A tempting way to live, wouldn't you say? Yes . . . until you grasp our Gospel; until you fix your gaze on Jesus; until you hear that the Son of God "was in the wilderness 40 days, tempted by Satan" (Mk 1:13); until you reflect on his response; until you tear his testing from the printed page and link it to your own. It could be a profitable prelude to your "40 days," put some bite into a listless Lent.

To make my point, I present to you a two-act play, with an epilogue. Act I is set in a desert some 1960 years ago. Act II is set in a city in the year of our Lord 1988. The epilogue? A personal word from your playwright.

I

Act I: a desert, the wilderness of Judea. Recall how the Jews of old saw the desert. It was not only an abode of wild beasts and demons; it was a place where the Jew made contact with Yahweh, where the Lord God met His people. And so you have God's wondrous words in His wooing of Israel: ". . . behold, I will allure her, and bring her into the wilderness, and speak tenderly to her" (Hos

3:14). Here it is that Jesus is at once escorted by the Spirit and tested by Satan.

The Son of God tested by Satan? It sounds so fantastic, like science fiction. Scripture scholars ceaselessly struggle with it.[1] Did the devil actually accost Jesus in some physical form, somewhat as three "angels" looking like men appeared to Abraham (cf. Gen 18:1 ff.)? How could Satan show Jesus "all the kingdoms of the world in an instant" (Lk 4:5)? Can we take it for a fact that a devil "took [Jesus] to Jerusalem and set him on the pinnacle of the temple" (v. 9)?

Good questions all, fascinating topics I recommend to you for a Scripture séance some enchanted evening. But at this moment you and I are not in class; we are at prayer, lost in wonder at a God-man tested, a Savior tempted. And he *was*. The New Testament Letter to the Hebrews leaves us no doubt on this score: "For we have not a high priest who is unable to sympathize with our weaknesses, but one who in every respect has been tempted as we are . . ." (Heb 4:15); and "because he himself has suffered and been tempted, he is able to help those who are tempted" (Heb 2:18).

But—a still more stimulating question—what evil thing was Jesus tempted to do, not simply in the solitude of a desert but all through his public ministry?[2] In one swift sentence: Jesus was tempted to use his power, his authority, as Son of God in his own interest, for his own purposes, apart from the mission given him by his Father. In striking fashion the three scenes in Judea's wilderness symbolize this. As you listen to Satan and God's Son, notice what unifies the three temptations: Jesus' three responses to Satan are quotations from the Old Testament book called Deuteronomy, from "passages that recall three events of the Exodus in which the Israelites in the desert were put to the test and failed. . . . Where Israel of old failed, there Jesus succeeds."[3]

Temptation 1. You're hungry; you haven't had a bite for 40 days. Don't be a fool. After all, you're the Son of God. Man, you've got power. So, "tell this stone to become bread" (Lk 4:3).[4] Satan is challenging Jesus: Forget your Father's design for you; the problem right now is bread; so, manufacture it. Jesus' response? "It is written in Scripture, 'Not on bread alone is man/woman to live' " (v. 4). Your problem and mine, good friends, is this: The sentence has turned into a stale proverb; we've forgotten its rich historical background. Jesus' retort is taken from the mouth of Moses (cf. Deut 8:3)—Moses reminding the Israelites of their desert experience, how in their hunger they sighed for the slavery of Egypt, "when we sat by the fleshpots and ate bread to the full" (Exod 16:3); how

Israel sought its food apart from Yahweh. Not so Jesus. His Father will feed him: "My food is to do the will of Him who sent me" (Jn 4:34).

Temptation 2. You want to rule the world, don't you? That's why you're here, isn't it—to proclaim a kingdom, a kingdom where you're the king? Right? Well, there you are: "To you I shall give authority over all this [over all the kingdoms of the world], and the glory that goes with it, because it has been made over to me; to anyone I please I can give it. So, if you fall down and worship me, it will all be yours" (Lk 4:5–7). Once again Satan is challenging Jesus, challenging him to accept world dominion from someone other than God, acknowledge as his master and lord someone other than his Father. Once again Jesus responds from Deuteronomy: "It is written in Scripture, 'The Lord your God shall you worship and Him only shall you serve (adore)' " (v. 8; cf. Deut 6:13). Once again he recalls Israel's desert experience. Enchanted by Canaanite cults, Israel was constantly warned by Moses not to chase after foreign gods; constantly Israel failed. Not so Jesus. In contrast to ancient Israel, he refuses to worship anyone, adore anything, save Yahweh, insists that his single mission is to see to it that his Father's kingship is established over each and all.

Temptation 3. You want to make a name for yourself, don't you—hear hurrahs and hosannas from the motley mob down there, maybe even get high-fives from the scribes and Pharisees? Well then, here's your chance, at the tip of the temple.[5] Play Superman: ". . . throw yourself down from here; for it is written in Scripture, 'He will give His angels orders about you, to protect you,' and again, 'On their hands they will bear you up, lest you strike your foot against a stone' " (Lk 4:9–11; cf. Ps 91:11–12). Once again Satan is challenging Jesus, this time to reveal himself with a flourish, with fanfare, showy display—what the people expected of a heaven-sent leader. Once again Jesus responds from Deuteronomy: "It is written in Scripture, 'You shall not put the Lord your God to the test' " (Lk 4:12; cf. Deut 6:16). Once again Jesus recalls Israel's desert experience. All but crazed with thirst, the people demanded "Give us water to drink" (Exod 17:2), murmured against Moses: "Why did you bring us up out of Egypt, to kill us and our children and our cattle with thirst?" (v. 3). Yahweh's answer was a miracle, water from a rock struck by Moses. Not so will Jesus have it: He refuses to demand miraculous protection for himself and his mission. No one may "demand such intervention from God merely to suit his fancy or whim."[6]

II

Three temptations, three rejections. Act I leads, without inter-
mission, into Act II. Some 1960 years have fled, and the Judean
desert is merely a memory. The date is 1988, and the setting is a
city—Tulsa, Washington, you name it. But right here a warning:
You dare not pass too facilely from Jesus' wilderness to our civilization. The temptations of Jesus are not recorded in the Gospels to
give us Christians a model for the temptations in our own lives.[7]
Satan tempted Jesus precisely as singular Son of God. That is not
our situation; not even a Jesuit will make such a claim.

Even so, Act II need not be canceled. For you too have a
mission, a commission, from God. Not the same mission as Jesus,
but still a mission that follows from his, is demanded by his. Your
basic charter is a pregnant paragraph in Vatican II's Decree on the
Apostolate of the Laity:

> The redemptive work of Christ has for essential purpose the salva-
> tion of man and woman; and still it involves as well the renewal of
> the whole temporal order. Consequently, the Church's mission is
> not only to bring to men and women the message of Christ and his
> grace, but also to penetrate and perfect the temporal sphere with
> the spirit of the gospel. In carrying out this mission of the Church,
> the laity therefore exercise their apostolate in the world as well as
> in the Church, in the temporal order as well as in the spiritual. . . .[8]

The point is, your very baptism laid on you a charge: not only
to "save your soul" but to transform the world on which you walk,
in which you work, to shape this earthly city into a city of justice, of
peace, of love. And where do you play this irreplaceable role? Not
purely or primarily in chapel or church; your distinctive arena is
our sin-scarred earth. Your mission territory is where you live and
move and have your being. Your home, of course; for the home is
the Church in miniature. But beyond that, your apostolic turf is law
office or legislature, media or medicine, public school or private
industry, executive suite or union hall, the hundred and one areas
of human living seldom open to the ordained.[9]

How do you bring Christ there or expand his presence? At times
by the power of the word: your word and God's. But more effectively
still, you transform your turf by the attraction of your lives. And
precisely here today's temptations raise their seductive heads.

Not, as I've said, not quite the temptations that assailed the Son of God. But there *is* a similarity. I too am tempted at times to use my powers, my gifts, my possessions just for my own fantastic self, for the sweet smell of success. It's a present danger, I assure you. A distinguished university, 350 years old, recently revealed the goals the incoming class had declared: (1) money, (2) power, (3) reputation.[10] A survey of 290,000 freshmen reports that, for three out of four, the top reason for going to college is financial success.[11] An article in *Esquire* suggests strongly that these days "money is the new sex."[12] A distinguished sociologist tells us fearfully that what imperils America, especially young middle-class America, is a resurgence of late-19th-century rugged individualism: Ultimately, I'm the only one who matters; there's only so much water in the well, so get to the well first; the race is to the strong, the swift, the savage.[13]

Temptations indeed. Not because money, power, fame are evils in themselves; they are not.[14] Where, then, is the seduction that can turn into sin? The temptation to amass money to pack only my own pockets, pile up power principally to lord it over the less powerful, enter halls of fame for the applause that pours over me. Run that route and you betray your God-given mission. Sing that song and Satan has impaled you on his pitchfork. By all means, with my warm blessing, make more megabucks than old J. P. Morgan, work your way to power structures from counting house to White House, sign more autographs than Bruce Springsteen or America's figure-skating sweetheart Debi Thomas. But never stop asking the crucial Christian question: Why? Why money? Why power? Why fame? To shape your acre of God's world in the image of Christ, or in your own image? To distance still further the haves from the have-nots, or to make life more human for children dehumanized by hunger, for the homeless chilled by winter winds and unfeeling hearts, for the aged pleading mutely for your love?

III

After Acts 1 and 2, a personal word from your playwright. What I have done is (1) re-express the experience of Jesus before his tempter and (2) sketch three tempting tendencies of our time, several seductions that symbolize today's city. My personal word to you, whoever you are, whatever the temptation to your human and Christian mission? I am not asking you to spend Lent wrestling with Satan, quoting Scripture to drive your devil away in shame. I am not asking you to desert the city for the desert. I *am* suggesting that you bring a bit of the desert into your city. I mean, some space for solitude, where the decibels are muted, where the beach is not for beer, where you can hear God speaking. Lent is for listening.

You see, God is wherever you are. A frightening thought if you're fleeing from God; a shot of adrenalin if you're looking for God. But you have to listen to God, let God talk. The Lord can talk to you in so many ways—not only when the word that is Scripture is read to you, but through Beethoven and the Beatles, through nuclear threat and chemical waste, through AIDS victims and bag ladies, through friends whose caring reflects the compassion of Christ and ayatollahs who identify America with Satan, through wealth and poverty, power and helplessness, fame and humiliation. But your ears must be open, attuned to God's whisper as well as God's thunder. Like the boy Samuel in the Old Testament, you have to say "Speak, Lord, for your servant is listening" (1 Sam 3:9)—not "Speak, Lord, and your servant will think it over." Lent is for listening.

God's word surrounds you. If you listen carefully enough, if you listen between the lines, you just might hear two voices: the siren voice of your own shrewd Satan, whatever sort of devil may be seducing you from touching the gospel to your turf; and the strong but gentle voice of Christ commanding or counseling what he wants of you, how he would like you to live each day the faith that brings you to his Sacrifice each Sunday.

Lent is for listening. I cannot promise it will be fun; I *can* promise it will be exciting. You may not live to be one hundred, but you *will* live each day "by every word that proceeds from the mouth of God" (Mt 4:4). Not a bad way to spend Lent; it sure beats giving up M & Ms.

> The First Church in Tulsa
> The United Presbyterian Church in the U.S.A.
>   and
> University of Tulsa
> Tulsa, Oklahoma
> February 17, 1988
>   also
> Dahlgren Chapel
> Georgetown University
>   and
> Holy Trinity Church
> Washington, D.C.
> February 21, 1988

4
THE DAY THE WORLD CHANGED
Passion/Palm Sunday (B)

- Isaiah 50:4–7
- Philippians 2:6–11
- Mark 14:1—15:47

It's a tough task I've set myself today. I want you to leave here with a crucial Christian conviction. I want you to leave here convinced that this week is the most important week of your year. Not because a lavender Lent is about to end. Not because Easter is acomin' round the corner and Wisconsin Avenue will be awash with bright colors. Rather because this is the week when the two most powerful of enemies clash, the real superpowers: life and death. This is the week when you should discover, or rediscover, how the whole world was changed for ever, and tie that discovery to your daily existence.

Sound a bit heavy? Well, it is. To make Christian sense of my song and dance, I impose on you three movements. I open with a story from the 20th century; I move back to the central story of human history; I return to today, to your story and mine.

I

My first movement: a contemporary tale. It's the story of one man—a man now in the twilight of his existence. He is quite content, because his life has been quite exciting. He has seen the world change—change often—and he has been part of it all. He saw the world change when panzers rolled over Poland, Nazi might mangled the Maginot line, Germans goose-stepped inexorably towards Moscow and Stalingrad, the *Luftwaffe* blitzed London night after night, and it seemed as if the Empire itself would be enslaved. He saw the world change when a horrifying A-bomb mushroomed

41

over Hiroshima and a hundred thousand humans tasted a fiery death. He saw the world change as two superpowers waged a chillingly cold war, as nuclear fear both endangered the earth and defended it. He saw the world changed by an eye—the eye of a camera—as TV ushered the globe into our pubs and parlors, pictured African apartheid and presidential politics, ballet and the budget, starvation in the sub-Sahara and seduction in the bedroom, Wall Street's Black Monday and the black death of AIDS. He saw the world changed by the graying of America and the annual destruction of 50 million innocents in the womb, by black power and our first, devastating defeat in battle. He saw the world changed by science, from the splitting of the atom to footsteps on the moon, from a heart transplant to birth in a surrogate womb. He saw the world changed by bytes in a computer.

All this he saw, and more. But for all the change he saw, one change he missed—the single most important way the world had been changed. Strange, because he was such a good man, so faithful a Christian. He had no false gods; kept Sunday reasonably sacred; cared tenderly for his mother and father; never took what was another's, whether life or wife, wealth or good name; fasted on Fridays in Lent; received Communion during the paschal season; even supported his pastor above the poverty line.

What, then, did he miss? Why, my second point!

II

You see, what is most significant in human living often lies beneath the surface. You see the scene, but fail to seize its significance. So too here. My good friend revered Good Friday, even walked the Way of the Cross between 12 and three while others were flipping Frisbees or frolicking at Fort Lauderdale. He knew that Jesus had died a dire death for him, out of love for him. But he saw no deeper than that. He had no idea that those three hours had changed the world, changed his world, for ever. An outrageous remark indeed, and it calls for clarification.

You must go back to Bethlehem, because Bethlehem and Jerusalem, Christmas and Calvary, crib and cross form one continuous story. When the Son of God touched this earth, He not only took the flesh of one teen-age Jewish virgin. As some early Church theologians trumpeted, "the whole of humanity was in Christ Jesus."[1] "He took the body of each of us,"[2] yours and mine, the flesh of every man, woman, and child, from Adam to Antichrist. In becoming one of us, in borrowing from us everything we are save for our sin, God's only Son wedded all of humanity to God.

I am not saying that the world became Christian at that moment, or at any moment since then. Six million Jews gassed in the Holocaust refute that; almost 500 million Moslems dispute it day after day. I *am* saying that, whether the world knew it or not, knows it or not, no human person could ever be the same once the Divine became human. In a way that baffles our limited intelligence, that impotent infant in Mary's arms contained all of us within himself, to reshape our sinful selves in his own image and likeness.[3]

But, in the Lord's limitless love, Bethlehem was only a beginning. The Christmas crib looked forward to Calvary's cross; the deathless Son of God was born to die; the Child wore our sinful flesh to nail it to twin beams of wood. Why? All I can answer is five immortal monosyllables in John: "God so loved the world" (Jn 3:16). And still I marvel: Why *this*? Of all the ways an all-knowing, all-powerful God could have destroyed the death in us, God chose . . . death. Not our death; the death of God's Son. In Jesus' flesh, life and death met in mortal combat. Life won out, but only by dying—dying to rise again. Against all the odds, the midpoint of history, the day the world changed for ever, is Good Friday.[4] God's life in us through God's death for us. It's weird, it's cool, it's everything we dare not believe . . . but must.

Did you ever read Flannery O'Connor's short story "A Good Man Is Hard to Find"? The central character is an escaped convict who calls himself The Misfit "because I can't make what all I done wrong fit what all I gone through in punishment."[5] Just before he shoots in cold blood a trembling grandmother who begs him to pray to Jesus, the Misfit utters a swift sentence, unaware how profoundly Christian it is: "Jesus thrown everything off balance."[6]

Yes, "Jesus thrown everything off balance." A cross of death is the tree of life. "If I be lifted up from the earth, I will draw all men and women to myself" (Jn 12:32). Friday is literally *Good* Friday. Calvary's tree is not tragedy but triumph. The "darkness" Luke says "covered the whole earth" from 12 to three (Lk 23:44) has been shattered by the light that is Christ. Beneath the cross we can sing with poet Gerard Manley Hopkins "The world is charged with the grandeur of God," because ever since that Friday "the Holy Ghost over the bent / World broods with warm breast and with ah! bright wings."[7] Because of Calvary you and I can echo the refrain of Eugene O'Neill's Lazarus risen from his grave:

Laugh with me!
Death is dead!
Fear is no more!
There is only life!
There is only laughter![8]

III

Now Jesus' story leads logically to your story and mine. To be like Jesus, to share God's own life, it is not enough to acknowledge that he died for us, not enough to spend Good Friday in mourning, not enough to mute our laughter from 12 to three. The world did indeed change when Jesus "breathed his last" (Lk 23:46); but it is a change you and I have to take to ourselves, take *into* ourselves.

You began the process in your baptism. Paul put it powerfully: "We were buried . . . with [Christ Jesus] by baptism into death, so that as Christ was raised from the dead by the glory of the Father, we too might walk in newness of life" (Rom 6:4). You feed that Christlife in each Eucharist. Jesus left no doubt on that score: Whoever "eats my flesh and drinks my blood has eternal life. . ." (Jn 6:54). You live that life when, as Vatican II urged, you "penetrate and perfect the temporal sphere with the spirit of the gospel,"[9] when you carry your Christlife wherever you labor and love, play and pray, dance and dream.

Still, I would be less than honest with you, less than Christian, if I did not stress this week what we call the "paschal mystery": Life springs most richly from death, living from dying. You see, the cross of Christ did not wither away on Calvary. The cross, a remarkable German theologian insisted, is "erected over history."[10] Crucifixion is writ large over human living. You see it from encephalitis in little ones a-borning to Alzheimer's disease in the aging; in the starving stomachs of the sub-Sahara and the stunted spirits of our own Appalachias; in two World Wars and babies blasted to bits in Belfast; in every mental ward and every vein of cocaine. You see the cross over uncounted beds of pain. And as the years fly by, you experience crucifixion ever so intimately in your own spirit and flesh. No need to spell that out.

But one thing does need spelling out. The crosses in your life—from adolescent acne through daily "installments in dying"[11] to a last tortured gasp—should not be for you simply an unfortunate by-product of human living. You dare not separate your days into "the good earth" and "the bad seed,"[12] enjoy the delights and endure or damn the disasters.

I am not asking you to *seek* for suffering—not even, like St. Teresa of Avila, to pray for "more, Lord." That can be either a high form of spirituality or a low brand of masochism. I *am* asking you to take whatever suffering comes your way—agony of flesh or anguish of spirit—and keep it from being wasted. I'm asking you to link your suffering to the passion of Christ, pin your nailed hands to his. I'm asking you to burn into your bones a sentence of St. Paul woven of mystery and love: ". . . in my flesh I complete what is lacking in Christ's afflictions for the sake of his body, that is, the Church . . ." (Col 1:24).

Only in such a vision does human suffering make Christian sense. It does not explain evil away, unmask the mystery; it simply lends a purpose to pain, transmutes sheer suffering to redemptive sacrifice. No longer are you putting up passively with what an impersonal fate prescribes. You are carrying Christ's cross to today's calvaries. Jesus is indeed our sole Redeemer; but the body that was bloodied then runs red now through the body that is his Church, his people, through your body and mine. In His unpredictable love, God has chosen to need us, to need you and me, to use us as channels of Calvary's grace. How? By word and work, of course; by your liturgy and your life; but most powerfully, by subsuming all these under the sacrament of suffering. The ultimate test? How sincerely, how utterly, can you murmur from your gethsemanes, murmur with Jesus and to your own little world, "This is my body, which is given for you" (Lk 22:19–20)?

Good friends: Holy Week is not simply history, "the week that was."[13] Holy Week is mystery, the week that is. Back then, the touch of God changed the world, changed it from a cross. This week, will Christ's cross change you—change your every dying into fresh living, change apparent tragedy into paradoxical triumph? If it does, don't be surprised if even your friends find you odd. They've rarely seen this kind of joy—rarely seen anyone flip Frisbees from a cross!

Dahlgren Chapel
Georgetown University
and
Holy Trinity Church
Washington, D.C.
March 27, 1988

EASTER

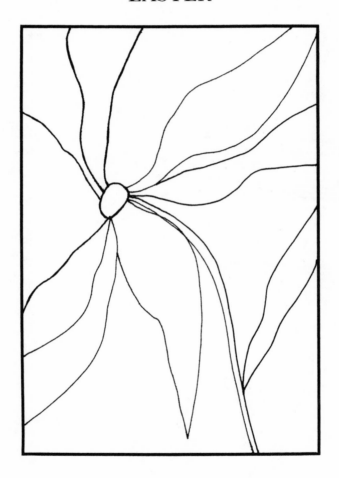

5
EASTER IS FOR EVER
Second Sunday of Easter (B)

- Acts 4:32–35
- 1 John 5:1–6
- John 20:19–31

Easter Sunday is a tough act to follow. A crucified Christ rising from the rock more alive than ever before, his risen flesh a triumphant cry: "O death, where is your victory? O death, where is your sting?" (1 Cor 15:55). A body so gloriously alive that even dear Magdalene does not recognize the love of her life until he merely murmurs "Mary" (Jn 20:16). Surely a moving meeting with his mother—not mentioned in any Gospel but, to paraphrase St. Ignatius Loyola, patent to anyone with a C-plus for intelligence.

Seven days have fled and already life seems different. All is suddenly all so ordinary. The job beckons imperiously and home life is humdrum again; professors are pushing for papers, students fingering the panic button; hunger and crack roam the streets once more. The liturgy is like it always was, and even the lilies are listless.

Utterly understandable. It does not mean that Easter was a dream, does not imply that we are back to what we were before the Son of God died for us. It does mean that the highlight on your personal computer must move a space. The stress is now not simply on Christ but more obviously on you. Precisely this is the lesson, the labor of love, today's liturgy lays on you—lays on me.

How make this real, how touch flame to it, how shape it into a song you can sing today? By plumbing the passages from Scripture that keynote today's liturgy. Three movements to my music, and in each movement a community holds center stage: (1) Jesus' own disciples, (2) the Jerusalem community after Pentecost, (3) the Christian community face to face with me now.

49

I

First then, Jesus' own disciples.[1] It is a puzzling picture John's Gospel paints. Here it is, resurrection day. John has already raced Peter to the tomb, has gone inside, has found it empty, and has told us himself "he saw and believed" (Jn 20:8). Magdalene has rushed from the rock to declare to the disciples "I have seen the Lord" (v. 18). But here they are hiding, huddled together behind locked doors, frightfully afraid. It doesn't make sense, and you'll be happy to know that Scripture scholars are as mystified as you and I.

At any rate, here they are, here in fear. Suddenly, here is Jesus too. We have no idea what that risen body looked like—a body that could pass through the barred doors of a room, as he had passed through the sealed doors of his tomb. But far more significant is what we do know of Jesus' Easter visit to his dearest friends.

First, "Peace to you" (vv. 19, 21). Not an ordinary greeting: "Hi'ya" or "Evening, boys." "Peace" assures the disciples they have nothing to fear from this uninvited guest, from this unexpected intrusion. More importantly, "peace" fulfills what Jesus promised so solemnly after the Supper: " 'Peace' is my farewell to you. My 'peace' is my gift to you, and I do not give it to you as the world gives it. Do not let your hearts be troubled, and do not be fearful. You have heard me tell you 'I am going away' and 'I am coming back to you' " (Jn 14:27–28). No wonder that "at the sight of the Lord the disciples rejoiced" (Jn 20:20). Do you remember another promise of Christ during the Last Discourse? "You are sad now; but I shall see you again, and your hearts will rejoice with a joy that no one can take from you" (Jn 16:22). In Jewish thought, peace and joy were marks of the time to come when God would bring about harmony in human life and in the world.

Second, "As the Father has sent me, so do I send you" (Jn 20:21). Disciples, those who *follow* Jesus, become apostles, those who are *sent* by Jesus. Sent to do what? To continue Christ's mission: "I came that [men and women] may have life, and have it in abundance" (Jn 10:10), in profusion, live God's life lavishly. But to carry Christ to others, the apostles need a God-given gift, the Gift of gifts. And so Jesus breathes on them: "Receive the Holy Spirit" (Jn 20:22), the Spirit he had promised their saddened souls the eve of Calvary: "When the Spirit of truth comes, He will guide you into all the truth" (Jn 16:13).

A fascinating scene, and I would love to bore you with it. But far more fascinating to me today is the sequel to that scene. Two of the Twelve were not in the bolted room when Jesus jimmied the locks. One was Judas; out of despair he had hanged himself. The other was Thomas, a disciple who endears himself to me for two reasons. On the one hand, his SAT scores in New Testament 101 were embarrassing; he had no idea what Jesus was all about. On the other hand, he loved Jesus, would do anything for him. When Jesus suggested a trip to a hostile Jerusalem lusting to stone him, the disciples were dismayed. All but Thomas: "Let us also go, that we may die with him" (Jn 11:16).

Then where was he when Jesus showed? Drowning his disappointment at a popular pub? Scuffing the dusty streets wondering how to fill his empty existence? Scripture doesn't say. But somehow the disciples got hold of him, crowded around him, shouted irrepressibly: "Man, did you screw up! While you were bugging out, we saw Jesus!" His reaction? "Unless I see in his hands the print of the nails, and place my finger in the mark of the nails, and place my hand in his side, I'll never believe it" (Jn 20:25). Harsh rhetoric indeed, but don't be too tough on Thomas. If the priests of your parish were to dash pell-mell into this sanctuary and shout "Jesus just barged into our TV room," what would *your* reaction be?

Happily, Jesus does not abandon his doubting disciple. Like the shepherd he described, the shepherd who left 99 sheep to seek the one sheep that had strayed, Jesus finds Thomas, finds him back with the rest behind locked doors. Again, how gentle of Jesus, how genial, how generous! No anger or resentment; only a unique invitation, an invitation he has tendered to no other: "Touch your fingers to my wounds. If touching is believing, then by all means touch!" For Thomas this is enough; doubt is dead; no need to touch. He proclaims the supreme profession of faith to be found in the Gospels: "My Lord and my God!" (Jn 20:28).

One profound problem here: Touching is not believing. Thomas' "cry from the heart"—the doubting disciple's "My Lord and my God!"—went far beyond the evidence. Like the eyes of the disciples on Easter eve, the fingers of Thomas could convince him that Jesus was alive and well; they could not persuade him that Jesus was his Lord and God. "No one," St. Paul proclaimed, "no one can say 'Jesus is Lord' except by the Holy Spirit" (1 Cor 12:3). At that emotional moment among the community of his disciples, Jesus could have said to Thomas what he said on a similar occasion to dear impetuous Peter: "Blessed are you. . . . For flesh and blood has not revealed this to you, but my Father who is in heaven" (Mt 16:17).

II

So much for the original community of Jesus' own disciples—disciples visited by the risen Lord, invited to witness his wounds, in one instance to finger them. There the stress was on faith. I mean the blessing of believing, the power of proclaiming, as Paul professed it, that "at the name of Jesus every knee should bend in heaven and on earth and under the earth, and every tongue confess, to the glory of God the Father: Jesus Christ is Lord!" (Phil 2:10–11).

Move now to a larger community of disciples, the Jerusalem community after Pentecost. Many of the old familiar faces are still there: Peter and John, Thomas and Matthew, the women who had followed Jesus so faithfully to Calvary itself—and, of course, his mother. But the community has mushroomed: three thousand baptized in a single day, unnumbered believers added day after day. Of these, Scripture should have startled you with that surprising sentence: "There was not a needy person among them, for as many as were possessors of lands or houses sold them, and brought the proceeds of what was sold and laid it at the apostles' feet; and distribution was made to each as any had need" (Acts 4:34–35).

No argument about it, this was a primitive form of communism. Luke's description leaves no doubt: "Now the company of those who believed were of one heart and soul, and no one said that any of the things which he possessed was his own, but they had everything in common" (Acts 4:32). You can, of course, have reservations about it. Jerusalem just after Jesus was a singular situation: a single community, relatively small, tightly knit, hardly a practical pattern for the Church once it overleaped the boundaries of its birthplace.

Argue like that and even a jesuitical type will agree. You may discount distant Jerusalem, find in it a phase doomed to fail—like the Jesuit settlements among the Guarani Indians you may have seen in the movie *The Mission*. But one clause in Luke's account you may not discount, a clause that should challenge each Christian community whatever our clime or century: "There was not a needy person among them." Challenge us because that naked fact is the prelude to a sobering theology in the Letter of James: "What does it profit, my brothers and sisters, if someone says he/she has faith but has not works? Can his/her faith save him/her? If a brother or sister is ill-clad and in lack of daily food, and one of you says to them, 'Go in peace, be warmed and filled,' without giving them the things needed for the body, what does it profit? So faith by itself, if it has no works, is dead" (Jas 2:14–17).

So, if the community that cowered in fear behind locked doors proclaimed a fundamental faith, "My Lord and my God," the community that burst those bolts to be fired by the Spirit fanned that faith into flame—a faith alive for one another: "There was not a needy person among them."

III

Those two communities lead into the Christian community face to face with me now. More accurately, the Christian community of which I am privileged to be a part. The problem, as I suggested early on, is this: How can we keep Easter alive? Must the honeymoon sink to the humdrum? Is this why we used to call today Low Sunday?

The problem is real. The response? Simple in principle, complex in the concrete. In today's technical jargon, you extend the highlight on your personal computer. How? From risen Christ to risen Christian. You still stress Christ, but no longer in solitary splendor, astride the stone that sealed his sepulcher. In mystery indeed, but no less really, you, each of you, rose in Christ, rose with Christ. That resurrection you realized in your baptism. Paul put it powerfully: "We were buried . . . with him by baptism into death, so that as Christ was raised from the dead by the glory of the Father, we too might walk in newness of life" (Rom 6:4).

Is "newness of life" too shadowy for you? Then hurry back to the first two communities. Fix your minds on faith and works, on "My Lord and my God" and "There was not a needy person among them."

First, faith. Your faith is not merely a matter of mind and memory. The Creed you will shortly confess does summarize much of what you accept on God's word: a Maker of heaven and earth, a God-man crucified and risen, a Spirit the Giver of life. But to come alive, your Creed, your faith, must move beyond brain and lips. Faith is your whole person given to God; living faith is an act of love. When Thomas cried "My Lord and my God!", he was not answering a quiz in theology. Those slender syllables were the outer shell of his heart. At that graced moment, knowledge reached its perfection. At that moment, to know was to love.

Such, I suggest, is your post-Easter task. Stir those Easter embers till they glow; stir them by touching love to sheer knowledge. If you want inspiration, thumb through Scripture, chock-full of folks whose faith was love, whose belief was alive. Abraham, leaving kin and country for only God knew where. Sarah, laughing till the tears come because she is pushing 91 and has been told she is going to have a baby. Noah, building a houseboat to ride out humanity's drowning. Moses, ferrying his people through the Red Sea as if it were Washington's Mall. The list goes on and on, till it climaxes in Jesus, dying not with experience of resurrection but only with faith in a Father who seems to have forsaken him.

Second, works. Here I have precious little to tell you. Not because there is little to tell; not because there are no needy on your street or across the seas. Rather because, once your faith comes alive, the love that quickens it will tell you where God wants you to work it out. New York's Cardinal O'Connor is at St. Clare's Hospital when a woman who has lost two children to AIDS sees a third die, and he realizes: "You're not dealing merely with a disease; you're dealing with a person." A Georgetown senior, aglow with God's love, tells me that, before she embarks on law for the poor, she must experience the poverty of Latin America.

The examples are legion, and the examples are exemplary. Still, one Pauline principle must pervade them all: You are a community, a community of Christ. However individual, however personal your service to Christ, you serve within and through a community. Keep one ear attuned to Paul: "As it is, there are many parts, yet one body. The eye cannot say to the hand, 'I have no need of you,' nor again the head to the feet, 'I have no need of you' " (1 Cor 12:20–21).

Good friends: A sparkling commercial insists "Diamonds are for ever." Not a gemmologist, I cannot comment. But this I do know: For a Christian, there is a still more enduring gem: "Easter is for ever." If . . . if your faith is fired by love, and your love thrusts you out to the needy among you, to the needy beyond you. Happy Easter!

Dahlgren Chapel
Georgetown University
and
Holy Trinity Church
Washington, D.C.
April 10, 1988

6
THE MOTHER OF ALL LIVING
Fifth and Sixth Sundays of Easter (B)

> Fifth Sunday:
> - Acts 9:26–31
> - 1 John 3:18–24
> - John 15:1–8
> Sixth Sunday:
> - Acts 10:25–26, 34–35, 44–48
> - 1 John 4:7–10
> - John 15:9–17

Each year I find Easter a strange season. Not because of what the Church positively preaches and Christians really remember. Rather because of what the Church rarely preaches and Christians apparently forget. We preach and remember so much: Jesus rising from the rock and Magdalene reaching to hold him; disciples receiving the Spirit of Jesus and Thomas demanding to touch his wounded flesh; two disciples joined by Jesus on the cheerless road to Emmaus, and Peter free-styling it to the shore where Jesus is broiling breakfast. But there is someone we seem to forget—perhaps because the Gospels speak not a syllable about her after the bloodstained murmur of Jesus to John: "Here is your mother" (Jn 19:27).

And yet, as Easter Christians, we *must* talk about her. If we do not, Easter is incomplete, May will not bud its "flower of the rarest,"[1] and even Mother's Day will commemorate only Eve as "the mother of all living" (Gen 3:20). So then, let me sing to you of Mary—in three movements: (1) Mary and Jesus; (2) Mary and Easter; (3) Mary and you.

I

I open with Mary and Jesus. Why? Because it is around our Lord that our Lady's whole life revolved. Because the moment our world began to change for ever, turn upside down, was when a messenger from God announced to a teen-age Jewess: "You will conceive in your womb and bear a son, and you shall call his name

Jesus" (Lk 1:31). From the moment Mary murmured "Let it happen to me as you say" (v. 38), Jesus was literally her life. Not that she neglected her neighbors. Soon after the angel went winging away, Mary sped perhaps 67 miles because her aging kinswoman Elizabeth was six months with child. Not that she ceased to be her own person. Listen to Mary scolding her 12-year-old runaway in the temple: "Son, why have you treated us like this? Look, your father and I have been terribly worried and have been searching for you" (Lk 2:48).[2] Listen to Luke after that rebuke: "[Jesus] went down with [Mary and Joseph] to Nazareth, and was obedient to them" (v. 51). Mary, in the tradition of good Jewish mothers, told the growing Son of God how to grow up!

When I say Jesus was our Lady's life, I mean that the child she bore in Bethlehem, the adolescent she nurtured in Nazareth, the man she freed for his journey to Jerusalem held center stage in her existence. She lived for him. And no human person, no man or woman, ever loved him as lavishly, as unselfishly, as she did.

It was dreadfully difficult, this unparalleled love. Why? Because Mary, like you and me, had to live her love on faith. The angel who announced to her that her child would be called "Son of God" (Lk 1:35) did not proceed to give her a theology of the Trinity, did not explain how this Son of God was different from all other sons of God. As Jesus had to grow in wisdom, so his mother had to learn slowly and painfully who he was, had to worry over him and wonder, had to listen to relatives screaming he was mad, watch her neighbors try to toss him over a cliff. No angel told her: "Mary dear, have no fear! No harm can come to him; his Father in heaven will see to that. Sticks and stones will never break his bones, rejection never break his heart." No angel told her he would be betrayed with a kiss, slapped and spat upon, condemned to a criminal's death, breathe his last on twin beams of wood before her very eyes. No angel consoled her on Friday: "Dry those tears, Mary: He'll be alive on Sunday."

And still, through all of this, not knowing what lay before her, not knowing what lay before her Son, Mary never took back the radical yes she had answered to an angel, had given to God: "Let it happen to me as you say." In death as in life, in his dying as well as in his living, it was always Jesus who centered her existence. At each moment from Nazareth to Calvary she lived what St. Paul would write much later: "I have been crucified with Christ; it is no longer I who live, but Christ who lives in me" (Gal 2:20).

II

All well and good, but what has Mary to do with Easter? Very simply, our Lady reveals, without words, what Easter is all about, what the paschal mystery means.

You see, Easter is not a one-man show—Jesus is alive, alleluia! Indeed he is alive; but he did not burst from the rock for his own sake, to prove something—like Houdini magically escaping from a box nailed shut. Here God's word comes through loud and clear: Jesus died *for us,* and he rose *for us.* He came alive to give us life. Not bare breath, mere muscle, sheer sinew. No, a share in God's own life. This is not empty rhetoric; God's life in you is as real, as vibrant as the blood in your veins. God's life in you is God within you: our Father, the risen Christ, his Holy Spirit.

It is because God is alive in you that you are not enslaved to sin, that you can listen when God calls and say yes, that you can love the Lord within you with all your heart and the person next to you as you love yourself. Because the risen Christ rests in you, you can carry crosses as heavy as his and still say with the Psalmist "Though I walk through the valley of deep darkness, I fear no evil, for you are with me" (Ps 23:4). Because the Holy Spirit is active in you, the God "who raised Christ Jesus from the dead will give life to your mortal bodies also" (Rom 8:11).

God alive in you now, you alive with God for ever—such is God's Easter gift. This is what we call redemption; this is the salvation Christ's dying/rising won for us. That much is hardly news to you. What may come as news is this: The most remarkable example of God's Easter giving, of the human person redeemed, is our Lady. Why do I say that? Because in our Lady we see to perfection what God's love can effect in a man or woman. At the first moment there was a Mary, God kept sin from ever touching her. A teenager, God empowered her to utter an utterly free yes to the most amazing request in human history: Conceive God's Son. From that moment till she left our earth Mary never said no to God—and that included the Way of the Cross. And now? As you sit here, our Lady lives in God's presence the way God has destined us one day to live: whole in soul *and* body, in spirit *and* flesh, her complete person a ceaseless, glorious, ecstatic yes to her Lord.

This, my friends, is Easter. And Mary is Easter in its fullness. Mary is, to perfection, what the Son of God was born to do, lived to do, died to do, rose to do.

III

So much for Mary and Jesus; so much for Mary and Easter. But what of Mary and you? Here let me speak frankly and plainly, come down to earth, your earth. Can one get to God, enter heaven, without touching Mary, without devotion to our Lady? Yes indeed. Patriarchs like Abraham did, leaders like Moses, prophets like Isaiah, holy women like Esther and Ruth, Susanna and the mother of the Maccabees. Millions of God-fearing Jews gassed in the Holocaust, children snatched from life in infancy, good Bushmen in the Kalahari desert, agnostics who follow their conscience religiously— all bear mute witness that it is possible to pass St. Peter and his pearly gates without having cuddled up to Mary.

But can *you?* I suspect you can; with God all things are possible. I simply submit: It's not a good idea, not a thoroughly Catholic "way to go." For all that only Jesus saves, Catholicism is not a me-and-Jesus religion. We who believe have been built by baptism into a community. And this community has three parts: the Church in pilgrimage on earth, the Church on tiptoe of expectation in purgatory, and the Church triumphant in heaven. This is the whole Church, the total Christ. With all these sisters and brothers you should be linked in love.

But linked in love especially with one: with Mary. For several awfully good reasons. First, because Mary is mother not only of Jesus but of his brothers and sisters as well. This is not pious pap. Good Scripture scholars will tell you that when the crucified Christ murmured "Here is your mother" (Jn 19:27), he was speaking not only to the apostle John but to all who by believing in Jesus are reborn in his image.[3] Here, good friends, is *your* mother, a mother who cares for each of you personally, a mother whose yes to an angel was a yes for you, a mother who knows what it means to be crucified, a mother who in this vast communion that reaches from earth to heaven is singularly powerful with her Son, a mother who cannot be deaf to our old familiar prayer: "Remember, O most gracious Virgin Mary, that never was it known that anyone who fled to thy protection, implored thy help, or sought thy intercession was left unaided." I am not asking you to worship Mary; that's for pious heretics. I am only asking you to say hello to your mother—a wonderful Jewish mother!

A second reason for warming up to our Lady: Mary will disclose to you, better than any theologian, the feminine side of God, the female face of God. I am not claiming that God is a woman;

divinity is neither male nor female. I *am* saying that Scripture's remarkable revelation of God as our Father has led the Christian centuries to imagine God as an austere masculine figure who dispenses justice with an iron hand, has led Christians to balance God the Father of justice with Mary the mother of mercy. No, my friends. The miracle of Mary is not that she makes God more lenient than God would like to be. Rather, in the way she lived, in the way she imaged God, in the very person she is and has always been, Mary reveals that it is God who is the Mother of mercy— caring and concerned and compassionate. She makes concrete, carries forward, what the Word of God discloses about God: In God originates all that is creative and generative of life, all that nourishes and nurtures, all that overflows with solicitude and sympathy, all we associate with mother-love.[4] Meditate long and hard on the complaint of the Israelites in Babylonian bondage: "The Lord has forsaken me, my Lord has forgotten me." The Lord's answer? "Can a woman forget her sucking child, that she should have no compassion on the son of her womb?" (Isa 49:14–15). And if you suspect jesuitical liberalism here, I refer you to Pope John Paul I (pope for only 34 days): God is not only Father but "even more so Mother, who . . . wants only to be good to us," loves us no matter how bad we are.[5]

A third reason why you should learn to love our Lady: I know no one who can lead you more surely to her Son. No statue of Mary is finished, no portrait of her complete, unless her hands are holding Jesus—at best, holding him out to you.

Finally—if none of the above grabs you—save yourself some embarrassment. Someday—tomorrow perhaps, or 50 years from now, or after a few impatient years in purgatory—you're going to *meet* your mother. Honest to God! I promise you. It would be so nice if you recognized her. Even nicer if you loved her.

> Cathedral of Mary Our Queen
> Baltimore, Maryland
> April 30 and May 1, 1988
> also
> Dahlgren Chapel
> Georgetown University
> and
> Holy Trinity Church
> Washington, D.C.
> May 8, 1988

ORDINARY TIME

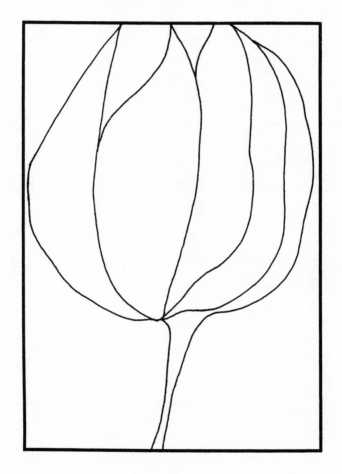

7

HELL IS NOT TO LOVE ANY MORE
Third Sunday of the Year (B)

- Jonah 3:1–5, 10
- 1 Corinthians 7:29–31
- Mark 1:14–20

One word lights up today's liturgy. Christian though it is, Christians are not overly fond of it. From Jonah through John the Baptist to Jesus and Paul, the word echoes harshly to us: "Repent!" It sounds so negative: Activate those hidden guilt feelings, calculate your peccadillos on your personal computer, renounce Satan and all his works and pomps.

Now the negative is not necessarily a no-no. If you're guilty before God, a gram of guilt is not out of order. If sin plays a large role in your life, face up to it. If Satan is playing the devil with your Christlife, bid him (or her) good-bye. But this afternoon I want to accent the positive in repentance. To repent, as the Gospel Greek has it, is to change your mind, to convert, to turn. Not simply turning *from* but, more importantly, turning *to*. Better, turning from *by* turning to. Three turnings, all linked: (1) You turn to yourself. (2) You turn to Christ. (3) You turn to others. A word on each, with a real-life story for each.

I

First, to repent is to turn to yourself, to look inside. Here a fire-and-brimstone preacher would be tempted to paint graphically the rot and corruption in the human heart. I have no gift for that, no desire. Another might tear a page from the book of Revelation, repeat the risen Christ's threat to the bishop of Laodicea: "I know your works: You are neither cold nor hot. Would that you were cold or hot! So, because you are lukewarm, and neither cold nor hot, I will spew you out of my mouth" (Rev 3:15–16). But only God has the right to speak such frightful language. I shall move away from the tepid, tell you of a red-hot Christian looking into himself. I mean that remarkable monk Thomas Merton.[1]

Aged 40, after 13 years with the Trappists, Merton had to ask himself: Should I leave? Why ask? For one thing, the cloister in Kentucky had changed chokingly: it "is as crowded as a Paris street." His old dream, to live as a hermit, tempted him ever more seductively; he needed greater freedom for private prayer, for contemplation.

But superiors would have none of this. Merton "fans" would be scandalized: his students, his readers, other religious. Trappist vocations would plummet. Merton stayed; but after a year he was still depressed, sought help in analysis, lived on the brink of a breakdown. He realized that all through his life a crucial question confronts the monk with fresh meaning and urgency: What are you doing here?

Against all the odds, Merton's inner conflict turned him outward to a world's sin and suffering, released him to a universe outside Gethsemani's gates, immersed him in passionate protest: against Vietnam and violence, against pollution, against racial injustice and nuclear war.

At 50, crisis flared up again. How live obedience when authority seems irrational? How deal with the perils and pressures of solitude? How harmonize his hermit side with his need for people and their need for him? The cost was high: stomach spasms, colitis, tensions that tied his "guts in knots of utter despair." No wonder he could write wittily to a troubled friend: "You think I got fun here? Man, you think more. You think I got no angst? Man, think again. I got angst up to the eyes."

Tempestuous years indeed. He did become confused, had to struggle with the life of a hermit, slipped in fidelity awhile. But in that decade of looking within he had grown much, discovered much. Illusions about religious life had been stripped away. He had gone through the loneliness of the desert, lost his way, found a more profound self that pervaded his final years, till he died so tragically and so young—accidentally electrocuted in Bangkok at 53—still looking for deeper and deeper identity.

And what of you? If you are not to stagnate, there are times—I cannot predict when—times when you must look within, ask yourself: What am I doing here? The problems are legion: God, work, people; church or family; desert or city. The problems will vary, depending on who you are, where you've been, where you're at. But turn inside you must, else you risk a living death, not even knowing you are dead. "Is this the way God wants me to live?" Oh, you may well answer: "Yes, by God yes! This *is* what God wants me to do, wants me to be." But you won't know that unless you look within, unless you risk discovering with Merton "I got angst up to the eyes."

II

Second, to repent is to turn to Christ. Pious pap? No, a perennial paradox: You must turn once *and* you must turn each day. Too abstract? Let me put a face on it: the man who, almost 16 centuries ago, changed the face of the Western world, laid the heritage of the old world at the feet of the new in a breathless synthesis. I mean St. Augustine.[2]

Till he was 32, Augustine was just another bright young man in tortured quest of truth and love. Born to a Christian mother but not baptized, with a superficial knowledge of Christ and Christianity, he confronted two major crises quite unprepared.

The moral crisis began at 15: "Arrived now at adolescence I . . . sank to the animal in a succession of dark lusts."[3] At 16 he came to semipagan Carthage; there "a cauldron of illicit loves leaped and boiled about me. I was not yet in love, but I was in love with love. . . ."[4] At 17 he took a mistress, lived with her for 13 years, had a son by her, surrendered her with sorrow: "My heart . . . was broken and wounded and shed blood."[5] His prayer to God? " 'Grant me chastity and continence, but not yet.' For I was afraid that you would hear my prayer too soon, and too soon would heal me. . . ."[6]

The intellectual crisis began at 18. It started with Cicero, who triggered his thirst for wisdom, whose majestic language made the simple Bible distasteful. He moved to the Persian prophet Mani, mesmerized by a free philosophy without the bridle of faith, pleasing his pride by freeing him from moral fault. Skepticism tempted him lightly. Neoplatonism captivated him. Even when he discovered what Neoplatonism could not offer, the Savior Christ and his grace, it was Augustine's intellect that was captured; his will was not completely conquered—the pull of the flesh was still too powerful.

The drama reached its climax in Milan, in a little garden.

"There I was, going mad on my way to sanity, dying on my way to life, aware how evil I was. . . ."[7] Pleasure plucked at his garment of flesh, murmuring softly: "Are you sending us away?" Torn by violent tears, he cried: "How long shall I go on saying 'tomorrow'?" Suddenly he heard a voice nearby, a sort of sing-song: "Take and read, take and read." He snatched up his Scripture, read the passage on which his eyes first fell, a passage from Paul to the Romans: ". . . not in reveling and drunkenness, not in debauchery and licentiousness, not in quarreling and jealousy; but put on the Lord Jesus Christ, and make no provision for the flesh, to gratify its desires" (Rom 13:13–14). Augustine tells us: "I had no wish to read further, and no need. For in that instant, with the very ending of the sentence, it was as though a light of utter confidence shone in all my heart, and all the darkness of uncertainty vanished away."[8] Almost nine months later, on the vigil of Easter 387, Augustine was baptized, the oil of confirmation completed his baptism, and he pillowed on his tongue the Christ he had fled "down the arches of the years."[9]

But baptism, at 33 or at birth, is only a beginning. For you as for Augustine, this radical, root turning to Christ makes a daily demand, a conversion to Christ that is constant. Ten years after his baptism Augustine had to confess that he was still wrestling with the lust of the flesh, the lust of the eyes, and the pride of life: with the memory of illicit love, the allurement of beauty sundered from Loveliness supreme, "the desire to be feared and loved by men for no other reason than the joy I get from it."[10]

Terribly true, but for you as for Augustine, turning to Christ each day is more than turning from temptation and sin. What was given you in baptism was life, a sharing in God's own life. From that moment, aware of it or not, you were a fresh creation, alive with the life of the risen Christ, empowered to know the living God and to love Him, empowered to hope against hope for a life that will never end. The Christian can proclaim with Paul: "It is no longer I who live, but Christ who lives in me; and the life I now live in the flesh I live by faith in the Son of God, who loved me and gave himself for me" (Gal 2:20).

But to stay alive in Christ, you must grow; for when you cease to grow, you begin to die. And how do you grow into Christ? Get to know him. Not a catechism Christ whom you memorize. Not simply the Christ of theology, revealed and concealed in concepts. Let him get inside of you. Listen to him thirstily as he speaks to you in his book and in his life, through his community and from his cross. Let him shake you and shiver you, tear you and strip you naked. Whatever you do, don't exile him to the edge of your existence, a shadow stalking your steps, the phantom of your opera.[11] Turn to Christ each day, if only to pray, with the father of the Gospel epileptic, "I do believe; help my unbelief" (Mk 9:24).

III

A third and final point. You see, turning to yourself and turning to Christ is not the whole story; you haven't turned quite enough. Repentance in its positive sense is not a private party—you and Jesus. You and I are part of a people, of a world for which Christ was crucified. To repent fully, we must turn to others. But again, no abstractions; only a life, a saint of the homeless and hopeless, now seven years dead. I mean Dorothy Day.

Long a Communist, Dorothy moved from Communism to Christ, from Union Square to Rome. A slow and painful journey, with strange turns in the road. She loved the Church, but "not for itself . . . it was so often a scandal" to her; she loved the Church because it made Christ visible.[12] And for Dorothy, Christ was crucifyingly visible in the poor and despised, the broken-down and the broken-hearted. For them she started houses of hospitality that spread across the country, breadlines in Depression days to feed the hungry, clothe the naked, shelter the homeless. She walked picket lines, struggled against segregation in Georgia, was jailed for supporting Mexican itinerant workers, squared off against a New York cardinal in defense of cemetery strikers. She argued passionately that "the poor do *not* have the Gospel preached to them."[13] To preach it to them, she lived with them, "with the criminal, the unbalanced, the drunken, the degraded . . . with rats, with vermin, bedbugs, roaches, lice. . . . Yes, the smell of sweat, blood, and tears spoken of so blithely by Mr. Churchill, so widely and bravely quoted by comfortable people."[14] Including me.

I am not suggesting that to repent you must mimic Dorothy Day, ape her actions—walk her picket lines, host her hospitality houses, bunk with the besotted, play the pacifist to the hilt. Here is where only Christ can summon with authority, can call with consummate conviction. But one charge I dare lay before all of you. It goes back to a spiritual reflection by Dorothy that has for title a declaration she derived from Dostoevsky: "Hell Is Not to Love Any More." It goes back to her autobiography, *The Long Loneliness,* and the note on which it closes: "We have all known the long loneliness and we have learned that the only solution is love and that *love comes with community*."[15]

Love comes with community. Indeed with community already created: a husband and wife in love, a loving family, a church committed to love, a parish pervaded by love, a campus that cares. But within and around all these is a community still to be created. I mean a community where old fears and new, old hates and new, no longer keep us from reaching out to one another, reaching out hands and hearts: black and white, the haves and the have-nots, pacifists and the Pentagon, the hale and the frail, Catholic and agnostic, somehow even prolifers and prochoicers—and yes, the AIDS-afflicted and those who see in AIDS the judgment of an angry God. But for such miracles to happen, we not only need God's generous grace. We have to turn Dorothy Day's dictum on its head. If it is true (and it is) that love comes with community, it seems equally true that community comes only with love.

How begin? Go back to Dostoevsky, back to Dorothy Day. Sear your spirit and flesh with one imaginative insight: Hell is . . . not to love any more.

Dahlgren Chapel
Georgetown University
and
Holy Trinity Church
Washington, D.C.
January 24, 1988

8
IF WE LIVE, WE LIVE TO THE LORD
Twenty-fourth Sunday of the Year (A)

- Sirach 27:30—28:7
- Romans 14:7–9
- Matthew 18:21–35

On this uncommon occasion, Sirach and Matthew are perilous passages. Their focus is on forgiveness, and I am only too aware that all of us who have lived together under the aegis of Ignatius have good reason to pray "Forgive us our trespasses. . . ."[1] This is strikingly true, I suggest, for a homilist who taught some of you, in rather despotic fashion, about the Fathers of the Church and the mother of God, and who should have been more of a model to you—not indeed in the Presley mode, but surely with the charism of Jesuits from Loyola to Arrupe.

Rather than pick at old scabs, let me fix on the text from Romans. It has an excitingly positive note, moves us from yesterday to tomorrow, reveals a vision splendidly Christian to all of us, wherever we are, whatever we've been and become. Listen to Paul once more:

> None of us lives to himself [or herself], and none of us dies to himself [or herself]. If we live, we live to the Lord, and if we die, we die to the Lord. So then, whether we live or whether we die, we are the Lord's. For to this end Christ died and lived again, that he might be Lord both of the dead and of the living.
>
> (Rom 14:7–9)

Here my hallowed three points must yield to two. Very simply, (1) Paul's words yesterday, (2) Paul's words today. Put another way, (1) Paul's appeal to yesterday's Romans, (2) Paul's appeal to today's Romans.

69

I

First, Paul's words yesterday, in the 50s of the first Christian century. Here he is, apparently in Corinth, at the peak of his powers, preparing Rome's Christians for his coming, explaining the gospel to them from the full richness of his experience of Christ, from the full maturity of his theology and spirituality. Towards the end of his letter he turns quite personal. There are Christians who are weak, and Christians who are strong. Weak in faith are those who are excessively scrupulous—about meat and wine, about fasting and the Sabbath. They have not grasped what it means to be upright in God's eyes *through faith.* In their immaturity they have to justify themselves "by additional practices that are only a form of fringe Christianity."[2] Strong in faith are those who see faith for what it actually is, who can distinguish between what is of major importance and what of minor.

How are they to interact, the weak and the strong? Engage in debate, in disputes, in ceaseless argument? No. Argument only "undermines confidence on all sides."[3] Look down one on the other, pass judgment? No. "Who are you to pass judgment?" (Rom 14:4) when "God has welcomed" (v. 3) both the weak in faith and the strong? On such matters, not of Christianity's inner core, Paul sees no evil in contradictory convictions.

Where, then, is the heart of the matter? For Paul, what counts most acutely is a Christian's motive. Whether your entrée is Caesar salad or Chateaubriand, whether your potion is Perrier or Port—it matters not, as long as what you do you do "for the Lord" (v. 6).

This is not a morality of naked intention. Paul's point is: As Christians, you Romans dare not live for yourselves. Oh yes, you have been set free by the liberating act of Christ, by his incredible cross—set free from enslavement to Sin, to Death, to Law. But set free not to serve self. Your fresh freedom enables you to live for your Lord, to serve God. Living or dying, you "are the Lord's" (v. 8), you belong to God.

That same liberating cross founds for Paul another freedom: to live not only for the Other but for others as well. Jesus died and rose again not for himself but for every man and woman from Adam to Antichrist. In Paul's pithy phrase, "Christ did not please himself" (15:3). So then, dear Romans, deal gently with one another, as Jesus is gentle with you. If you live for the Lord in scrupulous exactness, true to every jot and tittle, disdaining moral probabilism, playing it safe all the way, don't judge the free as lax, not living for the Lord. If your faith frees you from legalism, from anxiety about little things, from fear of a vengeful God, don't look down your Roman nose at the fearful, the scrupulous, the conservative. Both of you, weak and strong, must indeed live for God, as God gives you to live for Him or as your limited intelligence allows; but you must live for your sisters and brothers as well—the weak for the strong, the strong for the weak.

II

Thus far, Paul to yesterday's Romans. Now, what would our bald and bold, bowlegged and bewitching apostle say to today's Romans, specifically you and me? Christian living has grown confoundingly complex since Paul worried about circumcision and vegetarians. I do not know how he would advise a mother of ten about a hysterectomy, a childless couple on *in vitro* fertilization, the Albany legislature on Medicare for abortions. Nor is a homily quite the place to draw up a laundry list of major and minor doctrines, to specify Vatican II's "hierarchy of truths." At this moment I am far more interested in Paul's overriding principle: "None of us lives to himself [or herself], and none of us dies to himself [or herself]. If we live, we live to the Lord, and if we die, we die to the Lord. So then, whether we live or whether we die, we are the Lord's."

You and I have traveled varied roads since last we cavorted and disported in the Society of Jesus. Surely there is much that still severs us—and I doubt that the Apostle of the Gentiles would classify them all as minor. I suspect that we differ on what the Church of Christ should be and do, on how well or how ill the Society of Jesus has recognized and responded to the call of Christ. I would not be surprised if old scars have not disappeared, if some wounds are still open, if sad experiences rankle and fester. It is not unlikely that some of us are strong in faith, some weak—outside the Society and in.

Not unimportant, but at the moment not of supreme importance. What, then, *is* supremely important? Paul's crucial challenge: Set free by Christ, no longer slave to Sin and Death and Law, whom do you belong to, whom are you living for? Liberated from a life style less than liberating for you, whom now do you serve in freedom? Traveling as I do for much speaking (what some wag termed "the hoof-and-mouth disease"), I have been ceaselessly stunned, and humbled, to discover so many of you practicing more profoundly than I the centrally Christian sentence of Paul: "I have been crucified with Christ; it is no longer I who live, but Christ who lives in me; and the life I now live in the flesh I live by faith in the Son of God, who loved me and gave himself for me" (Gal 2:20). Whereas once I wept, selfishly, because your leaving diminished me, now, little by little, my tears turn to joy whenever I see that, like Paul, you have "died" only that you "might live to God" (Gal 2:19). And this amid trials and tribulations of whose depth and devastation you alone are aware.

The other side of the same coin is St. Paul's second facet of freedom in Christ: In living for the Other, are you living for others as well? "The faith that does justice" is not an in-house Jesuit prerogative. What John Paul II told the Latin American bishops at Puebla in 1979 is addressed to all who lay claim to being Catholic: "The Church has learned [in the pages of the Gospel] that its evangelizing mission has as indispensable part (como parte indispensable) action for justice and those efforts which the development of the human person demands. . . ."[4]

Not a pious platitude, to be stored simply in memory. First-rate sociologists insist that what we are experiencing today is a resurgence of late-19th-century rugged individualism, that in today's America what is of supreme importance is for me to get to the well first before it dries up, that in the last analysis the one reality that matters is myself; here is numero uno, here my ultimate responsibility.[5] To confirm that conclusion: Last year, when Harvard was celebrating its 350th birthday, its president revealed the top three goals the incoming freshmen had declared: (1) money, (2) power, (3) reputation.[6] It would not surprise me to learn that much the same goals dominate most college scenes today.

A homily does not allow for acute analysis and reasoned recommendations. Nor dare I detail what each of you in your (shall we say?) "existential situation" should do to counter the culture. But is it arrogant to suggest that far too few of us, Jesuits and former Jesuits alike, are in the forefront of the struggle for justice? This winter, as last winter, the homeless will huddle for warmth on Georgetown's grates, and I? I, like the priest in Luke's Gospel, will pass them by "on the other side" (Lk 10:31). Is it farfetched to fantasize that you and we, who share so much despite our separation, might somehow work together to make these streets on which we dance so lightly a human habitation for the hungry and the hounded and the helpless?

Frankly, I don't know. But I hope with all my heart that when we leave this chapel the words of consecration will have become our very own in a fresh sense, as all-embracing as the arms of Christ on Calvary: "This is my body . . . given for you" (Lk 22:20).

Loyola Hall Community Chapel
Fordham University
September 12, 1987

9

IN THE SHOES OF THE UNFORTUNATE
Twenty-fourth Sunday of the Year (B)

- Isaiah 50:4–9
- James 2:14–18
- Mark 8:27–35

Today's liturgy focuses on a rough human experience. So human that no human escapes it. It doesn't spare any of us—young or old, rich or poor, black or white, strong or weak, saint or sinner, Catholic or Protestant, believer or atheist. It's all around us, wherever our eyes fall, yesterday and today and tomorrow. It affects flesh and spirit, head and heart, bone and blood.

What is this experience? We call it . . . suffering. But today it is not simply suffering I want to address. I want to talk about the other side of suffering, our reaction to others' suffering. We call it . . . compassion. Literally, "suffering with." Why talk about compassion? Let me tell you why in three stages: (1) compassion and the human; (2) compassion and Christ; (3) compassion and you.

I

First, compassion and the human. Is compassion part and parcel of our humanity? If you are human, are you therefore compassionate? We like to think so. It seems so natural a reaction to human suffering. See a child struck by a speeding Saab, a blindfolded American held hostage in Lebanon, a homeless old man shivering against the winter cold, a pregnant young woman dying of leukemia—who among you would fail to feel compassion? It's instinctive, isn't it? You can't help yourself. In the face of suffering, compassion leaps forth from the very depths of human mercy.

74

Not so fast, good friends. If to be human is to be compassion-ate, then why is our world so wickedly wounded by war and hounded by hate? Why do a billion humans fall asleep hungry? Why is there such covert hostility between black and white, Muslim and Christian, the haves and the have-nots? Why do uncounted men and women feel alienated and alone? Why are we witnessing a resurgence of 19th-century rugged individualism, where the race is to the swift and the savage, and the devil take the hindmost? And how do you make human sense of the Jewish Holocaust, of South African apartheid, of Northern Ireland?

Go back to the word "compassion." It means that I "suffer with" another. A grief that afflicts you afflicts me; what burns you burns me.

> Compassion asks us to go where it hurts, to enter into places of pain, to share in brokenness, fear, confusion, and anguish. Com-passion challenges us to cry out with those in misery, to mourn with those who are lonely, to weep with those in tears. Compas-sion requires us to be weak with the weak, vulnerable with the vulnerable, and powerless with the powerless. . . .[1]

Is it surprising, then, that some see compassion as masochism, the compassionate person as abnormal? Be not surprised to hear that a compassionate society is a sick society. Listen to an article in *Harpers:*

> A genuine compassionate society, one that has succeeded in achieving the ideal of actually putting itself in the shoes of the unfortunate, will soon find itself marching in the direction of collective solutions inimical to individual freedom. . . . There is a real and awful danger of people actually beginning to identify with the world of suffering. . . . No healthy society should allow itself to see the world through the eyes of the unfortunate. . . .[2]

Along similar lines, three authors of a book on compassion[3] visited a caring Senator, the late Hubert Humphrey, to ask him about compassion in politics. Senator Humphrey picked up a long pencil with a small eraser at its end and said:

> Gentlemen, look at this pencil. Just as the eraser is only a very small part of this pencil and is used only when you make a mistake, so compassion is only called upon when things get out of hand. The main part of life is competition, only the eraser is

compassion. It is sad to say, gentlemen, but in politics compassion is just part of the competition.[4]

A pungent question for Christians: Is this your vision of reality: competition the pencil, compassion the eraser? From a sheerly natural standpoint the arguments in its favor are not easily dismissed. To confront the issue as Christians, you must look elsewhere. You must look to a perspective pithily put by the Son of God become one of us out of infinite compassion: "Be compassionate as your Father is compassionate" (Lk 6:36). Hence my second point.

II

If you take Scripture seriously, you will soon realize that our God is not some cold, distant, unapproachable Creator who got the world going and then left us to our own devices, to our own folly. Our God is the God of the Old Testament Psalms:

> The Lord is merciful and gracious,
>   slow to anger and abounding in steadfast love.
> He does not deal with us according to our sins,
>   nor requite us according to our iniquities.
> For as the heavens are high above the earth,
>   so great is His steadfast love. . . .
> As a father has compassion on his children,
>   so the Lord has compassion on those who fear Him.
>   (Ps 103:8–13)

This is the loving Lord who proclaimed to an Israel that felt Godforsaken, felt forgotten by God: "Can a woman forget her sucking child, that she should have no compassion on the son of her womb? Even these may forget, yet I will not forget you. Behold, I have graven you on the palms of my hands" (Isa 49:15–16).

In Jesus God's compassion took flesh. You see, Jesus is not just a remarkably compassionate man. He is, in Scripture's stark summary, "God with us" (Mt 1:23). God . . . with . . . us. In him God enters history as a suffering God, a God who wore our weakness, felt our fear, swallowed our caustic cup of rejection and loneliness. The compassion of Jesus is not a virtue he plucked now and again from a pigeonhole and applied to a needy case. For Jesus, compassion is not the eraser on the end of the pencil that is competition.

The whole package—pencil and eraser—is compassion. In Jesus, compassion is a synonym for incarnation. He lived as we live, died more cruelly than most of us die. Why? Because he wanted not only to know as God knows but to *experience* in our flesh what men and women go through each day—experience our joy and our hurt, our agony and our ecstasy. Only in this way could the Son of God *feel* what we feel, as we feel it.

> Here we see what compassion means. It is not a bending toward the underprivileged from a privileged position; it is not a reaching out from on high to those who are less fortunate below; it is not a gesture of sympathy or pity for those who fail to make it in the upward pull. On the contrary, compassion means going directly to those people and places where suffering is most acute and building a home there. God's compassion is total, absolute, unconditional, without reservation. It is the compassion of the one who keeps going to the most forgotten corners of the world, and who cannot rest as long as he knows that there are still human beings with tears in their eyes. It is the compassion of a God who does not merely act as a servant, but whose servanthood is a direct expression of his divinity.[5]

In one sense Hubert Humphrey may have had a point without knowing it: "compassion is only called upon when things get out of hand." What prompted the compassion of Christ was that things had gotten totally out of hand. After Eden the whole world, every human being, was out of kilter. But Jesus' compassion was not simply the patchwork the Senator had in mind. The Incarnation was not a band-aid project. Jesus came to heal the whole human condition, shape a new creation, men and women who could cry with St. Paul: "I have been crucified with Christ; it is no longer I who live, but Christ who lives in me" (Gal 3:20). The compassion of Christ was not sheer feeling. For him, to feel was to heal; and to heal was to turn humanity on its head, to transform the body of Adam into the body of Christ.

III

The compassion of Christ leads directly into my third point: compassion and you. To some extent, many of you exemplify, or will exemplify, Humphrey's crunch. You are caught between the rock and the hard place: inescapably involved in competition, yet profoundly committed to compassion. The article I quoted from *Harpers* warned you against putting yourself "in the shoes of the unfortunate," warned you, for the health of our society, not "to see the world through the eyes of the unfortunate." I acknowledge the danger if . . . if that is all you ever do with your feet and your eyes. A shoe that simply pinches, a tunnel vision—these can distort your sense of human living. This I do not commend. On the other hand, never to wear the footwear of the unfortunate, to look at life only through rose-colored glasses—this may well be destructive. It makes for two societies: the haves and the have-nots. It keeps you from being profoundly Christian, for it isolates you from the mind of Christ, who identified especially with the sick and the poor and the sinful: with Peter's fevered mother-in-law, with Lazarus begging for the crumbs of the wealthy, with a woman taken in adultery.

I cannot tell you how to wed compassion to competition. Here your concrete situation, your profound reflection, and your ear cocked to what Christ might be concocting for you—here are your richest resources for specific activity, not the abstractions of an aged theologian, and a Jesuit at that! Let me end, however, with a story that should stimulate your compassion.

This past June, in Nashville, an Anglican minister from San Francisco addressed the Catholic Health Association. To an audience that often wept openly Canon William Barcus said:

> I stand here with you—as a brother to you, a churchman, a man with AIDS. A man who regrets nothing of the love and goodness he has known, who stops now to notice flowers, children at play. . . . A man who loves his church from his heart, from every molecule in him.

In the course of his address Canon Barcus recalled a 1944 photo essay in *Life* magazine.

> It was about the red foxes of Holmes County, Ohio, who lived in the woods and ate mostly mice and crickets, but sometimes also chicken and quail. This, the story explained, "made the brave men of Holmes County angry because they wanted to kill the quail themselves." So one Saturday about 600 men and women and their children got together and formed a big circle five miles across. They all carried sticks and started walking through the woods and fields, yelling and baying to frighten the foxes, young and old, out of their holes. Inside this diminishing circle the foxes ran to and fro, tired and frightened. Sometimes a fox would, in its anger, dare to snarl back, and it would be killed on

the spot for its temerity. Sometimes one would stop in its anguish and try to lick the hand of its tormenter. It too would be killed.

Sometimes, the photo showed, other foxes would stop and stay with their own wounded and dying. Finally, as the circle came closer together, down to a few yards across, the remaining foxes went to the center and lay down inside, for they knew not what else to do. But the men and the women knew what to do. They hit these dying wounded with their clubs until they were dead, or they showed their children how to do it. This is a true story. *Life* reported and photographed it. It happened for years in Holmes County every weekend. . . .

I stand before you today [Barcus continued] as one weary of running, as one wounded myself, and I say to the churches, the churches first, and then to the government, the silent government, and then to the world: "What have you done to my people? What have you done to your own people—beautiful people. . . ?"

My people are being destroyed, and your people, and all our people together. Not only by an illness called AIDS, but by a darker illness called hatred. . . . The Christ, Jesus, the compassionate lord of life and lord of more forgiveness and lord of more hope is the one we have vowed to follow and be ultimatedly guided by. We must tell that to our smugly self-righteous brothers and sisters. . . . For if we do not, their souls will perish in the circle of misunderstanding and scorn they teach so many as they club and scream their disdain for the outsider, the misunderstood, the different. . . . Sadly, too many . . . with AIDS have wondered if they had any alternative but to go to the center of the circle and lie down and die. Where are you in that circle? Where are we? Where would Christ be? . . .

For all of us within an awakening church . . . I say to the world, "Help us. Join us." To you as church . . . I say from long despairing peoples of all kinds, "Help us. Please help us. Be the gospel alive!"[6]

Dahlgren Chapel
Georgetown University
and
Holy Trinity Church
Washington, D.C.
September 11, 1988
also
Academy of Homiletics
Drew University
Madison, New Jersey
December 2, 1988

10
MY WAYS ARE NOT YOUR WAYS
Twenty-fifth Sunday of the Year (A)

- Isaiah 55:6–9
- Philippians 1:20–24, 27
- Matthew 20:1–16

Ten minutes ago you listened to a passage from a prophet. As you listened, were you as troubled by the text as I am? Addressing His favorite people exiled far from Palestine, the Lord declares to them:

> My thoughts are not your thoughts,
>   neither are your ways my ways. . . .
> For as the heavens are higher than the earth,
>   so are my ways higher than your ways
>   and my thoughts [higher] than your thoughts.
> (Isa 55:8–9)

Lovely poetry, isn't it, utterly understandable? Of course God's ways are loftier than mine, God's thoughts more exalted than mine. After all, God is God, and I . . . I am a creature of earth, dreadfully limited in the thoughts I can think and the ways I can walk. Why make a federal case out of it? "Where's the beef?"

The problem surges up, ansgt arises, when you take Isaiah out of outer space, see God's poetry in its grim realism. To achieve that, let me do three things. First, I shall sketch the ways of God with the people of His predilection, the men and women of His singular love. Second, I shall ask how these "ways of God" fit with what we know of our God. Third, I shall muse a few moments on what all this might say to you and to me. Put another way, I shall move (1) from Scripture (2) through theology (3) to contemporary living.

I

First, the ways of God with the people of His preference. Thumb through Scripture. What sort of people did God first select as His favored flock, specially dear to Him, destined one day to give the world its Savior? Not a people of high culture, of *haute cuisine*. He chose a motley mob of unruly, runaway slaves, culturally undistinguished, frequently unfaithful, unpredictable, unreliable. How did God deal with these Hebrews He loved so passionately? He let them be led away in chains: into Egypt to slave under harsh taskmasters, into Babylon while their city was wasted and their temple destroyed. To Abraham, father of our faith, God promised a progeny without end, yet He commanded Abraham to slit his own son's throat in sacrifice. His faithful servant Moses had led God's people free of Pharaoh, through the Red Sea and the deadly desert, yet for a single act of faithlessness God barred him from the Promised Land: "You shall see the land before you, but you shall not go there" (Deut 32:52). When King David sinned with Bathsheba and murdered her husband, God forgave David, let him live, but . . . "the child that is born to you shall die" (2 Sam 12:14). Job, Scripture assures us, was "blameless and upright, feared God and turned away from evil" (Job 1:1), yet God allowed Satan to destroy his cattle and house and servants, his sons and daughters, allowed Satan to afflict him with a disease that never stopped hurting, murdered sleep, made him ugly to look at, so that Job from a community dump "cursed the day he was born" (3:1) and his dear, dear wife urged him "Curse God, and die" (2:9).

Had enough? Then turn to the New Testament, to the God of Jesus. Thumb through the parables, the paradoxes, the puzzles. To whom does Jesus liken his Father? To an employer who gives the very same pay to those who have worked a single hour and to those who have sweated a whole day. To an unjust judge who reluctantly gives a woman justice not because she deserves it but because she is making a damned nuisance of herself. To a miserly woman who scrapes the floor furiously because she has lost . . . a penny. Jesus' God enriches those who are already rich and snatches from the poor the pittance they possess. He lets the uncounted moral folk fend for themselves while He goes off looking for a single stray. He is "hell on wheels" to those who observe all 613 precepts of the law, but forgives prostitutes who swing by and simply say "Sorry, chum." A final surprise: Jesus gives divine approval to a dishonest manager who cuts his losses with some shrewd "insider trading."

Even if you understand all that, you will never begin to understand a God who loved you so lavishly that, to save you from sin and death, He had His own divine Son borrow your flesh from a teenage virgin and touch our scarred earth in a stable. Never begin to understand a God who loved you so prodigally that He turned a deaf ear to His Son's tearful cry, "Father, don't let me die!" (Lk 22:42). Never begin to understand a God who loved you so mysteriously that He allowed Roman soldiers to lash His Son with whips, crown his head with thorns, tie him to a criminal's tree till his heart could take no more. It's not the way you and I would have saved the world—not if *we* were God almighty, all-powerful.

No, God's thoughts are not our thoughts; God's ways are not our ways.

II

This raises my second point: How do these "ways of God" we encounter in the Word of God fit what we know of our God from centuries of research and reflection, from the ink and blood of our theology? The trouble is, most of us humans make God over into our own image. If God is Father or Mother, God must be a wondrous wedding of Bill Cosby and Mother Teresa, of Thomas More and Queen Victoria, of Ward and June Cleaver,[1] with an assist from 99-year-old Alf Landon. This is to turn reality on its head. When God is revealed to us as Father, it is not because He resembles the best fathers we know, not because He is modeled on human parents. It is God who is the model of all parenting, Parent par excellence.

True indeed, but it solves very little; if anything, it compounds our problem. It reminds me of a story told about that remarkable mystic and activist St. Teresa of Avila. As the story runs, Teresa was having a particularly hard time, experiencing an abnormal amount of anguish. Free with God as she was, Teresa complained in no uncertain terms: "How can you treat me this way?" God's response: "I treat all my friends that way." Teresa's retort: "No wonder you have so few!"

Because we are human, we can only think of God with very human thoughts, can only speak of God with stuttering syllables. And in large measure what most of us think and say about God is influenced, inspired, by our day-to-day experiences. On the grim side, the death of a dear one in a crib, in a car, of cancer; starvation in the sub-Sahara; war in Vietnam; Down's syndrome and multiple sclerosis; six million Jews gassed to death. And, perhaps just as powerful, the good things that happen to us: the miracle of a new birth or the gift of a long life; the love in a beloved's eyes or the joy in the life of the mind; friends who care deeply for you or work that pleasures you; prayers answered or hopes realized; rock 'n' roll or Handel's *Messiah*.

What theology tells us, and our faith confirms, is that in bad times as well as in good, in sickness no less than in health, in death as in life, God is there—and this God who is there is, has to be, a God of love, a God who loves you individually, a God who loves you despite your infidelities, a God who loves you even if you cannot understand how a loving God can let this or that happen.

For all our intellectual sweat, we have not solved the problem of evil. Why not? Because our minds, however brilliant, are too impotent to grasp our God. After half a century given almost totally to theology, I have gathered some fragments of the reality that is God. Precious fragments—and still God remains Mystery. For all that Jesus has revealed to us about his Father, about himself, about his Holy Spirit—and without it we would be groping in darkness—my intellect has only grazed our hidden God. And one of the deepest of divine secrets is the answer to the endless question "Why?" Why, dear God, did you let this happen? From the primeval rebellion in Eden, through the exiles of His people and the crucifixion of His Son, to two World Wars and the cancerous deaths of my father and only brother within three weeks of each other, I keep asking "Why?" and I can only tell you I do not know. What alone I know, what above all destroys despair and keeps hope burning brightly, is this: A God who gave His own Son to a crimson cross *for me* must remain a God of love through all my crucifixions and all the crosses erected over history.

III

This raises my third point: What might all this say to you and me, to contemporary living? Let me jet back to Job.[2] His is a fascinating story, crucial for a Christian spirituality, a spirituality of the cross. Job cannot credit the conviction of his friends: You must be suffering for your sins, else God is unjust. Job knows the accusation is absurd: He has never dealt in adultery or deceit, never been grasping or unjust. He has lived God's law as scrupulously as a human being can. How, then, can God treat him so harshly?

In Job's ceaseless wrestling there are two magnificent moments. The first is Job's act of faith, of trust. God has not really changed; He still cares. If Job's sufferings make no human sense, God has His own good reasons. But Job is still dreadfully desolate. He trusts God, but he cannot "get through" to God. The God who was once wonderfully present to him, this same God he can only experience as absent.

The second magnificent moment: God speaks to Job. He shows Himself to this tormented believer, this man who has demanded that God justify His ways. God speaks to him. But not to explain what He has done to Job, not to supply a theology of suffering. The real experience is simply the encounter: God lets Job find Him. And in the encounter Job finds rest from his wrestling. Not because he understands; no explanation has been given. Very simply, he has experienced God.

Here is a lesson it took me long to learn. There is a gigantic gulf between knowing *about* God and knowing God. Both are indeed good. The lifetime I have lavished on what God has told us *about* God—from the burning bush in Midian through the enfleshing of His Son to the signs of today's times—I treasure every moment of it, the near despair and the ecstasy of discovery. For, to quote a remarkable French theologian-in-a-wheelchair, "As for me, I want to gather up every small fragment of truth, wherever it is to be found, with the same care that I would use in picking up a tiny piece of a consecrated host."[3]

Admirable for theology, not quite enough for Christian living. For all I know *about* God, do I really know God? Can I say, like Ignatius Loyola, that I have truly encountered God, the living and true God? Can I say that I know God Himself, not simply human words that describe Him? Does the Father, His Christ, Their Spirit come through to me as real persons, real to me as you are?

How achieve this? There is no infallible formula, like Anacin or Rolaids. God speaks in a thousand ways: to Moses the "thunder" on Sinai (Exod 19:19), to Elijah the "still small voice" on Horeb (1 Kgs 19:12); the Word of the Lord from a pulpit, the flesh of the Lord on your palm; the faith of a friend, the despair of a dear one; an accident that shivers you, years of quiet fidelity. Naked genius will not do it; sheer intellect can get in the way. I recall the simple farmer who would drop into the village church each afternoon after work and simply kneel there. A friend who saw him questioned him in curiosity: "What do you say to God, and what does He say to you?" His reply: "I don't say anything, to Him, and He doesn't say anything to me. I just look at Him, and He just looks at me."

From such encounter comes love. And without love you are dead. But you will not love God because you have studied Him; you will love Him if you have touched Him—if He has touched you. The questions will not vanish; the "Why?" will not wear away. But, as with Job, within your "Why?" will be a profound peace. Not because the answers are now there for you to see. Rather because, as with St. Thomas Aquinas, theology must ultimately yield to adoration, and in the striking words of his Eucharistic hymn you too will sing:

> Godhead here in hiding, whom I do adore
> Masked by these bare shadows, shape and nothing more.
> See, Lord, at thy service low lies here a heart
> Lost, all lost in wonder, at the God thou art.[4]

Dahlgren Chapel
Georgetown University
and
Holy Trinity Church
Washington, D.C.
September 20, 1987

11
LAST OF ALL, SERVANT OF ALL
Twenty-fifth Sunday of the Year (B)

- Wisdom 2:12, 17–20
- James 3:16—4:3
- Mark 9:30–37

Young friends in Christ: Today's Gospel hides a sleeper. I mean, a single word that is supremely significant but could easily escape your ears. The most important word you heard this evening is a slender word: "If anyone would be first, he or she must be last of all and servant of all" (Mk 9:35). Servant. It didn't turn you on? Little wonder. Automatically we associate servant with low income and menial labor, with Topsy in *Uncle Tom's Cabin* or the old-time maid in apron and minicap, with the indentured servant in the colonies. My thesis is, "servant" is a synonym for "Christian." Let me unfold that theme in three swift stages: (1) A fact: You are already servants. (2) A theology: To serve is to image Christ. (3) A hope: May you always be servants.

I

First, a fact. Some of you are already servants, right here at the University of Richmond. I do not mean that you bow abjectly before authority, from president through faculty to campus minister. That could be not service but slavery. I mean rather a kind of service that impresses me mightily: Many of you give yourselves—your time and your energy, your head and your heart, your creativity and your compassion—to those who need you.

The examples are too numerous to mention all. Some of you serve at Freedom House, where you hear Jesus himself say: "I was hungry and you gave me food, I was thirsty and you gave me drink" (Mt 25:35). Some of you are Big Brothers or Big Sisters, aware of Jesus' remarkable assertion: "Whoever receives one such child in my name receives me" (Mt 18:5). Some of you tutor refugees who have watered Vietnam and Cambodia with their tears, for you believe what Jesus declared: "I was a stranger and you welcomed me" (Mt 25:35). Some of you serve others in worship: In profound humility you proclaim God's Word to His people, grace their palms or tongues with the blood of Christ, make music to the Lord.

II

These are sheer facts—impressive indeed, but in isolation mere facts. What impresses me even more than the facts is their Christian context—what I call theology. For you, to serve is to image Christ. It goes back to what Jesus said to his apostles: "[I] came not to be served but to serve"—in fact, "to give [my] life as a ransom for many" (Mt 20:28). Why else, do you think, did the only Son of God choose to be born of a teen-age Jewish girl in a stable? Why did God-in-flesh walk the roads of Palestine for three years healing the sick and raising the dead? Why did he make friends with prostitutes and the poor, with sinners and outcasts? Why did he let his enemies beat his back with whips, crown his head with thorns, nail him between two robbers, curse him till he gasped his life away? Because he loved every man and woman he had fashioned in his image; because he wanted to experience what he knew they were going through; because he cared—cared enough to live for others and to die for them. Because without his caring the whole world would literally have gone to hell.

Note especially that Jesus was a *suffering* servant—along the lines of the suffering servant so movingly portrayed by Isaiah: "He was despised and rejected by men, a man of sorrows, and acquainted with grief; and as one from whom men hide their faces he was despised, and we esteemed him not" (Isa 53:3).

Your role as Christians is to play the compassionate Christ wherever you live and move and have your being. To be a Christian, it is not enough to believe, to repeat the Creed each Sunday. The New Testament Letter of James is brutally clear on that score: "You believe that God is one; you do well. [But] even the demons believe—and they shudder in fear" (Jas 2:19). What else does God want? The same letter tells you graphically: "What does it profit, my brothers and sisters, if someone says he or she has faith but has not works? Can faith save him or her? If a brother or sister is ill-clad and lacks daily food, and one of you says to them, 'Go in peace, be warmed and filled,' without giving them the things needed for the body, what does it profit? So faith by itself, if it has no works, is dead" (Jas 2:14–17).

When you exit this Eucharist, you do not exit alone. You exit *with* Christ *for* others. Outside this chapel is a whole little world that needs you with your Christ. Your campus, like all campuses, teems with tensions, is a mélange of emotions: Teen-agers and young adults are weeping silent tears or flipping Frisbees gaily to the wind, are skiing high on love or worried sick over trouble at home, affection unrequited, the great grade rush. So many are just terribly lonely. And outside your gates are men, women, and children whose problems put the soap operas to shame, make "The Young and the Restless" seem tame.[1] You need not search with a spyglass; all you need is your naked eye—and a heart that cares.

III

This theology leads into my third point: my hope for you. You see, you will not cease to be servants when at last you clutch your diploma. Service at UR is indeed real, but in a sense it is good practice—an apprenticeship for the years ahead. For you, living itself should spell service. Service is not something you will leave to clergy types and social workers. Wherever you go, whatever you enter—classroom or operating room, counting house or Senate chamber, law court or board room, genetics lab or Op-Ed page, C.I.A. or NBC, wheresoever—you are to be servants by Christian vocation.

This is not pious pap, Jesuit exaggeration. Yours is an awesome responsibility. Only you, the laity, can play Christ day by day in every acre of God's earth. Not by preaching; not by changing law into gospel, medicine into faith healing, economics into a Christian calculus. Rather, by being the best that you can be, a wondrous wedding of technical competence and Christian compassion. By realizing that, despite the denial of killer Cain, you are indeed your "brother's keeper" (Gen 4:9), your sister's keeper. By affirming with your life that you are proud to bear the name "servant," even "suffering servant," for the sake of the other, of the less privileged and the downtrodden, of those the world despises as its refuse and its scum.

Let me end with one example. Two months ago, *Time* magazine ran an ethics article on what it called the NIMBY syndrome.[2] NIMBY is an acronym for Not in My Back Yard. It's a form of antisocial activism. Today you have more and more people who cannot care for themselves: "more homeless, more AIDS victims, more drug addicts, more prisoners, more garbage, more toxic waste."[3] Everyone admits, we have to take care of these. "But," as New York City's Mayor Edward Koch complained, "when you need a facility, they say, 'Not in my backyard.' "[4] Or, as some suggested about a proposed drug-treatment center, "Put it in Nancy Reagan's backyard!"[5]

Not only that. NIMBY has sparked violence. A foster home for infants is burned down; Molotov cocktails are hurled at homeless squatters; homes for the mentally handicapped are torched.

I am not suggesting a solution. The issues are complex: at times racial, but also political and economic, class conflict and understandable fear. I am simply insisting that your post-UR life will have to confront this type of dilemma—not only fiscal but ethical: "Who should bear the burden of the common good?"[6] The answers will not come easily; private right and common good are not swiftly reconciled. I simply submit that in such social conflicts you can play a creative role. In this age of rugged individualism you can highlight the role of servant. What would Christ have done? What is a suffering servant to do?

Good young friends: My hopes for your future as Christlike servants are high. But, a realistic warning: Don't wait for that future. Start serving now. Start serving here.

University of Richmond
Richmond, Va.
September 18, 1988

12
GODHEAD HERE IN HIDING
Twenty-eighth Sunday of the Year (A)

- Isaiah 25:6–10
- Philippians 4:12–14, 19–20
- Matthew 22:1–14

Today Isaiah intrigues me, and Matthew mesmerizes me. Why? Because each in his own way focuses on food, emphasizes eating. Not Domino's pizza, but a multicourse meal, a veritable belly stretcher. To describe God's kingdom to come, Isaiah imagines the Lord God gathering people from all nations and climes, from every race and walk of life, gathering them on top of Mount Zion for a sumptuous banquet, "a feast of fat things full of marrow, a feast of wine on the lees well refined" (Isa 25:6). Matthew compares God's kingdom to a marriage feast fit for a king's son. Old and young are invited, rich and poor, the happy and the sad, the good and the bad. Catered, of course, by Sutton Place Gourmet.[1]

Intrigued though I am, I shall not speak of a feast in the far future. I shall focus on a fabulous food here and now, a feasting that is our present pledge and promise of the banquet eternal. I do so because I have a three-tiered thesis about the Catholic Church. (1) The Mass, the Eucharist, is Catholicism in miniature. (2) The Mass, the Eucharist, is your community at its most Catholic. (3) The Mass, the Eucharist, provides a singular link between Catholic and catholic. A word of explanation on each of those affirmations.[2]

I

First, the Mass is Catholicism in miniature. Here, if anywhere, the Church Catholic comes together. Oh yes, we come together for much else: a lecture, a prolife rally, a protest against apartheid, a

90

reconciliation service. But the Eucharist is unique. Here alone the whole Catholic world gathers as one—ideally, all nine hundred million of us.[3]

It did not begin yesterday. It began one enchanted evening when Jesus told his special friends: "Do this in remembrance of me" (Lk 22:20). A remarkable liturgical scholar, Dom Gregory Dix, has described the effect of that command in rapturous phrases:

> Was ever another command so obeyed? For century after century, spreading slowly to every continent and country and among every race on earth, this action has been done, in every conceivable human circumstance, for every conceivable human need from infancy and before it to extreme old age and after it, from the pinnacles of earthly greatness to the refuge of fugitives in the caves and dens of the earth. Men have found no better thing than this to do for kings in their crowning and for criminals going to the scaffold; for armies in triumph or for a bride and bridegroom in a little country church; for the proclamation of a dogma or for a good crop of wheat; for the wisdom of the Parliament of a mighty nation or for a sick old woman afraid to die; for a schoolboy sitting an examination or for Columbus setting out to discover America; . . . because the Turk was at the gates of Vienna . . . on the beach at Dunkirk; . . . tremulously, by an old monk on the fiftieth anniversary of his vows; furtively, by an exiled bishop who had hewn timber all day in a prison camp near Murmansk; gorgeously, for the canonisation of S. Joan of Arc. . . . And best of all, week by week and month by month, on a hundred thousand successive Sundays, faithfully, unfailingly, across all the parishes of christendom, the pastors have done this just to *make* the holy common people of God.[4]

Indeed the Mass "makes" the Catholic people of God, shapes a community of Christ as nothing else Catholic can—neither letter nor law, neither catechism nor creed. For in the Mass the risen Christ, gloriously alive, is present in ways that take our Christian breath away. First, he is here when the faithful come in out of "the world." Already here—and not simply tented behind a veil. Already here because two or three, two or three hundred, two or three thousand are gathering in his name. Second, he is here when his word is proclaimed—when Moses blesses his people and Jeremiah trumpets his woes, when Luke announces God-born-of-woman and Paul preaches Christ crucified and risen. For, as the Second Vatican Council declared, "it is [Christ] himself who speaks when the holy Scriptures are read in the church."[5]

Third, the Mass fashions community uniquely through bread transformed. St. Paul put it pungently: "Because there is one bread, we who are many are one body, for we all partake of the one bread" (1 Cor 10:17). A unique bread. We can look upon a brittle wafer cradled in our fragile hands, and know that we are eyeing the swaddling clothes of God-made-man. We can touch the helpless Host, and feel that we are handling the hem of God's garment. We can taste the flavor of bread, and thrill that not bread but God-in-flesh is our food. A food that paradoxically is not changed into us; we are changed into Christ. In the felicitous phrase of Pius XII, "If you have received worthily, you are what you have received."

A unique bread, to shape a singular people. Simply because the Christ of the Eucharist is always one and the same Christ. For the Lord who locks himself in the tabernacle of my body is none other than the Lord who nourishes the child at home and the soldier overseas, the same Christ who feeds the Filipino, the African, and the Czech, the Italian, the Chinese, and the Swiss. Christ is not divided, not multiplied. There is not one body for me, another for my neighbor; one Christ who is my cuisine, another Christ the cuisine of Koreans. No, one and the same bread, one and the same body, one identical Christ for all.

Theologians have wrestled for centuries with four deathless words of a God-man destined to die: "This is my body" (Lk 22:19). We have delved into their depths unto frustration and contradiction, have spilt ink over them and even blood. Without surrendering the quest, we do best when in wearied rest we bend our minds and hearts with the simplest of the faith-full and sing full-throated to a hidden God as theologian Thomas Aquinas did:

> Godhead here in hiding, whom I do adore
> Masked by these bare shadows, shape and nothing more.
> See, Lord, at thy service low lies here a heart
> Lost, all lost in wonder, at the God thou art.[6]

II

If the Mass is Catholicism in miniature, the Mass is your community at its most Catholic. Fanciful? Not really. Oh yes, you do much else that is reasonably, arguably, persuasively Catholic. You struggle to understand a God whose ways are not our ways; with Jewish-Christian relations at times terribly tense; with divine revelation and our human response; with Christian marriage and pre-marital sex; with the assault on the womb and woman's rights; with legitimate authority and personal conscience. You try in your jobs, as Vatican II urged, "to penetrate and perfect the temporal sphere with the spirit of the gospel."[7]

But when the work week winds down and the weekend beckons, most of each Catholic community move to a Sabbath rest. "Rest" not as inactivity but in the sense of something different, restful, restorative. It does not exclude the liturgy that is Redskins football, 18 holes of frustration over an unco-operative Titleist, the wind in your face on the Chesapeake, parties and pubs, the Bolshoi or Rambo or Roxanne.[8] But in the midst of it all or at the end, you look to a pause that refreshes as no other, to a space where Spirit and spirit are freer to breathe and take wing. Oh I know, you discover the divine, as I do, wherever God's creative fingers have rested. You encounter God, knowingly or not, in every act of contemplation—what Carmelite William McNamara defined as "a long loving look at the real": as a solitary lark breaks the stillness of the dawn, as Potomac waters flow through your fingers, as a star streaks through a wintry sky, as a smile parts tender lips. Still, most move out to four-walled shrines, enclosed spaces where the covenant Christ struck with his blood is breathlessly recaptured—in symbol and song, in "the Word of the Lord" and a word from His unprofitable servant, in the flicker of a lamp and the clasp of a hand, in broken bread and ruddy wine overshadowed by the Spirit. And as you stream out into sunlight or dusk or deep darkness, with the Eucharistic Christ in your very marrow, some surely have grasped ever more richly the captivating couplet of John Donne:

'Twas much, that man was made like God before,
But that God should be made like man, much more.[9]

Do all Catholics discover such Sabbath rest? Hardly. We are still a pilgrim people, and some of our pilgrims march more slowly, march in different directions, march to a different drummer, or do not march at all. Some have been horribly hurt by Catholics who should care; others find less human love in Dahlgren than in the Dubliner, less of God's touch in Trinity parish than in Lafayette Park. Despite such distress, the deep spirituality within your community thrills me. Such profound oneness with a God you love above all else and with sisters and brothers you prize as images of God has to be grounded in the Eucharistic center of Catholic existence. It stems in large measure from a graced people that gathers each Sunday across the world in a single glorious act of community worship. It stems in some measure from a word of the Lord that can be grace-full even when, as with Balaam's beast, the Lord speaks through the mouth of an ass (cf. Num 22:28). It stems in incomparable measure from the sacramental presence of the risen Christ pillowed in your palms, nestling on your tongues, burning in your bodies.

Yes indeed, right here your community is at its most Catholic.

III

So far I have been parochially Catholic. Is the "C" all that provincial? Does a community whose heartblood is the Mass offer more than token tolerance to the larger world that does not share your Eucharist? In consequence, my third affirmation: The Mass provides a singular link between Catholic and catholic. It is precisely your Catholicism that makes you splendidly catholic. A paradox indeed.

An institution is catholic if its interests are pervasive, universal, all-embracing; if it can proclaim with the pre-Christian poet Terence, "Nothing that is human do I consider alien to me." Precisely here is the catholic challenge of the Catholic Eucharist.

You see, the Mass is not an occasion for narcissism, a chance for Catholics to fall in love with their own reflection, thanking God with the Gospel Pharisee that we are not like other men and women. The Christ who feeds us with his risen self forces us to focus on the hungers of the human family. In that context—millions of men, women, and children struggling desperately to live human lives, struggling even to live—talk about the Bread of Life can sound awfully empty, suspiciously hollow, unless we who feed on the Eucharistic Christ are ourselves eucharists for the life of the world. But only then are we eucharists when our feeding on the flesh of Christ takes us from church to world; when, like the Eucharistic Christ, we are *present* to others, present where they are, present in ways that respond to their needs—for food or freedom, for peace or truth, for the touch of a hand that heals or the murmur of a voice that cares. Like the Eucharistic Christ, *really* present—not merely our money or our minds, but we in person—restless to carry the compassionate Christ to those who share far more of his passion than of his resurrection, restless because as Catholics our richest life is not what we own but how we love, for it is love that gives life, love that promises someone somewhere a tomorrow more human, worth waking up to.

Eucharists for the life of the world? Yes indeed. But for your love to be catholic, you need not fly to Belfast or Beirut, to Chile or Chad, to Iraq or Iran. The immediate crisis, as so often, lies at your feet or along the Metro—the hundred acres of Georgetown's campus, the square mile of Holy Trinity parish, the 97 square miles of our District. Here are enough loneliness and lovelessness, enough anguish of flesh and spirit, enough trembling and terror, enough desperation and despair to wring from you every last breath of your love.

As you exit this sacred spot hosting the Bread of Life, pledge yourselves to be a kind of sacrament—I mean, vibrant symbols that speak to the fears and tears of a broken world. Vow not only to joy with all whose laughter is richly human, but to weep with all whose pain parallels your own. Take the first step wherever dislike divides; be willing to walk the extra mile. Challenge courageously a resurgent rugged individualism where the strong and the swift survive and the devil take the hindmost. Such must you be, for sacraments are not magic. You will be effective symbols to the extent that St. Paul's triad pervades you: "Faith, hope, love abide, these three; but the greatest of these is love" (1 Cor 13:13).

So then, good friends, as you move from Christ risen in your Eucharist to Christ still crucified on campus and in center city, echo to your sisters and brothers the pledge of Christ the night before he died, the pledge that alone can shape a city of justice, of peace, of love. As new eucharists, promise them: "This is my body . . . given for you" (Lk 22:19).

Dahlgren Chapel
Georgetown University
and
Holy Trinity Church
Washington, D.C.
October 11, 1987

13
I'M FALLING IN LOVE WITH GOD
Twenty-ninth Sunday of the Year (B)

- Isaiah 53:10–11
- Hebrews 4:14–16
- Mark 10:35–45

Two weeks ago a nun I do not know wrote me a fan letter. A rather long letter but, since I dote on compliments, I read it all, slowly, with relish. I'm glad I did. Not for the obvious reason. Rather because at the end our thoughtful sister told a swift, touching story. A sister in her community is 86. One day this aging sister stopped my correspondent and said very simply: "Please pray for me. I'm falling in love with God."

"I'm falling in love with God." Not a gurgle from the geriatrics ward; not a mewling from Medicare. A vibrant message for all of us—your homilist included. Hence this homily. Three stages to my song and dance. Stage 1 is a word from your Creator: How important is it to fall in love with God? Stages 2 and 3 are words from your not so humble servant: How in point of fact can you fall in love with God?

I

First, how important is it to fall in love with God? The 86-year-young sister of my introduction was not whistling in the dark. She was echoing a very ancient and surely the most significant command the world's Creator ever thundered to us earthlings. It goes back to that motley mob of unruly, runaway slaves God chose to be His people—culturally undistinguished, often rebellious, frequently unfaithful, unpredictable, unreliable. As Moses told them, "It was not because you were more in number than any other people that the

Lord set His heart on you and chose you, for you were the fewest of all peoples; but it is because the Lord loves you . . . that the Lord . . . redeemed you from the house of bondage, from the hand of Pharaoh king of Egypt" (Deut 7:7–8).

On this people of His predilection the Lord enjoined a solemn command: "You shall love the Lord your God with all your heart, and with all your soul, and with all your might" (Deut 6:4). And lest you be tempted to consign this command to a dead history, God's Son-in-flesh, when asked by a lawyer for "the first commandment of all," responded in almost identical words: "You shall love the Lord your God with all your heart, and with all your soul, and with all your mind, and with all your strength" (Mk 12:30).

This is not a polite request: "If you feel like it, would you be so kind as to love me?" This is an order—the most important command God will ever give you. You can keep all God's other orders perfectly—respect parents, sanctify Sunday, keep from killing, never lust after another's wealth or wife—but if you don't love God, sure as hell you're in deep trouble.

And the love God demands of you is not an ordinary love, not a matter of words, not something you act out on Sunday, fulfill by listening to a three-point homily. Have you ever loved anyone— man, woman, or child—"with all your heart, all your soul, all your mind, all your strength"? Then you have a fair idea of the kind of love God wants from you. Not simply a head trip, an act of faith, recitation of a creed; rather a love that burns you, consumes you, makes for ecstasy and agony, dark nights of the soul and self-surrender to whatever God asks.

II

But if love is God's command to all who believe, how in fact do you fall in love with God? Like all loving, the ways are beyond counting. Many of you, I'm sure, could tell me your own story of divine love. For those still searching or skeptical, still puzzled or confused, I suggest two avenues to love. Each should surprise you, may make you wonder whether your homilist is finally off his rocker.

One avenue I call contemplation. Not the popular sense of "contemplate," which you might instantly associate with "navel." Contemplation in its profound sense is just as real as your navel but immeasurably more exciting. My Carmelite friend William McNamara once called contemplation

> experiential awareness of reality . . . a way of entering into imme-
> diate communion with reality. Reality? Why, that means people,
> trees, lakes, mountains. . . . You can study things, but unless you
> enter into this intuitive communion with them, you can only
> know *about* them, you don't *know* them. To take a long loving look
> at something—a child, a glass of wine, a beautiful meal—this is a
> natural act of contemplation, of loving admiration. . . . To be
> able to do that, there's the rub. All the way through school we are
> taught to abstract; we are not taught loving awareness.

Never have I heard contemplation more engagingly defined: a
long loving look at the real. It's simply a different way of knowing.
Whether it's Beethoven's *Mass in D* or a ruddy glass of Burgundy, the
Mona Lisa smiling in the Louvre or Patrick Ewing soaring to the
hoop, an infant rising to birth from a womb or Christ Jesus descend-
ing to death in a tomb—whatever or whoever, you no longer analyze
it or argue it, no longer describe or define it; you are one with it. You
do not move around it; you enter into it. Dip your hand into Potomac's waters: You can say "Ah yes, H_2O," or you can simply let the
water trickle through your fingers in loving awareness. To contemplate is to rest in the real. Not lifelessly or languidly, not sluggishly or
inertly. Your whole being is alive, incredibly responsive, vibrating to
every throb of the real. Most of you experience it without realizing
it—as you watch a burning sun sink behind the hills, sit entranced
before *Swan Lake* or sway with Springsteen, meet the eyes of someone with whom you are wildly one. It's not study, not cold examination, not a computer. To contemplate is to be in love.

So should you regard your God. Theology, organized study
about God, is good indeed; I make my living at it. But better still is
contemplation. I am reminded of Eric Gill's outraged protest:
"Good Lord! The thing was a mystery and we measured it!"

But how realize your capacity for contemplation? Four ways.
First, some sort of desert experience. Not necessarily the physical
desert of the Bible, but any experience that brings you face to face
with solitude, with vastness, with powers of life and death beyond
your control; some experience—like illness or mid-life crisis—
where you opt for living or life destroys you.

Second, develop a feeling for festivity. I mean activity that is
not tied to other goals, to "so that" and "in order to." You take
usable time and withdraw it from utility. You simply enjoy. You
reject the 20th-century American article of faith: "Only useful activity is valuable, meaningful, moral."[1] You don't feel guilty if you

have nothing to "do." You admit with delight that you took yesterday "off," that you "did" nothing, that you just enjoyed. You raise
eyebrows at a party by asking not "What do you do?" but "Who are
you?" You remember Darwin's regret: "if I had to live my life again,
I would have made a rule to read some poetry and listen to some
music at least once every week."[2]

Third, don't try to "possess" the object of your delight—
whether God or a human you love, imprisoned marble or free-
flowing rivulet. With Walter Kerr you have to reverse an adage:

> A bird in the hand is *not* worth two in the bush—unless one is an
> ornithologist, the curator of the Museum of Natural History, or
> one of those Italian vendors who supply restaurants with larks. A
> bird in the hand is no longer a bird at all: it is a specimen; it may
> be dinner. Birds are birds only when they are in the bush or on
> the wing; their worth as birds can only be known at a discreet
> and generous distance.[3]

Fourth, read, make friends with, remarkable men and women
who have themselves looked long and lovingly at the real: Augustine of Hippo and Anne Morrow Lindbergh, Antoine de Saint
Exupéry and Catherine of Siena, Teresa of Avila and John of the
Cross, Thomas Merton and Thomas More, Mother Teresa and
Teilhard de Chardin—hundreds of women and men who have
smashed through boundaries and touched the very face of God.

Try it, good friends. Beyond sheer study, loving awareness: a
long loving look at the real. For a change, let science be silent. Let
your whole being—spirit and senses—revel in the real: in the things
of God, the people of God, God's very self. Don't analyze the or-
chid; smell it! Don't dissect your sisters and brothers; enjoy them!
Above all, don't misspend your life proving God exists; open yourself to God in love!

III

This leads into my third point, my second avenue to love of
God: God's images, people. And here I mean the most unlikely
images of God. It is a story of terror and hope.

In the Times Square area of New York, amid the porno
theaters and massage parlors, surrounded by pimps and prostitutes, drug dealers and speed freaks, stands Covenant House, in-

vention of Franciscan Bruce Ritter. Through its doors each year troop boys and girls by the thousands. Runaway kids. Street kids. Used-up, burned-out kids. Kids who had to keep from crying, however much it hurt, while they were sold like so much meat, forced to pose naked for filthy films, give their bodies to nice married men out on the town, smile while pimps and johns wasted their flesh and their spirit.

Father Ritter has written a small book with a profound title: *Sometimes God Has a Kid's Face*.[4] Listen to just one of the book's poignant episodes. Ritter is about to be filmed in a documentary about Covenant House; he gets into conversation with an 18-year-old street kid helping out with the documentary.

> "Thanks," he said. "Thanks for starting Covenant House."
>
> "Thank *God*," I said.
>
> "No," he said. "Thank *you*."
>
> "Don't you believe in God?" I said.
>
> Rick shrugged slightly. "Why should I?" he said. "God *never* did anything for me. . . . It's been pretty bad for me, Bruce. I'm a drifter—four years. . . . Have been since I was 14. There's not much about me that you would want to know. God either." He gave a grim little hurting smile.
>
> "You're *here*," I said, "and that's enough," I said. "We don't have to start anywhere else. I think God sent you here."
>
> "No, he didn't," Rick said. "I needed a place to stay. That's all. A john dropped me off. Not God. Why should God care about what happens to me? Why should I care about God?"
>
> "Did you ever fall in love with somebody?" I said. "Really in love?"
>
> He nodded slightly.
>
> "Did they ever ask you why you loved them? Did you have a reason? Did you need a reason?"
>
> "No," he said.
>
> "Neither does God," I said. "He doesn't need to have you love him back."
>
> "That's good," he said, "because I don't."
>
> . . . And then he gave me a rib-crunching hug. I hugged him back.
>
> "Thanks," he said.
>
> "Thank God," I said.
>
> "No," he said, "thank you."
>
> "Maybe thank God?" I said.
>
> "Maybe," he said. "It's easier to trust you, Bruce. You're here. I never saw God and I never will."

"Don't be so sure," I said. "You will," I said. "If *I* will you will," I said.

At the end [of the filming], the reporter asked me why I do what I do. "I do what I do because of God," I answered. "And sometimes, God has a kid's face."

It wasn't hard to play that scene. I just kept thinking of God and seeing Rick's face.[5]

That, good friends, is contemplation: a long loving look at the real.

"And so what?" you ask. Just a passionate prayer on my part. I pray that you may discover the delights of contemplation long before you retire; for at 65 it's easier to start jogging than to begin contemplating. I pray that if you have trouble finding God—in God's Word and works, in God's Bread—you will find God in kids. Not only in the gifted and the beautiful, but especially in the beaten and abused, the deflowered and the fearful, the sinful and the cynical, the raped and the restless, the defeated and despairing.

The problem, I fear, is that you and I will not find God there unless we meet God where they are—and that's not very pretty. It need not be Times Square, but neither is it the Kennedy Center. It's more likely to be the homes where GU students tutor, the street corners of the impoverished, the alleys where love is lust, the schools where crack is king, the jails for juveniles. Not easy places to crash, but that's where the image of God is defaced and disfigured, hidden beneath the grime and the grit.

It's not Disneyland, not Wonderland; but it's where God's chosen children are, and so it's where God is—by preference, as with Jesus. It's worth looking into, wouldn't you say? You'd not only be helping a crucified Christ; you'd be helping yourself. For you might end up pleading "Please pray for me. I'm falling in love with God."

Dahlgren Chapel
Georgetown University
and
Holy Trinity Church
Washington, D.C.
October 16, 1988

14
UNLESS YOU LOVE. . . .
Thirty-first Sunday of the Year (B)

- Deuteronomy 6:2–6
- Hebrews 7:23–28
- Mark 12:28–34

Your heady invitation to address your triennial national convention resulted in a homiletic headache. For today's sacred liturgy and your honor society[1] posed a perplexing problem. On the one hand, you have Deuteronomy and Mark: Yahweh and Yahweh's Son commanding you to love like crazy, as if loving is the coolest thing you could ever do. On the other hand, here is Alpha Sigma Nu, not I hope hostile to love, but the word does not appear in your constitution, your by-laws, your ritual of initiation. You do not define yourselves as a society organized for loving. Alpha Sigma Nu is not a "love boat."[2]

Still, I submit, the word stalks your society. Very simply, if you want to love God "with all your heart, soul, mind, and strength," if you would love your sisters and brothers "as [you love] yourself" (Mk 12:30–31), a remarkable way to show it is the triad that commands your charter: scholarship, loyalty, service. A word from your homilist on each.

I

Do you want to love "with all your mind"? One wondrous way is the road of the scholar, the student. Take theology. What is it? In theology you are searching for God. Not for a God who dwells only in light inaccessible, outside time and space. Rather for a God who has a history—a history shaped by every star and every stone, by each blade of grass, each deer in flight or bird on the wing, each human heart. For a God who shows Himself, not only in a burning bush millennia ago, but in today's passionate cry for freedom and today's quest for "roots." For a God whose pulsing image is every one of us. For a God who *became* one of us. And in theology, God-talk though it is, you are searching for man and woman. For, in the felicitous phrase of a second-century bishop, "God's glory is man/woman alive!"[3] Searching, therefore, for what it means to be human, what it means to live—yes, what it means to die.

But it is not only theology that touches our God. All genuine scholarship does, or can. If not the face of God, surely the trace of God, His footsteps. For, as Gerard Manley Hopkins sang, "The world is charged with the grandeur of God."[4] I do not mean that God is *why* you analyze the atom and the amoeba, walk on the moon and prowl the ocean floor, dissect the Dow Jones and the DNA that controls heredity. Each science has its own secular ends and purposes. My point is: In touching the things of God, you are touching the hem of God's garment. When you finger the pot, you touch the potter. If Rembrandt is still in his *Night Watch,* the God who shaped this earth is still discoverable therein. Baltimore Catechism number 1 was right on target. Question: "Where is God?" Answer: "God is everywhere." You will not sacrifice your science if, like ancient mathematician Archimedes, you dash naked into the street one day and cry "Eureka!" "I've found Him!"

But to *know* with all your mind is not enough. You have a power no IBM Word Perfect can match: You are commanded to *love* with all your mind. It is the perfection of knowledge—where knowledge is love, where what you know—Mona Lisa or a formula, law or medicine, man or woman or God—is part of you, intimate to you. Here is scholarship Gospel style. Eureka indeed, but eureka with love.

II

Do you want to love "with all your soul"? One wondrous way is the lane of loyalty. Loyalty, the dictionaries tell us, is fidelity—to a superior, to duty, to love, to a cause, to a principle. In your case, not a mindless "Yes, whatever you say." Your loyalty, your fidelity, the ritual of initiation makes clear, is "an intelligent commitment to Jesuit ideals of higher education."

Nauseatingly vague? Perhaps. How should you concretize it? Negatively, Jesuit higher education is not what a cynic once defined education to be: "the inculcation of the incomprehensible into the ignorant by the incompetent." Positively, we confront some confusion, because we discover development. The Jesuits of the 16th century were simply subscribing to age-old ideals of Western humanism, from Plato and Isocrates down. You were educated to the extent that (1) you could express clearly what you had thought accurately, and (2) you had an acceptable standard of right and wrong. After four centuries of change it is difficult today to distinguish what historian Philip Gleason glimpsed as two types of education: one "secular, scientific, and technical in spirit, particularized in vision, flexible in approach, vocational in aim, and democratic in social orientation," and the older Jesuit dream, "a system religious, literary, and humanistic in spirit, synthetic in vision, rigid in approach, liberal in aim, and elitist in social orientation."

To what Jesuit ideals are you committed? What specific identity can you identify with? What in the Jesuit educational vision can you love "with all your soul"? President Timothy Healy replied pointedly in his 1977 inaugural at Georgetown: "Any college that works toward an integrative curriculum, both in general education and in its majors; that labors to make sure its educated citizens carry moral, as well as intellectual, baggage; that commits itself in work and being to justice as the ground of faith—any such college will have something definite and different to offer its students and all America."

My ten years as theologian-in-residence here persuade me that, if today's Ignatian vision is to be realized in American Jesuit education, at least three needs are paramount.

First, our students must grasp profoundly and live joyously an integration succinctly expressed in the title of a minor classic by Benedictine Jean Leclercq: *Love of Learning and Desire for God*. Four years in a genuinely Jesuit college should be a gradual growth on two levels that are ultimately one: rich experience of created reality and close encounter with its Creator. Not just objective knowledge, professional competence, the great grade rush; rather, college as contemplation, what Carmelite William McNamara called "loving awareness—a long loving look at the real."

Second, it is we Jesuits, if anyone, who should incarnate the vision, put flesh on the skeleton, live it publicly and enthusiastically. Words in a catalogue, "aims and objectives," leave the soul cold, even the mind skeptical. If the Jesuit image you spy is unimaginative pedantry, unattractive spirituality, faith without justice, who will believe our rhetoric?

Third, if Georgetown is to remain Jesuit, Jesuits alone will not do. Essential to the vision are hundreds of staff and faculty many of whom have for good reasons resisted any temptation to be Jesuits. Of these, a fair number must share not only our authority but our intellectual and spiritual heritage, our living tradition, our mission. Not necessarily dotting every i, crossing every t, but surely sympathetic to our basic values. With such as these, from Boston to L.A., students beyond our counting will continue to love God, the images of God, and the things of God with all their souls.

III

Do you want to love "with all your heart"? One wondrous way is writ large over Alpha Sigma Nu. I mean service. Not just doing good to others, good though this obviously is. A Jesuit honor society honors this, but expects more of you than it does from Rotarians or the Elks. It expects you to reach out to the lonely aged and the retarded young, to the mentally ill and the delinquent, to street people and battered women, to the raped and the downtrodden, to illiterate Salvadorans and displaced Vietnamese—not simply because justice demands it, but primarily because love draws you, because love leaves you restless as long as your brothers and sisters cry mutely for bread or justice, because you are acutely aware of an awesome announcement of Jesus: "In so far as you did it to one of the least of these my sisters and brothers, you did it to me" (Mt 25:40).

I doubt that those who culled your credentials mulled over your motivation. I am not advocating that you alter your ritual. I recognize all manner of admirable motives in human service. You like people; a paraplegic tugs at your heartstrings; injustice makes your blood boil; compassion for the crippled you sucked at your mother's breast; your undeserved gifts give you guilt feelings; you never could resist an abandoned baby. Splendid! As long as your heart goes out to another, this is an act of love. But for men and women of your ideals the milk of human kindness is only a beginning. It is not *all* God asks of you. You are commanded—not invited, commanded—commanded not by a ritual but by God's Son in flesh—commanded to love those you serve as you love yourself. *All* those you serve: those who turn you off as well as those who turn you on; the pimped and the primped; the AIDS-afflicted as well as the hale and hearty; the drug addict and the all-American boy and girl; the bag of rags and the fashion plate. Your task, stimulated by Alpha Sigma Nu and enabled by grace, is to see in the less fortunate the image of God—begrimed and bruised beyond recognition, but still God's image, as was Jesus himself even when crowned with thorns, lashed with whips, pinned to twin beams of bloody wood.

Love them as you love yourself. A hard saying. Especially if you love yourself profoundly, passionately—as indeed God wants you to—and "the other" is less than lovable. And still you must. For, to quote St. Vincent de Paul, 17th-century apostle of charity, "Unless you love, the poor will not forgive you for the bread you give them."

Time to sum up, fold my theological tent, and steal away. On such as you, good friends, the "Jesuit" in our education largely depends. That is why this evening's liturgy is not just a neat spiritual garnish on a secular weekend. This ritual recalls a blessing and a burden. It reminds you that, if you are to be what you ought to be, all you can be, what Jesus called you to be, "the salt of the earth" and "the light of the world" (Mt 5:13, 14), you must put even richer flesh on your already rich ritual of initiation. You will be light to the world in an Ignatian sense only if you light the earth with your love: love God above all else, love all your sisters and brothers as you love yourself. You will be salt for the earth only if you salt it with your sanctity: simply a synonym for unconditional love.

This is not piosity; it is Ignatian realism, Gospel truth. Scholarship, intelligence, brilliance can be destructive; loyalty, blind; service, self-interest. Proof? Twentieth-century history, from the Holocaust through Watergate to computer crooks, insider trading, and the nuclear scandals highlighted in *Time*'s current cover story titled " 'They Lied to Us.' "[5]

What Alpha Sigma Nu expressly asks of you is indeed a wondrous way of life: scholarship for service. What the Gospel demands of you is scholarship for service out of love. It isn't impossible. It simply calls for *all* your mind, *all* your soul, *all* your heart. It can be fun, and quite rewarding: all this, and heaven too.[6]

Dahlgren Chapel
Georgetown University
October 29, 1988

15

THE NAME OF THE GAME IS RISK
Thirty-third Sunday of the Year (A)

- Proverbs 31:10–13, 19–20, 30–31
- 1 Thessalonians 5:1–6
- Matthew 25:14–30

Today's Gospel is uncommonly contemporary. It recalls last month's Wall Street—in reverse.[1] Two investors play the market shrewdly for their merchant boss, and they double their investments; no Black Monday there. But one fearful yuppie plays it close to the vest. Rather than invest, he keeps the capital in a safe place. Their employer returns from a month at the Club Med, praises the two nervy traders to the sky, screams at the nerveless nerd: "You lazy lout! You should have invested my money with the bankers. Out of my sight, once and for all!" (cf. Mt 25:26–27, 30).

Now the Gospels are not a guide to economics, how to "make it" in Fat City; the parables do not go up and down with Dow Jones. They are lessons in living—human and Christian living—lessons by way of story. Today's parable is a remarkable wedding of two paradoxical qualities: fidelity and risk. But to grasp what I am saying, you must follow me through three movements. We begin briefly with the three traders; from them we learn what it means to be faithful; and so we glimpse how rare fidelity is without risk.[2]

I

First, a glance at the Gospel, a peek at the parable.[3] What did today's parable mean 19 centuries ago? If it pleases you, you can do what Matthew and other early Christians did: They made an allegory of it. Who is the merchant? Christ. What is the journey he takes? He ascends into heaven. What is his return "after a long time" (v. 19)? His second coming, at the end of the world, to render to each of us according to our works. How does he reward the good? He ushers them into the Messianic banquet. How does he punish the wicked? He casts them "into the outer darkness" (v. 30), endless damnation.

I have no problem with that. The early Christians applied the parables to their own needs, and you have the Christian liberty to do the same. More important to me at the moment is what Jesus himself intended by the parable.[4] He was addressing the religious leaders of the Jews, addressing especially the scribes, teachers of Jewish law and tradition. A great deal had been entrusted to them—in particular, God's wondrous word. They would have to account for their stewardship. How had they dealt with God's word? Had they been "faithful" (vv. 21, 23), like the first and second servants? Or had they been "slothful" (v. 26), idle, lazy, indolent, like the third? Had they used God's word in harmony with God's will, traded on their trust, made it pay off? Or had they frustrated God's word by worrying about themselves, neglecting to use the trust, refusing to risk?

II

This leads swiftly to my second point: that vital word "faithful." It is a significant New Testament term. A twin meaning. On the one hand, the New Testament "faithful" are reliable, dependable, trustworthy. On the other, they are faith-full, full of faith. They can be trusted completely because they have entrusted themselves completely: to God and His Christ, to God's people, to God's creation.

Today, however, "faithful" is no longer a parlor word. Dogs are faithful; Federal Express is faithful; Marines are "always faithful"; but much of America is uncomfortable with it, from coaches to spouses. And yet, this is the distinguished title you and I bear: We are the Christian faithful. This perhaps more than any other single word sums up who we are as Christians. We are men and women who are full of faith and who keep faith. The term tells who we are, because the term tells whom we love. Let me explain.

We are Christian faithful, first, because we are committed to Christ. No commitment may take precedence over that. In baptism God "put His seal upon us" (2 Cor 1:22), the seal of the Spirit. Somewhat as a Roman soldier was branded with the seal of the emperor, somewhat as animals have been branded with their owner's mark, so Christians are stamped with the seal of the Spirit: We belong to Christ, and through him to the Father. Renounce it we can, with our lips or our lives, but the seal is ceaselessly there. From here to eternity we belong to Christ.

The problem is, how live the logic of this relationship? How be faithful to the Christ who owns us? A twin response: filled with faith and keeping faith. Filled with faith. Not only an intellectual confession: "I believe in Jesus Christ, God's only Son, born of the Virgin Mary. . . ." Important indeed, but not enough. My whole self must leap out to him—mind and heart, will and emotions. Such faith alone is alive, alive with love. Such faith alone is a Christian response to the love that was crucified for us, the loving person "apart from" whom I "can do nothing" (Jn 15:5).

Such faith makes it possible for me to keep faith. Because I have entrusted myself completely to Christ, he can trust me completely. Because I love him, I will be like him. And the more like him I am, the more likely I am to keep faith with him even unto crucifixion: "Not my will but thine be done" (Lk 22:42).

Second, we are Christian faithful because we are faithful to the Body of Christ, committed to the community of Christ. Precisely here lies the crisis of fidelity at its most crucial. What does it *mean* to be faithful to the community, to the Church? It would be fairly simple if all 900 million of us were of a single mind. But we are not; we are dreadfully divided. From contraception to the kiss of peace, from nuclear first-strike to Communion in the hand, from capital punishment to American capitalism, from remarriage after divorce to religion in politics, from priestly celibacy to women's ordination, from human rights to funding for abortion—on these and a host of other issues we Catholics are not only at odds; at times we claw one another like cats in a sack.

It is not that our wills are evil, our intentions bad. Oh yes, there are indifferent Catholics, Sunday Catholics, foxhole Catholics, social Catholics, birth-and-burial Catholics, way-out Catholics. But most of the faithful I have known through seven decades are precisely that: Christians who are trying desperately to be faithful. But it's a struggle: between the clear call from Rome and the crucifying confusion at home; between a Mass they drank in with their mothers' milk and a Mass that leaves them angry or just cold; between a liberty-loving culture that fashions them from the womb and a hard-nosed Church that refuses to move with their times; between commandments presumably from God and a conscience equally from God; between choices that baffle their minds and buffet their hearts.

How, then, be faithful—full of faith and keeping faith? A homily is not a computer: Press the right button and out pops the right response. I do not come to you with a hatful of answers. I simply submit that today's readings suggest how today's faithful can work out their faithfulness. Three suggestions: from contemplation on Proverbs, on Paul, on Matthew.

The word from Proverbs. You may not cotton to the "ideal wife" of Proverbs 31: her household chores, her rising at night (presumably her husband needs his sleep), even "*she* does *him* good" (Prov 31:12). But the soul of the portrait is a single syllable: "The heart of her husband *trusts* in her" (v. 11)). And the word from this wife to us is this: Fidelity is where you are; faithfulness is here and now. The wife of Proverbs was not peering over the hills at distant Syria, not planning how to be faithful in her senility. Fidelity was right there; fidelity was husband and children, servants and merchants, the poor and God. To each of these she had pledged herself, and she was a woman of her word.

And so for you. Fidelity is here and now; faithfulness is fall 1987. You have pledged yourself. To whom? To the Christian community: to live this day in holiness of heart, loving the other as Christ has loved you. Your baptism may have been "forced," amid wails of protest. Your presence here is a free, fresh commitment. From your humble "I confess to you, my brothers and sisters" to the "Amen" you murmur to "The body of Christ," you are saying to one another: I am part of you, I belong to you, you can trust me, rely on me. Not because your genes make you nice guys and dolls. Rather because the grace of our Lord Jesus Christ courses through you like another bloodstream.

The word from Paul: Fidelity is a Christ who comes in surprising ways. If you want to hear "Well done, good and faithful servant" from a Christ riding clouds of glory, then welcome him when he comes hungry and thirsty, lonely and unloved, in rags or in pain, imprisoned by all sorts of fears. To be faithful, all you have to do is touch each hand that stretches out to you. That's all. That's all?

III

The word from Matthew summons up my third movement: Christian fidelity calls for risk. Which of the three servants were called "faithful"? Not the servant who played it safe, hid his thousand dollars in the ground. Only the servants who took a chance, traded with the money their master had entrusted to them.

And so for you. The name of the Christian game is risk. To begin with, you commit yourself to a Christ you cannot see. Here you have left the secure world of scientific demonstration; here you do violence to what you see and hear, touch and smell and taste. You see a criminal on a cross, and you cry "My Lord and my God!" You hear words from a book, and they turn for you into the Word of God. You touch another's hand in love, and you sense the presence of Christ. You smell incense, and the Lord pervades your space. You taste bread, and you eat the body of Christ.

Risk? Of course! Because you do not have certainty and *then* commit yourself to Christ; you must first commit yourself in order to have any assurance at all. Risk because faith is not nice thoughts and feelings; it determines your life, who you are and what you do. Because he believed, Abraham was ready to sacrifice his son. Committed to crucifixion, Jesus did not suspect he would beg his Father to remove this cup if at all possible. Our Lady's yes to an angel was not preceded by a scenario "From Bethlehem to Calvary." Those who give up literally everything to follow the naked Christ naked— from ascetic Antony and friar Francis to Teresa of Avila and Teresa of Calcutta—do not know what tomorrow will bring. And we smaller folk, we too risk a cross if we live our Christian commitment. We know a cross will be there; the risk is, we do not know what shape it will take.

If we risk in committing ourselves to a Christ we cannot see, we risk perhaps more in committing ourselves to a Church we *can* see. For this is a pilgrim Church, a community on the way, not yet there; a body of sinful men and women, at times in startling contradiction to the Lord who heads it. Its outward face is not only spotted and wrinkled; it constantly changes—from a stone altar to a wooden table, from stony silence to squeals of peace, from Gregorian to guitar, from an all-male ministry to women in the sanctuary, from unquestioning obedience to strident resistance, from the simple confusion of the first Pentecost to the complexities of a new code of law.

And still it is Christ's community; here is where he expects us to experience him. And not only to endure it but to love it, to take it for better or worse, for richer or poorer, in sickness and in health, until death. Otherwise we are no different from the cautious servant. First, we play it safe, hedge our bets, stay out of trouble, don't get involved. Let the kooks feed the Ethiopians, argue about Nicaragua, hold hands at the Our Father. Second, when things get tough, we lay the blame on someone else: a harsh pastor, a Roman document on birth control, paranoid nuns in parochial schools, uninspired liturgy, marriage laws, priests in politics, Catholics who go piously to church but don't live it—the thousand and one reasons that keep us from looking within ourselves. We are victims; someone else is responsible for our failure. Third, we can indeed feel free, free of responsibility; we no longer have to do anything with our "talent," our faith. But the freedom can be an illusion. Without responsibility, there can be no Christian freedom.

My sisters and brothers: To be a disciple of Christ, you have to lose your life in order to find it. I do not know what life it is that Christ is asking you to surrender; wire-tapping is illegal even for Jesuits. I do know it is one thing to be faithful when the issues are stark and clear, when you know the way to go and what will end well, when it doesn't cost anything, doesn't threaten your way of life. It is quite another thing to grope in darkness, when you are not sure, when you're afraid, when discipleship costs, when the Lord simply says: "You have your gifts: my Church and your conscience, my grace and your good sense. Trade with them till I come."

You may indeed trade badly, choose poorly, decide wrongly. But when your Master returns, he will not ask how often you were right but how honestly you tried, not how brilliant you were but how loving, not how close to the vest you played it but how ready you were to risk all for him. Then will you hear from your Master, no longer "hard" (Mt 25:24) but "gentle" (Mt 11:29): "Well done, good and faithful servant. . . . Enter into the joy of your Master" (Mt 25:21, 23). But only if you risk.

Dahlgren Chapel
Georgetown University
and
Holy Trinity Church
Washington, D.C.
November 15, 1987

16
COME TO THE PARTY
Thirty-third Sunday of the Year (B)

- Daniel 12:1–3
- Hebrews 10:11–14, 18
- Mark 13:24–32

This afternoon I shall avoid today's Gospel. Not from fear—not even out of ignorance. My problem is, I preached from this pulpit on that Gospel six years ago. Not that I expect you to remember the homily, especially if you weren't here. Rather, the homily is printed word for word in my collection *Still Proclaiming Your Wonders*,[1] available from the Newman Book Store at a reasonable price. There you have it in a nutshell: all I know about the end of the world, the second coming of Christ, and the gathering of all the elect. End of commercial.

What then? The Gospel of this world's end suggests a related gospel—a subject we rarely talk about, infrequently preach about: our own end. I mean what will happen to us when we close our eyes in biological death. Three stages to my approach, three questions: (1) Will I really go on living after I die? (2) If I go on living, what sort of life will it be? (3) How make this life come alive in today's language, contemporary symbols?

I

First question: Will I really go on living after I die? Years ago, in philosophy classes, we spent endless hours trying to prove from sheer reason that your soul and mine never die. The arguments are not without merit, but you need a philosophical mind to appreciate them. Faith-full Christians respond more readily to St. Paul's rousing reaction to some Christians at Corinth who denied resurrection (1 Cor 15:12–19):

> Now if Christ is preached as raised from the dead, how can some of you say that there is no resurrection of the dead? But if there is no resurrection of the dead, then Christ has not been raised; if Christ has not been raised, then our preaching is in vain and your faith is in vain. We are even found to be misrepresenting God, because we testified of God that He raised Christ, whom He did not raise if it is true that the dead are not raised. For if the dead are not raised, then Christ has not been raised. If Christ has not been raised, your faith is futile and you are still in your sins. Then those also who have fallen asleep in Christ have perished. If for this life only we have set our hopes on Christ, we are of all men and women most to be pitied.

A powerful profession of faith. It demands your profound pondering. Meanwhile, allow me to unpack it a bit, phrase it so as to express the Catholic vision in my own words—and this after seven decades that moved from simple acceptance, through agonized questioning and critical re-examination, to my present peace of mind and heart.

First, some background you know full well. Because sin had ruptured man and woman from God, had severed man and woman from one another, had alienated man and woman from the earth on which they walked, had introduced a schizophrenia in each human person,[2] the Son of God took our flesh.[3] God's Son was born of a woman as we are—but laid in a feeding trough for cattle. God's Son grew up as we grow, learning from Mary how to love, from Joseph how to shape a plow—but without any of his neighbors suspecting who he really was. He left home as we leave, to do what his Father had sent him to do: preach repentance and forgiveness, heal the sick and raise the dead—but only for three swift years. He took flak from his own people for consorting with sinners of all sorts, was called crazy by his own kin. He changed bread and wine into his flesh and blood, so that he might be with us even after he died. He let himself be sold for silver by one of his closest friends, condemned on false charges, lashed with whips and crowned with thorns, nailed to twin beams of bloody wood. He died murmuring God's mercy on his enemies, love on all of us.

Why? So that we might live, happily or miserably, for a day or a hundred years, and then disappear into dust? So that uncounted thousands could die of hunger each day, babies be aborted or bombed to bits, good men and women waste away with AIDS, and that would be literally the end of them? So that we might taste what love is like and discover that death is more powerful than love? So that you might eat Christ's flesh, drink his blood, and bam! you're dead? Is this why God's own Son walked our earth and died for us, rose glorious from the grave and returned to his Father? If that were all, Christ's cross would be sheer tragedy; he might as well have stayed at home!

No, good friends. Not only does it fail to make sense, human or divine; it contradicts the very words of Christ. Why did he take our flesh? "I came that [you] may have life, and have it in abundance" (Jn 10:10). Why the Eucharist? Whoever "eats of this bread will live for ever" (Jn 6:51). Why did he die? "The Son of man must be lifted up [on the cross], that whoever believes in him may have eternal life" (Jn 3:14–15). He conquered death not for himself but for you and me; when he ascended to his Father, he returned home with us.

My first point is summed up in a single verse in John, a verse Martin Luther called "the gospel in miniature": "God so loved the world that He gave His only Son, that whoever believes in him should not perish but have eternal life" (Jn 3:16). That's the core of Christian faith. If it hasn't yet "grabbed" you, don't leave; just pray: "I believe; help my unbelief!" (Mk 9:24).

II

Second question: What sort of life will that afterlife be? In my childhood we grew up entranced by heaven, consoled by purgatory, scared green by hell. All sorts of images were fixed in our imaginations, from endless fun with angels to unquenchable fire amid pitch-forking devils.

To be realistic and Christian, you must begin with an admission of ignorance. We cannot really grasp what heaven is like, what we shall be like hereafter. The First Letter of John is clear on that: "Beloved, we are God's children now; it does not yet appear what we shall be, but we know that when He appears we shall be like Him, for we shall see Him as He is" (1 Jn 3:2). Thrilling indeed, but not very revealing. We do not know how God will "look" to us, what a soul is like outside the body, what our risen bodies will be like. I know I shall still be I, only (thank God) without the warts.

What do we know about heaven? For your information, heaven

is *not* an unrelieved, eternal yuk. "Bor . . . ing!" Heaven is a word, a less than thrilling word, for life. Heaven is being alive as you have never lived before. Alive with the kind of life God lives. Can you remember a moment when you felt so gloriously alive that you could scarcely stand it? Whatever it was—folding your first-born in your arms or scoring your first TD, total oneness with one other or a foaming mug of Michelob, molding a perfect figurine or shaping a brilliant idea, aware of Christ in the Eucharist or feeling him in your bones—whatever made you tremble with unrestrained excitement, multiply that to the nth degree and you will touch ever so lightly the joy that is life without end.

The problem is, we are still left to our imaginations; we've never experienced anything actually like it. St. Paul said we would "see face to face" (1 Cor 13:12); but the Trinity has no face. Mary Magdalene mistook the risen Christ for the gardener. What is beyond doubting is this: God will be there, no longer a hidden God, but . . . as . . . God . . . is. Father, Son, and Spirit. And with God all who have loved God with all their hearts: patriarchs like Abraham, prophets like Isaiah, remarkable women like Ruth and the mother of Jesus, Augustine and Aquinas, Thomas More and Thomas Merton, Teresa of Avila and Thérèse of Lisieux, your own mothers and fathers, your dearest friends. You've never seen a party like that one—and the party never ends.

Hell? We know even less about hell than about heaven. But three facts I must fix in your minds. (1) There is no proof that anyone is actually in hell. Perhaps some Jesuits are there, paying for crimes against the laity; but no proof. Don't take too seriously the *New Yorker* cartoon: Satan overlooking hordes of humans in hell and observing to one of his minions: "We do pretty well when you stop to think that people are basically good." (2) Hell-*fire* is an image—but don't get uptight about a combustion process with oxygen. Hell's deepest meaning is anguish, agony, sorrow, sadness. What sort of anguish? A fate far worse than fire: total frustration, endless alienation. My whole being cries out for God, and God is out of reach, for ever. There is no point in living, but live I must, unendingly. Fancifully, it's as if an eye knew that it could never see; an ear, that it could never hear; a withered hand, that it could never touch. Made for God, I am literally Godless. Made for love, I am literally loveless. Made for union, I am alone—days without end. (3) For your consolation, no one will ever be without God for ever unless he or she wants to be. C. S. Lewis expressed it as well as anyone: "There are only two kinds of people in the end: those who say to God, 'Thy will be done,' and those to whom God says, in the end, 'Thy will be done.' "[4]

Purgatory? I'll settle for it. It simply means that some of us, perhaps most of us, sinners that we are, may have to wait a bit before we "see" God; we're not really ready. But don't spend your Miller time trying to figure out what it's like. Simply, God will be preparing you for . . . life, for perfect joy. And you'll be at once happy and unhappy. Happy because you know you *will* enjoy God; unhappy because you have to wait, because you are restless for the Love that is all you want in life.

III

Third question: How make this afterlife come alive in today's language, contemporary symbols? Perhaps a story I read recently will help.

One day a saint was visited by an angel who asked her if she wished to see heaven and hell. She said yes and was immediately transported to hell. It was not at all what she had expected.

It was a beautiful place with many mansions. But then she heard terrible sounds of agony and pain. She followed her ears and found herself in a huge banquet hall. The tables were filled with delicious food, and all the residents of hell were seated at the tables.

They all looked normal except for one very important difference. They had long arms, maybe five feet in length. At the end of each arm, in their hands, were forks. But they could not get the food to their mouths because no one had an elbow. They howled with hunger before a banquet of food.

Next she was transported to heaven. It was not what she expected.

It was a beautiful place of many mansions—exactly like hell. But soon she heard sounds of rejoicing. She followed her ears and came to a huge banquet hall. The tables were filled with delicious food, and all the residents of heaven were seated at the tables.

The people were shaped exactly like the residents of hell— long arms and no elbows—but this fact caused them no difficulty. They simply loaded their forks with food and reached across the table to feed a friend. Everyone was fed.[5]

Good friends, that story is symbolic; it has a particular pertinence for your life and mine here and now. You see, God is ceaselessly inviting us to love. "When [we] . . . respond by feeding one another, [we] begin the banquet of heaven."[6] Heaven begins this side of the grave. You've heard it from the lips of Christ: "I was hungry and you gave me food, I was thirsty and you gave me drink, I was a stranger and you welcomed me, I was naked and you clothed me, I was sick and you visited me, I was in prison and you came to me" (Mt 25:35–36). What then? "Come, O blessed of my Father, inherit the kingdom prepared for you . . ." (v. 34). Come to the party. But the party begins now, feeding your sisters and brothers now, welcoming the stranger now, clothing the naked now, visiting the sick and the imprisoned now. R.S.V.P.

Dahlgren Chapel
Georgetown University
and
Holy Trinity Church
Washington, D.C.
November 13, 1988

MEDLEY

17
HIS BLOOD UPON US
Solemnity of the Body and Blood of Christ

- Exodus 24:3–8
- Hebrews 9:11–15
- Mark 14:12–16, 22–26

Today's liturgy focuses on a momentous monosyllable. A five-letter word. Other words, other symbols, have lost some or all of their power to shake us: a hug or a handshake, Uncle Sam and John Bull, a Nazi swastika or a bishop's mitre, the Democratic mule and the Republican elephant—even the Lamb of God and the Sacred Heart. Once they moved us mightily, changed human hearts and world maps, religion and politics. Time and culture have worn them away; they don't "grab" us the way they once did.

But one powerful symbol perdures from Cain to Antichrist. Our imagination is still riveted by . . . blood. And it is blood that the Church stresses across the earth to nine hundred million Catholics today. To make sense of this, let me (1) begin with a quick overture on ordinary human blood, (2) rise to a crescendo on Christ's blood, (3) come down to earth again with your blood and mine.

I

First, the blood we experience day after day.[1] Some of it is extraordinary. Who can forget Jacqueline Kennedy returning from Dallas to D.C. 25 years ago with the President's corpse, her pink suit still stained with his blood? Who can forget Corazón Aquino's husband, waked and buried in the bloodstained clothes he wore when assassinated at Manila's airport? Who can forget the blood-red vestments of Salvadoran Archbishop Romero murdered at the altar? Whose eyes cannot still redden with the blood of Robert

Kennedy and Martin Luther King? And who can face the 58,156 names sculpted on the Vietnam Memorial and not see red?

But, good friends, blood is not a personal preserve of the heroic. Blood is so ordinary we forget it is your life stream and mine. Without blood no part of your body can live. Without blood you could not breathe; without blood Domino's pizza would stick in your gullet; without blood food would turn you into a huge garbage can; without blood you could not fight off a common cold. And let me clue you in on one more miracle: If you could lay your total blood system end to end, it would reach around the equator four times—about 100,000 miles![2]

II

Now a homily is not a class in Blood 101. The point of my overture is this: Blood is indeed writ large and deep into our sheerly human experience; but paradoxically, it is part and parcel of our religious existence as well. Here too blood is a striking symbol of life—but this time life without compare. Each of today's three readings should enter intimately into your spirituality, your oneness with God.

Take the excerpt from Exodus. Moses establishes a permanent bond between the Lord and His people—a bond the Bible calls a covenant. How is the bond sealed, the covenant cut? By a ritual of blood. Why blood? Because to the Hebrews blood was a specially sacred symbol; for blood was the seat of life's mystery. And so half the blood of the animal victims was poured on the altar—the altar that stood for God; half was poured on the people. And Moses said: "This is the blood of the covenant which the Lord has made with you in accordance with all these words" (Exod 24:8).[3]

For the Hebrew people this solemn compact with God sealed in blood was no small matter. In entering the covenant, they pledged fidelity—they would be faithful to all the conditions of the covenant. What conditions? At rock bottom, the Commandments: no false gods, Sabbath reserved for God, honor to father and mother, no murder or adultery, no stealing or false witness, no coveting what belongs to another.[4]

And how did the people respond to what the Lord demanded? "All the people answered with one voice and said: 'All the words which the Lord has spoken we will do'" (Exod 24:3). Not a mere matter of words. By this ritual of blood, the people called down on themselves a bloody end if they proved faithless to their pact with God. Shall we say they took the Sinai covenant seriously?

Take the reading from Hebrews. Its background is Old Testament sacrifice. In sacrifices blood was an essential element. In every sort of sacrifice the priest poured blood on the altar and all around. Now the Lord God accepted the immolation of animals, accepted blood sacrifice, but under one condition: if the sacrifice was offered, as Abraham offered, in a spirit of faith. What counted before God was not what met the eye but what was hidden in the heart.[5]

What the New Testament Letter to the Hebrews declares is pivotal to your piety, to your life in Christ. Each word is shaped of wonder: "If the sprinkling of defiled persons with the blood of goats and bulls and with the ashes of a heifer sanctifies for the purification of the flesh, how much more shall the blood of Christ, who through the eternal Spirit offered himself without blemish to God, purify your conscience from dead works to serve the living God" (Heb 9:13–14). In temple worship men and women could be reconciled to God through an animal's blood, as long as in this symbol they offered themselves to the God who gives everything the life it has. How much more likely is it that you and I can become one with God by offering to God the blood of God's Son!

That text finds its Christian center in today's moving Gospel from Mark. For those words "to the Hebrews" were written to a Christian community in danger of renouncing Christ, of returning to the Judaism they had abandoned, of recanting the covenant Mark's Gospel proclaims, the last will and testament of our Lord Jesus Christ at the Last Supper four decades before: "He took a cup, and when he had given thanks he gave it to [the Twelve[6]], and they all drank of it. And he said to them: 'This is my blood of the new covenant . . .' " (Mk 14:24).

The *new* covenant. A solemn compact sealed not with a signature, not with the blood of a bull, not with your blood and mine— sealed and signed with the blood of God made flesh for us. Little wonder that the New Testament is dotted with that monosyllable. A monosyllable that gets monotonous. How did he make peace? "By the blood of his cross" (Col 1:20). How did he make expiation for our sins? "By his blood" (Rom 3:25). How is it we are redeemed? "Through his blood" (Eph 1:7). How were we brought near to God? "In the blood of Christ" (Eph 2:13). What gives us confidence to enter God's sanctuary? "The blood of Jesus" (Heb 10:19). How did Jesus sanctify us? "Though his own blood" (Heb 13:12). How

were we ransomed from the futility of our fathers? "Not with perishable things such as silver and gold, but with the precious blood
of Christ" (1 Pet 1:18–19). And so on and so forth.

III

All right then: There is a spectacular blood that keeps us alive in
flesh, and a still more astonishing blood that makes us alive in Christ.
So what? So this. A compact, a contract, an agreement is never a one-
sided affair. It is a free engagement between two parties. The new
covenant Christ cut with his blood is two-sided: You and I, the whole
Christian community, have signed that covenant with Christ. You
may not have known what you were signing when a priest poured
water over your unsuspecting infant head. Now you know it. When
you approach this altar and touch the blood of Christ to your lips,
you are affirming at once a dignity and a responsibility.

A dignity. As the years roll on, I am increasingly amazed that a
God who doesn't really need me has drawn me into a covenant, a
compact, an agreement. With simply no deserving on my part, with
nothing to commend me, God has shaped me, shaped me like God,
has sent the Son of God to bleed for me, to buy me with his blood,
has gifted me with divine life, has made it possible for me to love
God with all my mind and heart and strength, possible to love those
who hate me, possible even to pour out my lifeblood for others with
the kind of love Jesus experienced on Calvary. Whatever my fail-
ings, whatever I lack in gray matter or tanned muscle, in achieve-
ment or prestige, in money or neon lights, I am loved by the same
God who fashioned the primal pair, the same God who loved Israel
like a mother, the same God who loved me long before I came to be.
The God who is always faithful to His promises has pledged to
remain faithful to me whatever I do, however faithless I prove. The
proof? In the Old Testament: "Can a woman forget her sucking
child, that she should have no compassion on the son of her womb?
Even these may forget, yet I will not forget you. Behold, I have
graven you on the palms of my hands" (Isa 49:15–16). In the New
Testament, St. Paul's summary of our dignity: "The Son of God
loved me and gave himself for me" (Gal 2:20). What more, in God's
name, do I need?

With that dignity, however, a responsibility. Few are called to
reflect the gory scene on Calvary: "One of the soldiers pierced

[Jesus'] side with a spear, and at once there came out blood and water" (Jn 19:34). It does happen: in South Africa and the North of Ireland, in countries stomped by the Russian Bear. But for most of us it demands St. Paul's challenge to the Christians of Corinth, torn asunder by cliques and factions: "Let a man examine himself, [a woman examine herself,] *and so* eat of the bread and drink of the cup" (1 Cor 11:28). Examine what? Examine if communion in the blood of Christ sets me with Mary and John squarely beneath a cross. Examine whether a bloodstained Calvary and a bloodless Eucharist have transformed my blood, have transformed me, into a symbol of life. Examine whether I am no longer shocked by the shocking assertion of radical H. Rapp Brown, "Violence is as American as apple pie." Examine what I, what we as a community born of Christ's blood, do to stanch the violence in our hearts, the violence in our homes, the violence on our streets. Examine how we respond in fact to the command of Christ, "Love one another [everybody] as I have loved you" (Jn 15:12). Examine how sincere we are when we pray the prayer without which our Lord's blood would have made no sense: "Father, forgive them . . ." (Lk 23:34); how sincere when we call out in each Eucharist "Forgive us *as we forgive*."

Frankly, I know not how to bring this down to earth, down to your earth. You have to listen not to my abstractions about blood but to the Lord whose blood alone can bring peace. Allow me simply to close with a story—a story that actually happened not long ago in the Middle East.

In the Hashemite Kingdom of Jordan, in a tiny town named Mafraq, two Bedouin youths got into a fight, fell to the ground in their fury. One lad pulled out a knife, plunged it fatally into the other's flesh. In fear he fled for days across the desert, fled the slain boy's vengeful relatives, fled to find a Bedouin sanctuary, a "tent of refuge" designed by law for those who kill unintentionally or in the heat of anger. At last he reached what might be a refuge—the black-tented encampment of a nomad tribe. He flung himself at the feet of its leader, an aged sheik, begged him: "I have killed in the heat of anger; I implore your protection; I seek the refuge of your tent."

"If God wills," the old man responded, "I grant it to you, as long as you remain with us."

A few days later the avenging relatives tracked the fugitive to the refuge. They asked the sheik: "Have you seen this man? Is he here? For we will have him."

"He is here, but you will not have him."

"He has killed, and we the blood relatives of the slain will stone him by law."

"You will not."

"We demand him!"

"No. The boy has my protection; I have given my word, my promise of refuge."

"But you do not understand. He has killed your grandson!"

The ancient sheik was silent. No one dared to speak. Then, in visible pain, with tears searing his face, the old man stood up and spoke ever so slowly: "My only grandson—he is dead?"

"Yes, your only grandson is dead."

"Then," said the sheik, "then this boy will be my son. He is forgiven, and he will live with us as my own. Go now; it is finished."[7]

Dahlgren Chapel
Georgetown University
and
Holy Trinity Church
Washington, D.C.
June 5, 1988

18
SHE HOLDS HIGH MOTHERHOOD
Homily for a Marian Year Vespers

- Luke 1:26–38

If you were alive and well in the wild and woolly 60s, you must have noticed that "things they were achangin'." Not only from booze to pot, from faculty burn-outs to student burn-downs, from "My country right or wrong" to "No, no, we won't go," from postwar freedom to post-Christian license, from white slavery to black power, from male domination to female liberation, from age-old colonialism to revolutionary republics.

Not only that; "things they were achangin'" in the Catholic Church. A new world and a world-wide council of bishops changed the face of Catholicism. Catholics and Protestants were talking civilly to one another—across back yards and theological tables, from the grass roots of Iowa to the gilded walls of the Vatican. The Church was no longer a tight little island battered by unbelief and stormed by secularism; it was part and parcel of the world it inhabited, open to that world, yearning to serve it, holy indeed but sinful too, always in need of reformation. The Mass was changing from a stately Latin few understood to a graceless English a child could grasp, from organ to guitar, from stress on the Sacrifice to equal value for the Word. Priests and sisters were questioning their calling, starting the mass exodus that would decimate our rectories and religious houses. The laity were flexing their Christian muscles, recognizing that they were as much "church" as the mitred few.

Much of the change was commendable, and I for one rejoiced. But almost insensibly, not quite recognizing it, we were losing a fair bit. Here I am not concerned with doctrine or morals, with liturgy or law. My concern is devotion—or, if you will, devotions. I mean

127

the affective, warm, somewhat private, deeply personal part of Catholicism that is not a requisite for life eternal but can help us to be at once more Christian and more human. We may argue about statues and vigil lights, about novenas and the Way of the Cross, about Benediction of the Blessed Sacrament. What I see as tragic beyond dispute is what brings me here this evening: We lost our Lady.

Let me address three issues here, ask three questions, play successively historian, theologian, and homilist. First, how come we lost our Lady? Second, why was it such a tragedy? Third, what should we do about it?

I

First, how come we lost our Lady? How did it happen? There is no simple, single answer. Some insist that the villain was the Second Vatican Council. Instead of devoting a complete document to Mary, the bishops "hid" her in the last chapter of the Constitution on the Church—long after it had discoursed at length on the hierarchy, on laity and religious, even (God save the mark!) on "the eschatological nature of the pilgrim Church." Some say we yielded, perhaps unwittingly, to Protestant pressure, centuries of non-Catholic claims that Catholics had put Mary on a par with the one only Redeemer Christ; so, we "put her in her place." She would no longer be "our life, our sweetness, and our hope." Some iconoclasts surely wanted to discard the accumulated baggage of the past, get the Church out of the Middle Ages, emphasize the essentials: word and worship, sacraments and sacrifice. No need to pray to St. Joseph holding his lily, light a candle for the dead, make the Nine First Fridays to assure your salvation, finger a mindless rosary, bless yourself with holy water, fast on Friday, strafe the sanctuary with smoke, kneel for Communion, confess in darkness a laundry list of peccadillos. We're beyond that. It was good enough for our immigrant forebears; it's not for us, educated, sophisticated, men and women of a new era, who walk on the moon and talk on TV, have smashed the atom, create life in a test tube, can nuke the world in a matter of minutes.

In this context our Lady suffered. So many who wanted a document on Mary never read the revolutionary eighth chapter of the Constitution on the Church, never discovered why Mary is singularly precious for our life of faith. So many who wanted Mary put in her place left her no place at all. And those who looked askance at Catholic devotional practices seemed to forget that Catholicism is not a religion of cold reason, of abstract intelligence; it is a religion of the whole person, heart as well as mind, emotion as well as understanding, passion as well as purpose. For all practical purposes, in our day-to-day living we have lost our Lady. No longer, with Jesuit poet Gerard Manley Hopkins, do we compare the Blessed Virgin to the air we breathe, no longer sing with him:

> . . . men are meant to share
> Her life as life does air.
> If I have understood,
> She holds high motherhood
> Towards all our ghostly good
> And plays in grace her part
> About man's beating heart,
> Laying, like air's fine flood,
> The deathdance in his blood;
> Yet no part but what will
> Be Christ our Saviour still.[1]

II

This moves me to my second question: Why is such a loss so tragic? After all, didn't we get rid of some pious superstitions, medieval relics: that Jesus administers justice but Mary ministers mercy; that in a pinch only the mother will get you out of hell? Didn't we finally subordinate the rosary to the liturgy, Mary to the Mass, the mother to her Son?

Perhaps, but in the process all too many rushed pell-mell, helter-skelter, to an un-Catholic extreme. They lost, or never possessed, a priceless tradition that 20th-century theologians had recaptured from the early Church and medieval times: Mary is a type or figure of the Church. What Mary was and is, that the Church and each individual Christian is expected to be. Put another way: Mary is the first Christian disciple. More than that, she is the model, the most remarkable model, of what Christian disciples should be, what *we* should be. This demands some explanation.

In the New Testament, to be a disciple is to be a follower: specifically, to follow in the footsteps of one Master, Christ. Not to imitate him in externals—walk in sandals, talk Aramaic, cure a military man's son, raise a widow's only child from the dead. Essential to discipleship is to have the *mind* of Christ. And what was that? In his own simple, profound response, "I seek not my own will but the will of Him who sent me" (Jn 5:30). It is the mind he taught us in the Our Father: "Thy will be done, on earth as it is in heaven" (Mt 6:10). It is the mind he lived through bloody sweat in Gethsemane: "My Father, if it be possible, let this cup pass from me; nevertheless, not as I will, but as you will" (Mt 26:39).

Such was the mind of Mary. It is splendidly summed up in Nazareth, when God asks her if she will bring into the world, give her flesh to, "the Son of the Most High" (Lk 1:32). She is puzzled, of course; what teen-age girl, what woman of any age, would not be? She asks one question, a natural question: How? "How . . . , since I have no husband?" (1:34). Once she hears "The Holy Spirit will come upon you and the power of the Most High will overshadow you" (1:35), her answer is swift, unreserved: "Be it done unto me according to your word. Let it happen to me as you say" (1:38). Your will be done.

There it is, in a nutshell. If that was the hour when the Son of God took flesh, it was also the hour when the first Christian disciple was born. And yet, that hour of rapture was but a beginning. As with all other mothers, so with Mary: She did not know where her yes to God, her yes to motherhood, would take her. Dear angel Gabriel did not leave her with a script: not a word about a feeding trough in Bethlehem, flight by night into Egypt, three obscure decades in Nazareth, three short years "in the world," townspeople who tried to throw him over a cliff, relatives who shouted he was mad, a jeer-strewn journey to Jerusalem, a traitor's kiss, disciples abandoning him, a criminal's condemnation, a crown on his head and lashes on his back, twin beams of bloody wood. Not a single word. And no angel promised this mother: "Fear not; your son will rise again."

Did Mary worry about her Jesus, weep and bleed for him, lie sleepless and afraid? The Gospels do not say so (or only once [Lk 2:48]), but you'd better believe it; she was not a robot. And still, through those three decades and more, Mary never took back that initial, radical response: Whatever you want, Lord. That is what gives rich Marian meaning to an episode in Luke that could confuse you, an incident that has misled many a believer down the centuries. Remember the woman who cried to Jesus from the crowd: "Blessed is the womb that bore you, and the breasts you fed on"? Remember Jesus' response? "Blessed rather are those who listen to the word of God and keep it" (Lk 11:27–28). Not the back of his hand to his mother; quite the contrary. Simply, Mary is even more blessed because she ceaselessly said yes to Yahweh than because she gave birth to God's Son. Of course it was a unique, glorious, ecstatic act, lending her flesh for ever to the Son of the Most High. But Mary's most admirable gift to God was not the sheer tabernacle of her body. More blessedly still, she laid at God's feet her freely uttered yes—from Nazareth, through Bethlehem, to Jerusalem and beyond. Whatever you want, Lord. She never took it back.

Now precisely for that reason the fathers at Vatican II enclosed our Lady within a document on the Church: ". . . the Mother of God is a model of the Church in the area of faith, of love, and of perfect union with Christ."[2] She does not sit on a golden throne in splendid isolation, while we bend low before mystery that is meaningless for our lives: before an immaculate conception that was never ours, a virginal motherhood unique in history, a glorious assumption not preceded like ours by the corruption of the grave. Mary makes sense, contemporary sense, as a link between Christ and the Church. This very human Jewish woman stands before you in the flesh she gave her Son, stands before you not like a lifeless statue but as a living example, God's finest example, of what it means to be a disciple, how you should live here and now if you want to follow Christ. Not only you individually. This is what the Christian community must be and do if it wants to be the Church of Christ.

In a word, our Lady, mother of the Church, stands before each and all of us who claim to be Christian, ceaselessly urging on us what she said to the servants at Cana's wedding feast: "Do whatever he tells you" (Jn 2:5). She speaks not from book learning but from living experience; for in the story of humankind no sheerly human being has listened to the word of God more intently, has said yes to the word of God more unreservedly, has done the word of God more perfectly . . . even unto crucifixion.

III

This leads into my third question: Granted all this—granted we have lost our Lady and the loss is tragic—what should we do about it? After all, this is not a class in theology, despite the appetizer you've just ingested. Do you merely leave Holy Trinity enlightened in mind about Mary, with perhaps a fresh conversation piece for a Catholic cocktail party? Good indeed, but not good enough. Like the crowds who flocked to John the Baptist, you ask: "What then shall we do?" (Lk 3:10).

First and obviously, you do, or resolve to do, what our Lady did, what she told the waiters at Cana: You do whatever the Lord tells you. But this lesson most Christians learn quite apart from Mary, learn it from her Son: learn it from the Our Father ("thy will be done, on earth as it is in heaven" [Mt 6: 10]), learn it from Jesus' agony in the garden ("Father, if thou art willing, remove this cup from me; nevertheless not my will, but thine, be done" [Lk 22:42]). And even if our Lady does confirm, strikingly, impressively, what our Lord taught us by word and in deed, is this all there is to it? Abstract knowledge? Is this reason enough for a Marian Year?

I say no. For what is tragic in what we have lost is that we have lost not simply a principle but a person. And not a person who once was alive and now is dead. We have lost a lady who at this very moment is more alive than you and I are, is as alive as is her risen Son, gloriously alive, not only in soul but in her body as well, splendidly whole, now as God wanted her to be when choosing her to mother the Messiah, when shaping her free from sin, when setting her beneath the cross, when lifting her from earth to heaven.[3] She is Number One in a Christian body we have likewise lost, the Church in glory, the communion of saints, of the holy men and women who have lived their yes to God on earth and live with Him days without end.

Now Mary's presence in that Church triumphant is not a static, frozen, plaster-saint presence. The yes she murmured to an angel, the yes that gave us God's Son in our flesh, that same yes she carried with her when she left our tortured earth; that yes *is* Mary. And in the Catholic tradition our Lady's endless yes is powerful with her Son. No words are necessary; she need not plead for us on bended knee. Her yes to God was a yes for us, and in God's sight it remains, and will remain till time is no more, a powerful prayer for us to her risen Christ. That is why we pray, or used to pray: "Remember, O most gracious Virgin Mary, that never was it known that anyone who fled to thy protection, implored thy help, or sought thy intercession was left unaided."

In this context, what we ought recapture today is a warm relationship to the mother of Jesus. She is not our Redeemer; only Jesus is. We do not imitate the charming piety of the Italian peasant woman finally convinced by a Communist that there is no God. Her response? "All right, so there is no God. But we still have the mother of God!" Her logic limped, but her instincts were right on target. We have to play the child again, for Mary is *our* mother too. Recall the scene on Calvary. "When Jesus saw his mother there with the disciple whom he loved, he said to his mother: 'Woman, here is your son.' In turn he said to the disciple: 'Here is your mother' " (Jn 19:26–27). Highly symbolic, good Scripture scholars insist. The "beloved disciple" is not simply the apostle John, the individual son of Zebedee and brother of James. The "beloved disciple" is the Christian, all Christians: Those who believe in Jesus are reborn in his image. As sisters and brothers of Jesus, you too have Mary for mother.[4]

If that is so, then you and I had better begin treating Mary as our mother. Now the way you live such a relationship is not spelled out for you in Scripture; no single way is imposed on you by Rome. Times change and cultures vary; one person's meat is another person's poison. Some go for pilgrimages: to Fatima or Lourdes, to Czestochowa or Guadalupe, to Walsingham or Medjugorje. Others light candles, kneel through novenas, crown Mary Queen of the May. Still others let beads slip insensibly through their fingers, while they praise Mary repeatedly for her yes to God and ask her intercession "now and at the hour of our death." At least we used to.

For me, most meaningful is continual contemplation, with rosary or without. Let reason desist, argument be still, theology fade. Let the mysteries of Mary and her Christ inhabit the screen of your imagination: the face of Mary before a reverent angel or an apologetic innkeeper; her eyes drinking in her newborn baby. Feel how Mary felt when her relatives shouted he was mad, when her neighbors tried to cast him from a cliff. Agonize with her as thorns crown his brow and whips lash his back. Be there as she cradles his lifeless flesh in a living Pietà. Joy with her when the risen Jesus stands before her with all his love in his eyes.[5]

This is not gushy sentimentalism; this is Christian realism. Here is the flesh-and-blood human who, after her Son on the cross, murmured the most radical yes in recorded history; the woman who lived most perfectly the ideal of Christian disciple; the mother not only of Jesus but of his sisters and brothers, holding "high motherhood" even now "towards all our ghostly good." No need to apologize for Mary, to remove her statue as a threat to the tabernacle; for she always holds Jesus in her arms, holds him out to you and me. Our task is to warm up to her, to fall in love again. And we had better love her. After all, we're going to have to live with her . . . for ever.

Holy Trinity Church
Washington, D.C.
February 3 and April 17, 1988
and
Dahlgren Chapel
Georgetown University
April 17, 1988

19
HOPE . . . IN THE LORD
Homily for a Baptism

- Ezekiel 34:11–12, 15–17
- 1 Corinthians 15:20–26, 28
- Matthew 25:31–46

Good friends: You will pardon me, I trust, if I address my homily directly to the main character, the principal actress, the leading lady, the star in today's drama.

I

Last month, Hope Chang Woolsey,[1] on the 19th day of October, without your knowledge and without your consent, your mother and father did something to you that is at once wonder-full and fear-full. They initiated you into the human community.[2] It was a moment filled with wonder, because another image of God had been shaped. One of countless billions indeed, from the fashioning of the first Adam to the final Eve. And still unique, because there had never been this "you" before, and there never will be again. And so someone singularly precious came forth to us that day, to lengthen our laughter and season our tears with your own. That day you gave to a whole little world such fresh hope, such a lift of the heart, as none but the newborn can give. Your birth into the human community was an unspoken hope that because of you we just might be more human, more obviously a people of God in love with the Lord and *all* His human images.

And yet, that moment so wonder-full was also quite fear-full. For your father and mother were initiating you into a community of contradictions—where images of God not only die for one another but kill one another; where love mingles with hate, faith with

135

infidelity, hope with despair; where at any given moment half the world is at war hot or cold; where a cross is erected over history; where despite the miracles of technology the threat of annihilation hangs over us by a hair, like the fabled sword of Damocles.[3] Limited as we are, loving you though we do, we know not what your parents have initiated you into, what this world holds for you as you grow into the child, the adolescent, the woman.

II

Yes, dear Hope Chang Woolsey, it is not only wonder-full but fear-full, this initiation into the human community. That is why this afternoon we celebrate a second initiation. Without your knowledge and without your consent, the Church will initiate you into the Christian community. It is indeed a moment filled with wonder, for it is a new birth. When the waters of baptism bathe your brow, another image will be shaped: an image of Christ.[4]

You see, right now, as I speak, you are something of a paradox, hard to believe. On the one hand, you are beloved of God; you were so from the moment of your conception. On the other hand, you are not yet what the Father of Jesus Christ wants you to be: You are not-yet-in-Christ. The Christ who was born for you, who lived for you, who died for you, who rose for you—this Christ has not yet taken possession of you. In a few short moments he will. At that moment miracles of grace will begin for you. The power of Christ will cast out the power of Satan, the Spirit of love drive out the spirit of evil. Your loving Lord will pour into your whole person a threefold power that is dormant today but will quicken into action as your limbs grow, as your mind matures, as your heart expands.

I mean, first, the power to believe. Not only to give a firm assent to propositions: "I believe that there is one God in three divine Persons; I believe that the Second Person of the Blessed Trinity became man and died for our salvation." I mean, even more importantly, the power to give yourself totally, in full awareness of its perils, to the Christ within you. I mean, second, the power to hope—to hope even against hope; through all the bittersweet of human and inhuman living, to keep repeating with the Psalmist "O my God, in thee I trust" (Ps 25:2); the power to "walk through the valley of the shadow of death" and "fear no evil" (Ps 23:4) because God—Father, Son, and Spirit—lives in you, loves you, carries you in the palm of His hand. I mean, third, the power to love—not in

some vague, fantasy-island fashion, but to love God and God's images as Christ our Lord loves his Father and you—loved them even
unto crucifixion.

You may one day read what Jesuit poet Gerard Manley Hopkins sang of you long before you were born, the close of a superb
sonnet on our imaging of Christ:

> Í say more: the just man justices;
>   Keeps gráce: thát keeps all his goings graces;
> Acts in God's eye what in God's eye he is—
>   Christ. For Christ plays in ten thousand places,
> Lovely in limbs, and lovely in eyes not his
>   To the Father through the features of men's faces.[5]

Yes, Christ will play to the Father through you, through the faith,
the hope, the love he pours into you today, the gifts that will enable
you to act in God's eye what in God's eye you are: Christ.

Wonder-full indeed, especially because this second initiation is
so fear-full. For we are initiating you into a community of contradictions. As you grow up, I am afraid you will often be scandalized. We
are proud to call ourselves a community of faith, the Christian
faithful; yet you will find many of us long on propositions, short on
self-giving; less suffering servants than lip servants, serving many
masters: possessions and power, fame and comfort. We call ourselves a community of hope; yet you will be disenchanted to discover how many of us put our hope in the genius of man and
woman, in hardware and software, in the weapons of war, the
power of politics, the dominion of the almighty dollar. We call
ourselves a community of love; yet who looks at the barbed wire in
Belfast, apartheid in South Africa, bloated starvelings in Ethiopia,
the slums of our cities, and thinks of us as a community whose life is
love?

Thank God, however, that despite our inner contradictions,
the community that welcomes you is not just another sin-ridden
establishment. There is a Presence here that is not of this world, a
Presence that pervades and invades us, a Presence that breaks
through our smallness and our sinfulness, makes us better than we
are—a Presence that is remarkably real because it is a person, a
living, pulsing, risen person. Here, Hope Chang Woolsey, in this
community, you can, and I hope you will, find Jesus: find him in
our gathering together as we do today, find him in the word we
proclaim, find him in the bread become his body, in the wine blush-

ing into his blood; find him in the smiles that crease our faces, in the love we lavish on you.

III

You know, Hope Chang Woolsey, I find it wonder-full that you grace our community on this festival day—the feast of Jesus Christ our King. For today we are consecrating you to a king whose kingdom is literally "out of this world," who is king not of states but of hearts, who will never compel your love but only draw you by his own crucified love, whose kingdom, the Preface of the Mass will proclaim, is "a kingdom of truth and life, a kingdom of holiness and grace, a kingdom of justice, love, and peace."

Today, I am sure, many of us will bring you a variety of gifts. Splendid! But there is one gift no one of us should forget to bring. In turning *you* to Christ in love, we should turn *ourselves* afresh to Christ. Only thus can we justify the risk with which we burden you: the risk of becoming one with us, with our community. Only thus will the burden become a blessing, the fear in our hearts be cast out by the wonder of it all: the Christ who plays to the Father through the features of *our* faces. Such is my hope, the hope that your very name inspires in me.

Jesuit Community Chapel
Georgetown University
November 22, 1987

20

MY BODY, GIVEN FOR YOU
Homily for a Mass of the Resurrection

- 1 Corinthians 15:12–19
- John 11:17–27

Today[1] I find no place for prolonged preaching. Today I remember, I regret, and I rejoice.

I

Today I remember. Each of you has his or her own memories; forgive me if I can speak of Edward Bennett Williams only as *I* remember him. And my memory is short: It spans fewer than five years. What do I remember?

I remember a man for others. A man who wedded a love for law with the law of love. Brilliant, yes; but more importantly, he cared. Cared not only for well-heeled clients but for the beggar who lay in wait for him at Holy Trinity; not only for his noble Knights and Ladies of Malta but for his hapless Orioles;[2] not only for his firm but for his family; not only for a Buchwald[3] but for a Burghardt as well.

I remember a man of courage—incredible courage. Only his dear ones and his doctors know in detail how deeply death was etched into his flesh, into his every day, this past decade. Few realize what it cost him to live not for tomorrow but for today—and to live each day fully, with peace on his strong brow and humor in his eyes.

I remember a Catholic Christian. I mean a man who loved his Christ, the Christ with whom he was crucified on his cross of cancer. Loved his Church with a passion, while acutely aware of its scarred and wrinkled humanity. Loved his Eucharist, where he

139

drew ceaseless strength from the flesh and blood of his Lord. Loved even his Jesuits, split his affection rather evenly between Worcester and D.C., between Crusaders and Hoyas.[4]

II

Today I regret. I regret that I came to know Ed so late in life— St. Augustine's lament, "Late have I loved thee."[5] I envy you who watched him grow, as Jesus grew, "in wisdom, in stature, in favor with God and with men and women" (Lk 2:52). I regret that I never saw him in action: defending the famous and the infamous and the defenseless, mesmerizing a jury or a commencement, coming to grips with a Redskins co-owner or a U.S. President.[6] I would like to have shared over the years his inner life, his life with God in the sanctuary of his heart, the way he related to Agnes and the children, of whom he spoke to me with such pride and affection.

I regret that Ed has been taken from us. Though death was long writ large on his flesh, the final cross, "Into thy hands I entrust my spirit" (Lk 23:46), still tears my heart. Not so much because I shall never again hear his hearty hello: "Numero uno" he would hail me—a supreme salute from so superb a speaker. Rather because his death diminishes us all. All of us are the poorer for his passing. Grace has been taken from our midst. Not sinless, surely; not flawless, of course; with apologies to Shakespeare, not necessarily "the noblest 'Roman' of them all."[7] Just a man who inspired me to be better than I am, and often showed me how—without a word.

I regret that I was unable to stand beneath his cross, like John on Calvary, the day he left us. I regret that I was unable even to help consign his body gratefully to the Lord whose image he strove so mightily to be.

III

I remember; I regret; and still I rejoice. I joy in the strength he passed on to me in his very weakness; for he proved to me the truth of St. Paul's paradox: "The weakness of God is stronger than men" (1 Cor 1:25).

I joy not merely in my memory of him but in his vibrant presence in who I now am. Because of Ed, I am a more human man, a more courageous Christian, a Jesuit more like Jesus, a more passionate priest.

I joy in the living images of our Lord he has left us: Joe and Ellen, Bennett and Ned, Dana and Tony and Kimberly. If not quite "chips off the old block" (each of you is unique), you are still part and parcel of his flesh and spirit—his legacy to us.

I joy, above all, in my Christian conviction that at this moment Ed is more thrillingly alive than he has ever been. He bears out the stubborn refusal of Jesus to put our dead "on ice" till the last day, his stirring declaration to Martha inconsolable over her dead brother Lazarus: "Whoever . . . believes in me shall never die" (Jn 11:26). Edward Bennett Williams is alive! That, good friends, I believe with all my heart. For your strength and consolation, I pray that you do too.

On behalf of GU's Jesuits, I thank you, Agnes, for sharing Ed so unselfishly with us. Our gratitude can be expressed no more richly than in the Church's central act of thanksgiving: the Eucharist which Father Collins, Father George, and I are offering this evening for Ed—the Sacrifice where we will murmur with our lips what Ed ceaselessly thundered with his life: "This is my body . . . given for you" (Lk 22:19).

Jesuit Community Chapel
Georgetown University
September 21, 1988

21
FAITH, INTELLIGENCE, JUSTICE
Centennial of a New Orleans Academy

- Ezekiel 34:11–16
- Ephesians 3:14–19
- John 15:9–17

How shall I celebrate your centennial? If the Academy of the Sacred Heart were just one human person, a lady grown old graciously, there are prescribed amenities, social courtesies, that would see me through. I would discount the wrinkles and express pleasure that she is still with us, unexpectedly but delightfully alive after one hundred years. I would bend over the rocker, take the gnarled, veined, liver-blotched hands in my own, and the two of us would reminisce with a mint julep over her lives and her loves.

But Sacred Heart is not just one person, not just a gracious old lady; she is an institution. And a homily is not a history, anecdotes from ancient annals to make you feel good. Indeed, a homily has for purpose to celebrate God's wonderful works in the story of salvation, and, to our delight, one of God's wonderful works is . . . Sacred Heart: the Heart that was born in Bethlehem 19 centuries ago, and the heart that began to beat in its image in New Orleans a single century past.

You do well, therefore, to glory in your history. Neither cataracts nor hardened arteries should keep our gracious lady from warm memories. The problem is, 1887 is not so much a memory as a challenge. It projects a perennial institutional issue: yesterday and tomorrow, tradition and reform, continuity and change. The challenge to your second century, I suggest, lies in three areas that have dominated Sacred Heart education since 1800. The areas are ageless, but the context for the challenge has changed, and this forces from you a fresh form of response. Let me speak to you of (1) faith, (2) intelligence, (3) justice.

142

I

By "faith" I do not mean simply the age-old Act of Faith: "O my God, I firmly believe that thou art one God in three divine Persons, Father, Son, and Holy Ghost. I believe that thy divine Son became man and died for our sins. I believe these and all the truths which the holy Catholic Church teaches, because thou hast revealed them, who canst neither deceive nor be deceived." Important, of course; for Catholicism expresses itself, its faith, in formulae that are inexpressibly rich, formulae that are part of "the faith." Important, but not sufficient for salvation. Remember the New Testament Letter of James: "You believe that God is one; you do well. Even the demons believe—and shudder" (Jas 2:19). To come alive, faith has to be instinct, infused, with love. It is the faith of which you have just heard from Paul's prayer for the Christians of Ephesus: ". . . that [the Father] may grant you to be strenghtened with might through His Spirit in the inner man and woman, and that Christ may dwell in your hearts through faith; that, being rooted and grounded in love, you may have power to comprehend with all the saints what is the breadth and length and height and depth, and to know the love of Christ which surpasses knowledge, that you may be filled with all the fulness of God" (Eph 3:16–19). Your faith is you, given totally to God—your mind and heart, your will and emotions, your bone and blood—given to God more completely than you give yourself to any human being, however closely knit to you in love.

Why is such a faith significant? When St. Madeleine Sophie Barat founded your Society, the historical context was a crimson revolution, a rebellion of the masses. In its quest for liberty, equality, and fraternity, the French Revolution in large measure exalted freedom over faith, reason over revelation, even celebrated the feast of Goddess Reason in Notre Dame Cathedral. During the Reign of Terror the blood of the Church flowed freely. You had to love God with all your heart and mind, all your soul and strength, because your life was at stake . . . literally.[1]

In our time the challenge to faith is different. The problem has been impressively posited by German theologian Karl Rahner:

> Every age has its own task before God; the task of today's world is to believe. For today it is not this or that belief, this or that article of the faith which is called into doubt, but faith itself, man's capacity to believe, man's ability to commit himself completely to a single, unambiguous, demanding conviction. . . .[2]

Today your faith is under assault not so much from the masses as from the intellectuals. You are not likely to endure the rack, to grovel beneath a guillotine, simply because you are a stubborn believer. You can profess your faith propositions in the French Quarter or on the lakefront, can love God openly with the fearless freedom of Jesus himself, and little blood, if any, will flow. All you have to face, all you have to fear, is pity or contempt, laughter or irritation, hostile argument or uncaring silence.

II

You will grasp what I am getting at, realize your role in response to today's faithlessness, if you link with your faith a second area of Sacred Heart's educational tradition. I mean . . . intelligence. In that tradition, faith has always struggled for understanding. For faith, in the Catholic vision, is not a mindless possession. Part of the total person given to God totally is your intelligence. And a thrilling, fantastic way of giving your faith-filled mind to God is the effort you initiated at Sacred Heart: the struggle to discover and appreciate the things of God (His trace in all creation), the people of God (His image on the face of all humanity), and God Himself.

Those who inherited your tradition before you rarely carried on the search in idyllic tranquility. In Europe your 19th-century ancestors confronted currents that seemed on the surface to contradict so much that was Catholic: in politics, the movement from a sacral to a secular society; in science, the apparent threat to a Creator God from evolution; in Scripture, the assault on the historical authenticity of God's Word.

Today your faith confronts three forceful foes. If I may borrow, without fear of costly consequences,[3] the language of Jesuit John Courtney Murray, there is, first, "the godless man of the Academy," of the university, whose will is to "explain the world without God." There is, second, "the godless man of the communist world revolution," the godless man of Marxism, whose will is to suppress God. There is, third, "the godless man of the Theater," the theater of the absurd, the godless man of the arts, who "wills the absence of God."[4]

Now the godless man and woman of the Academy, of Marxism, of the Theater may well pose a threat to your personal faith. After all, uncounted Catholics have succumbed to their siren songs. But on this your centennial I am not particularly concerned to protect your baptismal beliefs against the attacks of the atheist. I want to accentuate the positive. I am far more absorbed by apostleship, by a vision of the apostles your own Academy summons you to be, apostles to the godless in all their shapes and forms. Not simply a dream, not sheer fantasy, reverie. I thumb through your *Profiles of Outstanding Alumnae*,[5] brief sketches that are said to "symbolize all former students."[6] I see a political activist and a preservationist, a physicist and a physician, a civil servant and an English scholar, a TV editor and a magazine editor, a rural-development manager and a liturgical musician, a newspaper columnist and a mayor, a sociologist and a city councilwoman, an attorney, an author, an artist. And so many of these are mothers as well. Here are women who wed faith and intelligence, who live Vatican II's impassioned appeal to the laity: "to penetrate and perfect the temporal sphere with the spirit of the gospel."[7]

These alumnae of your Academy are not anomalies, exceptions to the rule. They represent what an impressive number of you actually are, what all of you ought to be if you are to confront a fresh atheism with a faith that seeks understanding. Otherwise your attractive Academy makes little human or Christian sense: one hundred years spent, at extraordinary expense, in preserving your personal faith, in mounting a fortress mentality that keeps American culture from poisoning you, from ever touching you. No. The future of your Church and of your culture rests in large measure on your ability, on your yearning, to infuse your world with the dream of Jesus expressed the night before he died: "that they may know thee, the only true God, and Jesus Christ, whom thou hast sent" (Jn 17:3). And you do this not primarily by professing your faith; you do it by confronting your acre of God's world with the intelligence that makes faith persuasive—the intelligence that may cut into the 1.6 million annual American assaults on the womb, may help persuade the superpowers that an uncontrolled arms race can only end in a nuclear hell, may finally bond black and white as brothers and sisters in the Lord.

Today's Gospel strikes a subtle blow for an apostolate of intelligence. "No longer do I call you servants [or: slaves], for the servant [or: slave] does not know what his/her master is doing; but I have called you friends, for all that I have heard from my Father I have made known to you. You did not choose me, but I chose you and appointed you that you should go and bear fruit and that your fruit should abide . . ." (Jn 15:15–16). Our Lord has left you incredible insights into the mind of his Father. It is your privilege and your function, as friends of God-made-man, to plumb those insights, to touch them to our technological times, and so to humanize an emerging America that, on its own admission, is captivated by three goals: money, power, and fame.

III

This leads logically into a third area of Sacred Heart's educational tradition: justice. Not a bloodless "Give to others what they deserve, what they have a strict right to demand because it is chiseled into human law or required by moral reasoning." Rather, the justice proclaimed in Old Testament and New: Feed the hungry and slake the thirsty, clothe the naked and house the stranger, console the sick and comfort the enchained because this is the way God has acted toward you. Because this is demanded by the Heart of Jesus that was pierced with a lance because he loved—loved without reserve or discrimination, loved the prostitute and the prodigal, loved the penitent thief *and* the unrepentant, loved Judas as well as John.

Such has been your Society's charism since 1800. Can you ever forget Mother Philippine Duchesne, bent and broken, leaving St. Louis at 72 to live among fierce Indians—too weak to work but ceaselessly at prayer, so that the Indians named her "The Woman Who Always Prays," even honored her in grisly fashion by hanging scalps outside her hut?[8] Can you forget what Superior General María Josefa Bultó wrote to her Sisters in America in 1968, to celebrate the sesquicentennial of the day Mother Duchesne "kissed passionately the rich soil of your beloved country"?

> Enlightened and strengthened by faith, may you go to all men, the ignorant, the poor, the suffering, be Christ to them. It is for this that you have left all things, your home, your loved ones. . . . Our responsibility as educators in this field [social justice] is an all-important one. We cannot shirk it. Each one of our students should leave us with [an] anxiety for social justice, [a] determination to make this world a better place, in an evangelical spirit, in fraternal love.[9]

Today most of the Academy's alumnae live in graceful comfort. No sin in that. Jesus loved Lazarus and his sisters, though they seem to have lived rather well. He announced salvation to wealthy Zacchaeus, though the little fellow gave to the poor only half of all he possessed. The fact remains, America's agony is not only AIDS but still "the cry of the poor." In 1985 the leading killer of children in affluent America was poverty. A child-death study estimates conservatively that 10,000 American children die each year from poverty— this compared to 8,000 from traffic, 3,000 from cancer, 1,800 from heart disease. And while 15 percent of white children are born poor, 45 percent of black children are born into poverty.[10] Poverty makes for second-class citizens, for stunted minds and bodies, for men and women who rummage for food in garbage cans, warm themselves in winter on sidewalk grates. Poverty makes a shameful sham of the American proposition "All are created equal."

Women of the Sacred Heart have been impressively generous in giving of their substance to the disadvantaged, the downtrodden, the despairing. What you must join to your generosity is the insight of St. Vincent de Paul, 17th-century apostle of charity: Unless you love, the poor will never forgive you for the bread you give them. What you must add to your giving is self-giving, the "I" that touches not poverty but a person, the "I" that welcomes the sufferer somewhat as John Paul II embraced a child afflicted with AIDS. It is then that you can echo with a special stress the words of the Lord you heard from Ezekiel: "*I* will seek the lost, and *I* will bring back the strayed, and *I* will bind up the crippled, and *I* will strengthen the weak. . . . *I* will feed them in justice" (Ezek 34:16). For then you will have responded as a living, throbbing, compassionate person to God's challenge in Isaiah:

> Is not this the fast that I choose:
> to loose the bonds of wickedness,
> to undo the thongs of the yoke,
> to let the oppressed go free,
> and to break every yoke?
> Is it not to share your bread with the hungry,
> and bring the homeless poor into your house;
> when you see the naked, to cover him,
> and not to hide yourself from your own flesh?
> Then shall your light break forth like the dawn,
> and your healing shall spring up speedily;
> your righteousness shall go before you,
> the glory of the Lord shall be your rear guard.
> Then you shall call, and the Lord will answer;
> you shall cry, and He will say "Here I am."
> (Isa 58:6–9)

Women of the Sacred Heart: It is clearly not merely a memory you celebrate today; it is a promise as well. *Your* promise—to the Sacred Heart and to the world you walk. A promise that your past is prologue. A promise in three parts. (1) A promise that the Sacred Heart in whose likeness the Academy has shaped you will always be, by God's gracious giving, the Heart in which you place your deepest trust, the high model of your loving *faith*. (2) A promise that this faith of yours, penetrated with love, will continually seek more profound *intelligence*, ceaselessly yearn to understand the things of God, the people of God, yes the living God Himself. (3) A promise that this intelligent faith will not stay sterile, will increasingly be a faith that does *justice*, that looks on each Lazarus who lies at your gate with the compassion of Christ, that deals with the disadvantaged as the Lord God has dealt with you.

Good friends, you are indeed a blessed breed, a favored flock. For the days that have fled, I thank you; for the days that lie ahead, I envy you. I pray, with today's Gospel, that Christ's "joy may be in you, and that your joy may be full" (Jn 15:11).

St. Louis Cathedral
New Orleans, Louisiana
October 2, 1987

22
DARE TO RISK
Canonization of Philippine Duchesne, RSCJ

- Isaiah 52:7–10
- 2 Corinthians 5:14–17
- John 12:20–26

Earlier in our century that prince of paradoxes G. K. Chesterton wrote: "A saint is one who exaggerates what the world and the Church have forgotten." That sentence makes sense not only of a hermit Antony locking himself in an Egyptian tomb, a black Martin de Porres asking his superiors to sell him into slavery, all those saints who slept rarely, bathed never, ate reluctantly. It is thrillingly true of all those men and women who were "eccentric" in its literal sense: They deviated from the center, from usual practice, the ordinary way of doing things, established methods. Put another way, they stood where your dear deceased friend John Courtney Murray placed himself—what he called "the radical center." In a word, while utterly faithful, they were willing to risk.

Such, I submit, was Rose Philippine Duchesne. On this solemn, festive occasion[1] let me spell out my thesis in three stages: (1) risk and your saint, (2) risk and your Church, (3) risk and you. In other words, today we remember, we reflect, we resolve; we look back, we look within, we look ahead.

I

First, risk and your saint: We look back, we remember. Now a homily is not a history; it must center on the Mystery—on Christ and the Body of Christ. Besides, you know your history far better than I. Still, the story of your saint is significant if you are to understand not only her but the Church and your place therein. I focus on the risk that was Rose.

To risk, the dictionaries tell us, is to expose yourself to loss or injury, to disadvantage or destruction. Such was your saint. I remember that she began awfully early. She risked her father's wrath when she entered the Visitation novitiate and argued with her family from behind a grille. She risked the wrath of the French Revolution when she ministered to men and women destined for the guillotine. She risked the wrath of the state when she returned to the convent and put on the habit, only to find herself and her love alone amid the religious ruins. She risked the displeasure of your dear Father Varin, when he came to discuss with her the new Society of the Sacred Heart. To the impatient 34-year-old woman he said: "You know, God always acts slowly." Her swift retort: "On the contrary, Scripture says He runs with giant bounds."[2]

But those risks were preparation—our Lord was preparing Philippine for the American apostolate dear to his heart and hers. I remember how this novice of 35 met her Sacred Heart superior, all of twenty-five. Amid all the wisdom Madeleine Sophie Barat passed on to Philippine, one gem is the riskiest of all: "You know that the greatest of treasures is the cross. A large portion is reserved for you. . . . You must suffer, and suffer without consolation."[3]

I remember how, 14 years later, a year short of 50, the supreme risk of Philippine's life began: to transmit the spirit of her Society to the New World. On the Feast of the Sacred Heart 1818, the small sailing vessel *Rebecca* came to anchor 20 miles below New Orleans and Philippine knelt in the dark to kiss the soil her heart had craved for years.

I remember how swiftly the cross was erected—the cross that embraced her for 34 years. Strangely, no word of welcome from the bishop—explained even then by the postal service. The news that not cultured St. Louis was to house her school but tiny St. Charles, which Philippine saw as "the tomb of her hopes."[4] So little contact with the "noble savage" for whose salvation she had crossed the sea. The school itself was a risk: Philippine found English an enigma; books and paper, quills and pencils, were at a premium; bone-chilling cold and pitiful food; liberty-loving children without the obedience of Sacré Coeur in France. "Perhaps [God] wants His missionary nuns to sanctify themselves by failure."[5]

I remember how St. Charles closed, and the sisters moved to Florissant. Now a small log cabin less human than St. Charles. But here the risk took encouraging shape: a boarding school, promis-

ing students, progress in learning, poise and courtesy—even a pi-
ano from France. And wonder of wonders, novices, vocations. Yet
always the cross: yellow fever caught on a ravaged vessel; cyclone
and flood at Florissant; calumny ("They say everything about us
except that we poison our children"[6]); even the risk of keeping the
Missouri Mission Jesuits alive—cooking for them, sewing for them,
going without basics for them, so that the De Smets could bring
Christ to victimized Indians. The scary radio serial of my adolescence "The Perils of Pauline" cannot compare with the perils of
Philippine!

I remember the St. Louis school that pioneered parochial and
public school systems there. It too had its cross for Philippine:
poverty and illness, the mystery of English, an old and tired heart.
While she watched her most faithful companion die in agony, Philippine's hair turned white.

I remember that Philippine was 72 when she realized her
heart's desire: an Indian school in Kansas. But as always, with love
came crucifixion. This woman whom the Potawatomi revered as
"the woman who prays always" could not teach them God's ways by
word, for the language was too difficult and her health was dreadfully frail. Wanting only to die among them, she was denied even
this. One year, and back to St. Charles. "It seems to me that in
leaving the savages I have left my element, and that henceforth I
can do nothing but languish for the heavenly country from which
happily there will be no more departures."[7]

What do I *not* remember? A single word of self-pity. Dismay
yes, but never despair. Feelings of failure yes, but never surrender.
Sadness indeed, but through it all a profound joy in her belief that
it is God "who gives life to the dead and calls into existence the
things that do not exist" (Rom 4:17). Father Murray phrased it
profoundly to your sisters back in 1941: Her "depressing sense of
inadequacy" before her task and ideal "did not take the heart out of
Philippine Duchesne. Rather, it put a heart into her, the Heart of
Christ, patiently obedient unto death, even to the death of the
Cross. In deepest union with Christ she went on."[8]

When she died at 83, Philippine could not have seen what her
"failures" would achieve: in North and South America, from Aus-
tralia to Zaire. Oh, she knew what God could and would accom-
plish: "You will see that when I am dead everything will prosper."[9]
Not that she had a vision of the future. She simply lived what the
Son of God had told her from the shadow of his cross: "I say to you,
unless a grain of wheat falls into the earth and dies, it remains alone

[merely a grain of wheat]; but if it dies, it bears much fruit" (Jn
12:24).

II

Second, risk and your Church: We look within, we reflect. You
see, Philippine Duchesne is not a saint primarily because she is
different; she is a saint because she symbolizes in striking fashion
what the whole Church is called to be: not only utterly faithful but
willing to risk.

Philippine reminds us that the Incarnation itself was a risk.
Never has the world seen, never will it see, the risks that were
Bethlehem and Calvary: the Son of God born in a stable, God-in-
flesh dying not with proof of resurrection but with faith in his
Father. If ever our earth witnessed apparent failure, it was this man
who preached eternal life and was crucified like a common criminal. The point is, Jesus not only *said* that to bear fruit the grain of
wheat must die; he *was* the grain of wheat par excellence. From his
death our life was born.

Philippine reminds us that Christ took a terrible risk when he
had Calvary continued by men and women, all feeble and fallible,
some craven and corrupt. The Church is a risk God took, and only
by risking can the Church carry Calvary forward. Risk has been our
destiny, our story, from the day the Holy Spirit rested on the apostles like tongues of fire, the day bruised and beaten apostles "left
the council, rejoicing that they were counted worthy to suffer dis-
honor for the Name" (Acts 5:41).

Philippine reminds us that the Body of Christ has spread
through the world because countless men and women afire with
the Spirit dared the impossible. Not only the canonized: 13-year-
old Agnes challenging the Roman Empire with her blood; Boniface
reforming the face and faith of Germany; Augustine and Aquinas
reshaping the Christian intelligence of the West; Francis of Assisi
and Jane Frances de Chantal, Ignatius Loyola and Madeleine Sophie, founders and foundresses of religious congregations large
and small. Not only the uncanonized in neon lights: Thomas Merton and Dorothy Day and Mother Teresa. With these the unsung
millions, ordained or not, lay or religious, married or single, who
have spent tears and sweat and blood to touch Christ to their acre
of God's world.

Philippine reminds us that we too, all of us, are asked to walk in their footsteps, simply because these are the footsteps of Christ. Not to do exactly what they did; each age, each spot, has its unique problems, and each of us is called individually. But all of us are called to risk, because each of us is called to be Christ where we are.

Philippine reminds us that the Church of Christ languishes where the mass of Christians are content to do what they have to do, are satisfied with a minimum, do not realize that they are commanded—not invited, commanded—to love God with their whole heart and mind, soul and strength, commanded to love every human person as much as they love themselves. She reminds us that we are all called to be saints.

Philippine reminds us that the joy which, Christ promised, no one can take from us is impossible without the cross—Christ's cross and our own. The Christian message is still life through death; only by losing your life for Christ's sake will you find life.

Philippine reminds us that we are not called to be successful but to be faithful, and to be faith-full is to risk, literally, all.

III

Third, risk and you. By "you" I mean the Religious of the Sacred Heart. Not exclusively, for others dream your dreams and participate in your apostolates. I simply want to be daringly direct.

I have known you for half a century—ever since that day in '38 on Convent Avenue in New York when the new kid on the whiz block, rising young Jewish philosopher Mortimer Adler, addressed the graduating class on, I believe, "Measure, Weight, and Number." I have been privileged to touch you from Purchase through St. Louis to San Francisco. I have watched you struggle to link fidelity to your foundress with the demands of a new age—education then and education now. I have seen you change (the word has an honorable Christian history). Not only in externals—turtlenecks and pocket money, travel and TV—but change that cuts at the vitals of your vocation. You know the neuralgic changes more intimately than I—from a new Manhattanville to a general chapter that focused your apostolate on peace and justice, on a preference for the poor, on the Third World.

You have dared to risk, to expose your Society to loss, injury, disadvantage, even destruction. Knowing some of you, I know how delighted many of you are in your re-formation. But not all your friends have been happy—not even all your own sisters. If your

Society is anything like mine—and from your birth you have been remarkably close to us—there are those among you, as among us, who have felt such anguish in changes so drastic that they cry out: "This is not the Society I entered, not the Society in which I vowed obedience." And for some the pain is so poignant, the hurt so heart-wrenching, that they must bid farewell as to a loved one who has died.[10]

It is not the right of a homilist to *appraise* your risk. Time alone will reveal to your heirs and descendants whether the risk was worth the price. What moves me mightily is your *readiness* to risk. To risk all for the heart of Christ as you hear it beat today, for the Church as it summons you at this moment in its mission, and for the most impoverished among God's people.

Here I return you to your dear Philippine. Time alone has put her "failure" in perspective. If you could tear her away for a moment from her endless partying with the angels, if you were to fix her gaze on the Children of Mary in America and on the countless children of God you have served these 170 years, if you were to say "See what your risk has wrought, what your 'failure' has fashioned," Philippine would glow with delight but answer "*Moi?* I? Not really. I merely let God be God. For all my love for the 'noble savage,' I never told God 'It's the Potawatomi or it's no go.' "

Good friends of the Sacred Heart: Your own Sister Cooney, in a profound meditation on Philippine,[11] asked what she would be doing if she were among us today. After all sorts of possible activities, from the victims of civil war in Nicaragua, through the feminist revolution in the States, to the deadly disease of AIDS, Sister Cooney recalls two temptations you must resist in a time of transition: disowning the past and simply repeating it. No, she insists, you have a much more difficult task. You must assimilate the past so as to move creatively into the future: "an enormous and exhausting and often frustrating, ever hopeful and obstinately determined effort of creative imagination."[12] Philippine would agree. "Be faithful but free. Dare to risk. Dare to be Christ—not to the Paris of 1800 or the Sugar Creek of 1841 or even the Manhattanville of 1938. Dare to be Christ to your own world, as God gives you in community to see it. Above all, let God be God. Let the heart of Christ be your heart."

National Shrine of the Immaculate Conception
Washington, D.C.
November 17, 1988

23
LEARNING, FREEDOM, FAITH
Homily for a University Bicentennial

- Jeremiah 9:23–24
- Galatians 5:1, 13–14
- Matthew 5:13–16

In today's liturgy a peril lurks. The peril is formalism. A Catholic institution—of course we open the bicentennial with a Mass. But, having paid due deference to the Lord, let's get on with celebrations proper to a university. Let's tackle academic freedom and nuclear deterrence, plumb religious pluralism and critique Catholic education, celebrate our "moral minority" and raise Christian fists for human rights, play *Romeo and Juliet* in the Quad and dance beneath the stars.

I'm afraid it will not wash; it's too simplistic. Like any masterly overture—the overture to Mozart's *Don Giovanni*—this liturgy should put you into a proper frame of mind for all that follows. The overture to Georgetown's grand opera is played by a prophet, an apostle, and God's unique Son—by Jeremiah, by Paul, and by Jesus. They suggest successively three ongoing facets of GU education: (1) what is the height of human knowing, (2) what it means to be free, and (3) the burden your years here lay on Hoyas for life. In other words, the three themes of your bicentennial: learning, freedom, faith.

I

First, the height of human knowing. The Hilltop has changed in startling fashion since John Carroll welcomed little William Gaston to the Academy, when "Georgetown's lowest division was open to any literate eight-year-old of respectable behavior."[1] Latin and

Greek have yielded pride of place to economics and linguistics; females grace and race corridors once sacred to a single sex; uniforms have given way to blue jeans; the ban on "publick houses" and "gaming tables" has been lifted; the rod has been replaced by sweet reason; few Hoyas still rise at 5 and retire at 8:30; daily Mass is no longer a command performance.

Still, one staple continues to command the Hilltop. Education at Georgetown springs unspoken from the song of Jeremiah: "Thus says the Lord: 'Let not the wise glory in their wisdom, let not the mighty glory in their might, let not the rich glory in their riches; but let those who glory glory in this, that they understand and know me' " (Jer 9:23–24).

This is not a slogan for a seminary. It follows on an insight superbly sung by Jesuit poet Gerard Manley Hopkins: "The world is charged with the grandeur of God."[2] It is not only an altar or a cross that speaks of the Lord. A whirlwind reflects God's power, a mountain mirrors God's majesty, surging waves God's irresistibleness, a star-flecked sky God's breath-taking loveliness.

That is why Georgetown's curriculum and classroom, your struggle to comprehend creation, is implicitly an effort to grasp creation's Creator. Here your mind has come to know what is true; your senses, to delight in what is beautiful; your will, to love what is good. You have struggled with ideas: wrestled with philosophers from ancient Greece to modern Britain; parleyed with politicians from the Soviet State and the Middle East, from China and Central America; marveled at matter through a microscope, at galaxies through a telescope; cruised through cultures other and older than your own; winged your way back millions of years to the very origins of human living. You have fallen in love with beauty: from Sappho to Shakespeare to Sandburg and Spielberg, from Apollo Belvedere to Rembrandt to Gauguin and Grandma Moses, from Greek choruses to Bernstein and Agnes de Mille, from medieval mystery plays to *Chariots of Fire* and *The Phantom of the Opera*.[3] You have grappled to grasp what it means to be good: on Capitol Hill and Wall Street, with nuclear warheads and African apartheid, in board room and bedroom. In all this you have, however unaware, touched the God who is eternal Truth, who is Beauty ever ancient ever new, who is Goodness in three Persons.

Pervading all this is your conscious search for God. I mean, in a theology which glories now not in being queen of the sciences but their humble servant, ever suggesting that there is more to human living than the most sophisticated microscope can discover: God wearing our flesh. And in the Eucharist even the 4.0 among you bend your minds and hearts with the simplest of the faith-full and sing full-throated to a hidden God as theologian Thomas Aquinas did:

> Godhead here in hiding, whom I do adore
> Masked by these bare shadows, shape and nothing more.
> See, Lord, at thy service low lies here a heart
> Lost, all lost in wonder at the God thou art.[4]

Despite Descartes, mathematics is not the highest form of knowledge. But neither is theology; for theology speaks *about* God. The highest form of knowledge is to know God—where knowledge is love. Georgetown is one with Aquinas when he writes: "There are two ways of desiring knowledge. One way is to desire it as a perfection of oneself; and that is the way philosophers desire it. The other way [of desiring knowledge] is to desire it not [merely] as a perfection of oneself, but because through this knowledge the one we love becomes present to us; and that is the way saints desire it."

II

The prophet turns us to the apostle, Jeremiah to Paul. If, as Jesus declared, "the truth will make you free" (Jn 8:32), what is this freedom to which Christ has called you? What are the enslavements Paul has in mind? Not directly South African apartheid or sub-Saharan drought, Middle East war or Cambodian refugees, black poverty or killer crack, AIDS or the pimping of adolescent America. Then what? Listen again to Paul: "Do not use your freedom as an opportunity for the flesh, but through love be servants of one another" (Gal 5:13). For Paul, the freedom Christ brings springs you from a twin slavery: slavery to sin and to self. Sin: the "sin of the world" and the sins of your own concocting, social sin and political sin. Self: where all living revolves around me—my aims and my ambitions, my successes and my failures, my injured ego and my acid indigestion, my image and my power.

No way, Paul protests; "through love be servants of one another" (Gal 5:13). That resounding cry Georgetown's rocks (her *saxa*[5]) re-echo. Not sin, not self, only service. This is not to condemn the top three goals proclaimed by America's incoming collegians: money, power, fame. These are not ethical evils in themselves. They take their morality from a single syllable: Why? Why money, why power, why fame?

Georgetown insists that if you wish to be free with the freedom Christ brings, these may never be ends for you—that way slavery lies; they must be means. Money, megabucks, however hard-earned, is a gift to you—a gift from the God who made it all possible by giving you life and breath, talent and toughness, a gift not to be clutched in hot little hands but to be given, to be shared, to lift the less-gifted from the grime and the grit, to slake their hunger for bread or justice, for peace or freedom, for knowledge or understanding—yes, for God. Power, influence—from rock 'n' roll through E. F. Hutton to the power houses in Washington—is a possession plagued with peril but potent with promise. Not because it satisfies a lust for control, but because it lets you be a servant, lets you minister to your sisters and brothers, lets you imitate the God and Father of us all, whose power is identical with His love, identical with His goodness, identical with His self-giving. Reputation, fame, is not yours to ape Narcissus, the mythological youth who fell in love with his own image. Fame allows the other to know you, to know what you are like, and so to lie at your golden gate, like poor Lazarus in the Gospel, and be fed at least with the crumbs from your table (cf. Lk 16:20–21).[6]

This is the freedom from a suffocating self that hundreds of Hoyas experience here day after day as they reach out to the lonely elderly and the retarded young, to immigrant children and juvenile delinquents, to the physically handicapped and the mentally ill, to soup kitchens and women's shelters, to street people and the raped. This is the freedom Mother Teresa experiences every day at the curbstones of Calcutta and across the world. Listen to her in her powerful simplicity:

> One day I was walking down the street and I saw a man sitting there looking most terrible, so I went to him and shook his hand (and my hand is always very warm), and he looked up and said, "Oh, what a long, long time since I felt the warmth of a human hand." He brightened up, he was so full of joy that there was somebody that loved him, there was somebody who cared.[7]

Such freedom from slavery to self possesses two paradoxes. First, it lets you be you, lets you be Christ, without the wearing weight of self-worship. Second, it is an indispensable contribution educated Christians must make to destroying the divisions that devastate our planet. If apartheid begins in hearts apart, if, as Vatican II declared, "peace is the fruit of love,"[8] then an endless outpouring of Hoyas who "through love [are] servants of one another" (Gal 5:13), servants of all others without distinction, can help bring it to pass that one person or a thousand, one city or a nation, will cry out, as Martin Luther King did, "Free at last, free at last! Thank God Almighty, we are free at last!"

III

This leads into my third, perhaps most important point: the burden your years here lay on you for life. "You are the light of the world. . . . Let your light so shine before women and men that they may see your good works and give glory to your Father who is in heaven" (Mt 5:14–16). A burden you may not refuse: "Thank you, Lord, but no thanks. I don't have time. I've a dozen children to raise, I've bought Trump's Twin Towers, I have some insider trading to do." No, "let your light shine. . . ."

What light? In one monosyllable, your faith. Not sheerly a creed you recite on Sundays: "I believe . . . I believe . . . I believe." Not a crutch on which you can lean if you are intellectually crippled—a weak substitute for hard proof. Christian faith, Catholic faith, Hoya faith is a whole way of life. It is an engagement of your total self, a covenant with God sealed in the blood of Christ, a contract you can break only at terrible risk.

Such faith is a tough faith. Tough, first, because the bedrock of your belief is a cross—a cross erected not only over Calvary but over history. A cross on which not only God's Son hung but on which you and I must sooner or later hang. Each of us cries with St. Paul: "I have been crucified with Christ" (Gal 2:20). "Far be it from me to glory save in the cross of our Lord Jesus Christ, by which the world has been crucified to me, and I to the world" (Gal 6:14). "I bear on my body the brandmarks of Jesus" (Gal 6:17). A cross carried with profound joy, a living rebuttal to Nietzsche's caustic critique of Christians: "You do not look redeemed."

A tough faith, second, because you must at once embrace the world you walk and work, and challenge it. You do not embrace the sin it contains, the vast and frightful pornography to which it is linked. You embrace it because it was made to mirror God, to reflect divinity. You embrace it because here your likeness to Christ must unfold, because here lies your Christian and human task: to move your acre of God's world a bit closer to God's kingdom. Technology is not evil, as none of God's creation is evil—business, the body, politics, poetry. But it does demand to be sanctified; you must direct it to justice, to peace, to love. Here is how your light shines: attractive to the world because you are so splendidly human, a challenge to the world because you are more than human, because Christ so clearly lives in you.

A tough faith, third, because it is a faith that does justice—with a preferential option for the poor, the less privileged, the powerless. A faith that is restless as long as in our "land of the free" young minds are stunted by slums and bellies are bloated with hunger, as long as a million unborn are aborted each year and all too many elderly die alone and unloved. Not yours to preach justice from a pulpit; rather to let the corridors of influence and the skid rows of degradation see in you the risen Christ of today: competition wed to compassion, intelligence to love, wealth to wisdom, power to service. This is faith in action, the faith the New Testament Letter of James proclaimed: "I by my works will show you my faith" (Jas 2:18).

A recent cover story in *Time* magazine had for question "Who Was Jesus?"[9] People are yearning, *Time* told us, for a "tangible, real, vital" Jesus.[10] Such is the Christ your living faith must reveal to your world: a divine person as real and as human, as wise and as caring, as youthful and as ageless as . . . George Burns.

Good friends: To know God, in personal intimacy and in the works of God's art; to use your freedom not to satisfy self but to serve the other; to live a faith that is founded on a cross, challenges the world it loves, and does justice—such is the beauty and the burden of the education that began modestly with John Carroll, has grown in awareness through two hundred years, and, God willing, will reach fresh heights in Georgetown's third century. For this task, God needs you. For this task, God speed you.

Georgetown University
October 2, 1988

24
ALL ONE IN CHRIST JESUS
Labor Day 1988

- Genesis 2:4–9, 15
- 2 Thessalonians 3:6–12, 16
- Matthew 6:31–34

On this day so beloved of labor that we refuse to labor thereon, you have listened to three inspired readings. All three have to do, in some way, with work. In the first, the Lord God sets the first man in a garden "to till it" (Gen 2:15), to work it. In the second, the apostle Paul counsels a Christian congregation in Greece on work and idleness, on the laborer and the drone. In the third, Jesus tells you not to worry about where tomorrow's pizza is coming from, the next suit or shoes; today's troubles are enough.

I find these readings stimulating. Why? On the one hand, each says something immensely important for workers in any age. On the other hand, each has to be brought into a particular age, a specific moment, this moment. For, as Pope John Paul II phrased it in his encyclical on work, "fresh questions and problems are always arising, there are always fresh hopes, but also fresh fears and threats."[1] So, let's work on these challenging texts, struggle to discover what God might be saying to you this Labor Day 1988—saying to each of you individually, saying to all of you as a working community.

I

First, the opening pages of Genesis. A thrilling background for your vocation as workers. And by "workers" this morning I mean all who are actively engaged in producing something, in achieving some end. Not only "labor" but management as well. And I find justification for this in God's own Book; for Genesis has a remarkable conclusion to the story of creation: "And on the seventh day God finished His *work* which He had done, and He rested on the seventh day from all His *work* which He had done" (Gen 2:2). The first worker of all was God, and without raising a hand, without raising a sweat, God shaped a universe. All of you are workers, and the first chapter of your story as workers was written by a working God.

Now this same God took the first man He had fashioned and put him in a garden He had Himself planted. Not only to enjoy it, to lie on lush grass and count the stars, but to work it, to make flowers grow afresh, to give it new life—in imitation of God the original gardener. Above all, to work it with delight, from morning till night. Sweat indeed, but good, rich, enjoyable sweat—the sweat that calls for a Pepsi or a Bud. What God planned for Adam He intended for us. Three prime purposes: (1) In our work we should become more and more like God; for in work we should, like God, be ceaselessly creating the earth, making our acre of God's world a better place for human living, for our sisters and brothers. (2) Through the work we do we should become more and more human, grow inside and out as men and women. (3) In work we should be building the kingdom of God that Christ our Lord took our flesh to proclaim, the rule of God over human hearts that he died to achieve.

Now sin has made this ideal more difficult—Adam's sin, social sin, political sin, our own sins. For much of humanity, work since Adam's exile from Eden has been turned into toil, a day of dull drudgery. "Work," a worker complained, "work is a drain down which I'm pouring my life." It is not godlike, not even human. "Most of us," Studs Terkel wrote 15 years ago, "have jobs that are too small for our spirit. Jobs are not big enough for people."[2]

In consequence, good friends, a first Christian task for you. Only a favored few become Leo Iacoccas or Sandra Day O'Connors, Donald Trumps or Mother Teresas. No matter. Put your heads and hearts together, your intelligence and your love—women and men, front office and assembly line—and you can create a climate where each one of you will reap satisfaction from what you do, take pride therein, feel that your turf is greener because of you, someone somewhere is the better for your labor, and you yourself are more human.

II

Second, St. Paul's tough language to a Christian community: "If anyone will not work, let him not eat" (2 Thess 3:10b). How do you react to Paul's principle? American Christians, I suspect, could come to blows on that one. For some, Paul is right on target. Why should my hard-earned money go to the lazy? Others find Paul much too callous. After all, many are simply unable to work, many cannot find work however hard they try.

No need for Christian infighting. Paul was not laying down a universal principle. He was addressing a community in which a fair number, if not all, were expecting the world to end soon, looking for Christ to come quickly. The result? Some saw no point in working. Why build bridges for a world about to disappear? Why till the earth when, as Paul himself put it, "the dead in Christ will rise first; then we who are alive, who are left, shall be caught up together with them in the clouds to meet the Lord in the air; and so we shall always be with the Lord" (1 Thess 4:16–17)?

Yours is a different problem altogether. If Paul were alive today, if Paul were to write a Letter to the Sooners, what would he say? His text might well be the State motto carved into the marble of your Capitol: "Work overcomes simply everthing."[3] Work and you've got it made. But at that point Paul might well be stumped. What do I say to Sooners who want to work but the work isn't there? How does work overcome simply everything when perhaps nine percent of your work force is out of work? What do I say when John Steinbeck's fictional drought of Oklahoma's 30s has become the raw reality of your 80s—*The Grapes of Wrath*?

A homily is not a class in economics. Although I hail from Washington, I have no economic solution for a depressed economy. Yet this much I can say: A depressed economy is not God's will for His Sooner people. But a depressed economy may point up what *is* God's will for His depressed people. What St. Paul proclaimed to the Christians of Corinth can be transferred to all of you in this house of God—in fact, to all workers in Oklahoma. You are one body. Varieties of gifts indeed, many parts, but one body nevertheless. "The eye cannot say to the hand, 'I have no need of you,' nor again the head to the feet, 'I have no need of you.' On the contrary, the parts of the body which seem to be weaker are indispensable. . . . God has so adjusted the body . . . that the members may have the same care for one another. If one member suffers, all suffer together; if one member is honored, all rejoice together" (1 Cor 12:20–26).

If one of you suffers, all of you suffer. No man, no woman, is an island. No one of you can say to any other, "I have no need of you." Here, surprisingly, lies your hope—your Christian hope, your human hope. Suffering should bring you together—not to wring your hands in collective misery, not to mourn at an economic wake, not to curse Congress or OPEC. Rather, to pool your remarkable resources—head and heart, imagination and organization, courage and compassion, politics and prayer—so as to shape not a workers' paradise, not necessarily a land flowing with gas and oil, but what the U.S. bishops called "a new American experiment: partnership for the public good."[4]

In consequence, good friends, a second Christian task for you, intimately linked to the first. Come together! In a sense far richer than the original Red slogan, I say to all of you: "Workers, unite!" For justice and jobs; for a revived economy and a living wage. Not selfishly, as rugged individualists. But most of all because you are one body with many members. Because as members of one body you care—care for one another, care deeply, care enough to share, care enough to carry a sister or brother on your own bruised shoulders.

III

Third, the startling counsel of Jesus: "Do not be anxious, saying, 'What shall we eat?' or 'What shall we drink?' or 'What shall we wear?' . . . Your heavenly Father knows that you need them all. But seek first His kingdom and His righteousness, and all these things shall be yours as well" (Mt 6:31–33). Can Jesus really be serious? Dare I preach this to the billion who bed down hungry each night across the world? Dare I preach it to the millions who exist below the poverty line in the United States? Dare I even preach it to the jobless in Oklahoma? Trust in God, love the Lord, and you'll get everything you need? Nonsense, our experience retorts. Some get what they need, others do not. And the dividing line is not whether you worship the one true God or neglect Him.

There is mystery here. Understandably so, for we are trying to fathom the mind of God—a God who *is* Love and still allows the children of His love to suffer, doesn't do a blessed thing about Middle East oil or the unemployment rate. We are probing the problem of evil—evil that has mystified mortal minds since Adam was exiled from Eden. It baffles me too, believe me; I do not come to you with a hatful of answers. Let me simply suggest a way of looking at today's Gospel that just might prove of profit to you. I want to turn your eyes back 19 centuries, to the earliest Christian communities.

You see, for all their "dissensions" and "quarreling" (1 Cor 1:10–11), most early Christians were conscious of being a community, the body of the risen Jesus. They were men and women who cared. And those who put their trust in God did experience what Jesus promised. No stomach was bloated from hunger; no lips ever cracked with thirst; no flesh shivered in nakedness. Why? The community saw to that. Listen to Luke on the congregation in Jerusalem: "There was not a needy person among them, for as many as were possessors of lands or houses sold them, and brought the proceeds of what was sold and laid it at the apostles' feet; and distribution was made to each as any had need" (Acts 4:34–35).

My point is, Jesus was not laying the whole Christian burden on his Father: Pray "Give us this day our daily bread" and manna will descend from heaven as from a silo. God can indeed rain Big Macs on you, can irrigate the Sahara desert with a single sacred syllable, can warm all flesh with sheepskin. If anything is possible, God can do it. But in practice, apparently the good Lord leaves much of that to His people, to the community, to you and me. So then, when I see bellies bloated from hunger in Tulsa or Washington, when the strong hands of good people cannot find work, might it not be time to stop asking questions about a God whose ways are clearly not our ways, and turn our thoughts to the Christian community that is not really Christian, not really a community, unless it cares? We may argue till hell freezes over about God and the problem of evil; but philosophy and our frustration with a strange God should not be a cop-out from the compassion that calls us to play Christ to our crucified sisters and brothers.

In consequence, good friends, a third Christian task for you, closely allied to the first and second. Fashion a community. Not just thousands of Christians who happen to be workers. Rather, thousands of workers who trust so thoroughly in God's care for you that you see to it yourselves that no brother or sister has to be anxious about tomorrow—tomorrow's bread, tomorrow's coffee, tomorrow's shoes—yes, tomorrow's children. The Jesus of yesterday's Jerusalem is the Christian community of today's Tulsa. It is you, all of you together, who must heal the sick and comfort the afflicted, feed the hungry and clothe the naked, find work for the unemployed and destroy those who deal death with coke and crack.

What have I been preaching to you, to Oklahoma's Christian workers? In a nutshell, what Paul preached so powerfully to the Christians in central Asia Minor about the year 55: "As many of you as were baptized into Christ have put on Christ. There is neither Jew nor Greek, neither slave nor free, no male-and-female; for you are all one in Christ Jesus" (Gal 3:28). The troubling question, the question you alone can answer, is: Are you actually one? If you can respond with a resounding yes, then you can sing lustily the ending of your State song: "You're doin' fine, Oklahoma—Oklahoma, o.k."

Christ the King Church
Tulsa, Oklahoma
September 5, 1988

25

LOVE OF LAW, LAW OF LOVE
Homily for a Red Mass

- Wisdom 2:12, 17–20
- James 3:16—4:3
- Mark 9:30–37

For those of you who, unlawyerlike, have sat mutely through many a Red Mass[1] homily, have never shot up to shout "irrelevant and immaterial," a word to relax you. I shall not lecture you on things legal; my "thing" is theology. I shall not numb you with the natural law; this is worship, not a workship. I shall not argue *Roe* v. *Wade*, indefensible though I see it.

On *any* occasion, the hope of a homilist is to link human living to divine giving, to help you realize what certain Greeks in the Gospel asked of the apostle Philip: "Sir, we would like to see Jesus" (Jn 12:20–21). On *this* occasion, my hope is somehow to link God's love for you to your love for law, to help you see Jesus the lawgiver with new eyes. With apologies to Jesus, I too have come not to abolish the law but to bring it to fuller expression in you. How? By taking a tip from today's three readings. They speak, in swift succession, of justice, of wisdom, of service. And so shall I.

I

First, justice. The word is central to your vocation. You see to it that just laws foster the common good, that human rights written into law are protected, that the scales of Lady Justice are not weighted in favor of the rich and powerful, that men and women remain innocent until proven guilty, that the punishment fits the crime. A proud profession indeed, for without you "America the beautiful" would be a nation in anarchy, a country uncommonly

167

unfree. "Equal before the law" is still an ideal, but largely because of you we are creeping slowly towards it.

But the just man or woman that is the American lawyer or legislator, the American judge or jury, is not the just man or woman revealed by God.[2] Oh yes, Yahweh ordered Israel to "execute justice" (Jer 7:5), flung this challenge to a chosen race: "What does the Lord require of you but to do justice . . . and to walk humbly with your God?" (Mic 6:8). Still, the justice God asked of Israel was not an ethical construct, not a legal enactment. It did not mean merely: Give to each what is due to each, what each person has a strict right to demand, because he or she is a human being, has rights that can be proven from philosophy or have been written into law. No, Old Testament justice was a whole web of relationships that stemmed from a covenant—Israel's pact with God. The Israelites were to father the fatherless and watch over the widow, keep from oppressing the alien or shedding innocent blood, not because the orphan and the widowed and the outsider and the guiltless deserved this, but because this was the way *God* had acted with *them*. In freeing the oppressed, they were mirroring the loving God who had freed *them* from oppression, had delivered them from exile in Egypt and bondage in Babylon. In loving the loveless, the unloved, the unlovable, they were imaging the God who wooed Israel back time and again despite her infidelities, betrothed her to her Lord for ever (cf. Hos 2:14–23). Israel's justice was to image not the justice of man, not the justice of woman, but the justice of God.

So, too, for the New Testament. The early Christians, like their forebears, had covenanted with God. This covenant demanded that they treat one another, treat all others, treat friend and enemy as *God* wants them treated, the God who "makes His sun rise on the evil and on the good, sends rain on the just and on the unjust" (Mt 5:45). And precisely because God acts this way.

What should all this say to you? Although your professional life is the law, you dare not limit your life to living by the law. The love of law should lead to the law of love. Why? Two reasons. (1) Because human law, precious though it is, cannot save you, cannot make you one with your God. Only love can do that—love of God above all that is not God, love of other humans as you love yourself. (2) Because the equality you mete out at the bar of justice is not enough to unite black and white, man and woman, the haves and the have-nots, the restless young and the rest-home aged, the crack pushers and the police who imprison them. Only the Sermon on the Mount can do that, not Blackstone's *Commentaries*.

A first challenge, then: to link in your lives Lady Justice and the Judeo-Christian just; to give to each what each deserves and to give to all more than they deserve; to give to each what you have covenanted with the law to give, and to give to all what you have covenanted with the Lord to give.

II

How do you manage this mission impossible? The Letter of James suggests how: by a "wisdom from above" (Jas 3:17). From above. You will not do it because you have the legal leverage of a Thurgood Marshall or a Sandra Day O'Connor, the I.Q. of a Ramsey Clark or a Robert Bork. Good indeed, enough for the blindfolded lady with scales and a sword; not enough for the Lord of love. You need the wisdom Paul preached to the Christians of Corinth in powerful contrasts: "Has not God made foolish the wisdom of the world? For since . . . the world did not know God through wisdom, it pleased God through the folly of what we believe to save those who believe. . . . We preach Christ crucified . . . the power of God and the wisdom of God. For the foolishness of God is wiser than men, and the weakness of God is stronger than men. . . . We impart a secret and hidden wisdom of God . . ." (1 Cor 1:20–25; 2:7).

I am not denigrating the profound knowledge within your profession. After all, the incompetent jurist is surely as perilous to human persons as the incompetent priest. And Vatican II made it pellucidly clear that every branch of secular learning has its own proper methodology, its authentic independence. Much as Western jurisprudence reflects many gospel values, the law is not the gospel—not even "L.A. Law" or "Matlock."[3]

But if I am not elevating stupidity over intelligence, what is this "foolishness of God" that is wiser than our accumulated human wisdom? It is simply . . . Christ crucified and risen. He does not replace Blackstone or the Bill of Rights—no more than he rejected the prophecy of Jeremiah or the philosophy of Plato. As with justice, so with wisdom: Important as your wit and wisdom are if we Americans are to escape the law of the jungle, if we are not to do unto others before they do it unto us, it remains true that the wisdom of earth cannot raise us to heaven. Even my treasured theology is inadequate here. It can tell me *about* God; it cannot by itself link me to my Lord in love.

What, then, are you to do? Live two lives—one on weekdays, in

the grime and grit of lawlessness, of murder and the Mob, of cocaine
and conspiracy, of child abuse and insider trading; the other on
Sundays, warmed by church and God, Communion and a rare uplift-
ing homily? I say no. In the Christian vision, you can touch your
God-given destiny, can achieve what you were born to be, only if
your love of law is linked to your dying and rising with Christ. I do
not mean that you fuse jurisprudence and Christian dogma; that
would create a bastard science. I mean rather that ideally your love
of law, of equal justice for all, of an America genuinely "the land of
the free," should stem from the love that a crucified Christ has
lavished on you, from the awesome fact that "you were ransomed . . . not with perishable things such as silver or gold, but with
the precious blood of Christ" (1 Pet 1:18–19). I mean that ideally
each decision you make on the level of human law, the justice you
mete out on the basis of human wisdom, your prosecution and your
defense should be in a genuine sense an act of love—the love of a
man or woman who has risen with Christ and therefore you love the
other, even the guilty, those you exile from society, as profoundly as
you love yourself, as intensely as Christ has loved you. An awesome
attitude indeed, especially as you sit before or beside those who do
not reverence law and order as you do. Otherwise you risk the pungent question of Christ: "If you love [only] those who love you," how
do you differ from the unbeliever (cf. Mt 5:46–47)?

A second challenge, then: not to leave compassion to defense
counsel but to integrate the cross—your own and others'—into all
your legal lives. I am not trying to turn you into "bleeding hearts." I
am not presuming to empty our prisons. I do submit that to image
the Christ who despised the sin and still cared for the sinner—the
Son of God who wore our flesh and was crucified for every sinner
from Adam to Antichrist—your day is not ended when you have
meted out justice, when a trial is over and the "bad guy" has lost.
Behind bars or on the streets is someone for whom the Son of God
died. Does the foolishness of God mingle with the wisdom of man
in your heart and mind? When justice is done, is there still room for
compassion?

III

That question impels me to my third point. It begins with
perhaps the pettiest dispute in Scripture. Twelve grown men, selected by God-in-flesh to be his intimate friends, his kitchen cabi-

net, argue like little children about . . . who's the greatest! And Jesus stuns them with the paradoxical response: "If anyone would be first, he must be last of all and servant of all" (Mk 9:35).

Service . . . it has an honorable history. It goes back to ancient Athens, where the Greek word we translate as "liturgy" meant a burdensome public office or duty which the richer citizens discharged at their own expense—a service for the polis, for the people or the state. Service goes back to the Suffering Servant, to the Son of God who told us he "came not to be served but to serve"—in fact, "to give his life as a ransom for many" (Mt 20:28). Service goes back to the best of popes, who gloried in the title "servant of the servants of God." Service goes back to lawyers like your patron St. Thomas More, who died merrily on the scaffold declaring himself "the king's good servant, but God's first."

In the public eye, to eyes of earth, you are indeed men and women of distinction. But in God's eyes you are distinguished in the first instance not because you practice a proud profession, but by your reply to a two-edged question: Are you a servant? And if so, whose servant?

Not an easy question for you to answer. After all, aren't you masters of what you survey, in control, with authority—at times over life and death? No matter. Remember the striking words of Jesus to his disciples the night before he died for us: "You call me Teacher and Lord; and you are right, for so I am. If I then, your Lord and Teacher, have washed your feet, you also ought to wash one another's feet" (Jn 13:13–14). In the Christian vision we are all servants. Not because we do servile tasks—wash windows or dig ditches, baby-sit or change diapers. Rather because the Christian, every Christian, is, like Jesus, "a man or woman for others." God's second great commandment comes to Jew and Christian through Moses and Jesus in identical words: "You shall love your neighbor as you love yourself" (Lev 19:18; Mt 22:39).

And so for you—bench, bar, schools of law—you are servants. And you serve not an abstract quality called justice; you serve your own flesh and blood. It is a strange, unsettling service. For some of you serve by prosecuting the insider trader and the murdering mafioso; others, by defending them. Sometimes you serve by shackling a sister or brother for months or years, sometimes by lifting the shackles that imprison them. Some of you hassle us for the IRS, others keep corporations from being taxed to death. Constantly you confront one another; ceaselessly you bedazzle juries with your rhetoric; now you may even compete for bodies on the boob tube.

I do not object, believe me. I simply submit that, whatever your specialty, you owe yourself, your profession, and your God an annual evaluation. The two-edged question: Are you a servant, and whom are you serving? I rejoice when I read that 40% of a Los Angeles firm's 480 attorneys did pro bono work last year and that the firm paid for such work. I rejoice when I read that "Columbia University law students have been flocking to a program of summer legal-aid work, though it means forgoing the opportunity to make $1,200 a week as interns at major firms." I rejoice when I read that "Tulane University law school has made 20 hours of legal service a graduation requirement." But I weep when I read that "only 17.7% of the nation's 659,000 private attorneys perform" pro bono work. I weep when I read that "more than 80% of the legal needs of the poor goes unattended."[4]

I am not suggesting that pro bono or legal aid is your only service; I have already insisted that all of law ought to be a form of service. I do submit that representing the poor at some cost to yourself is a splendid way to imitate the Suffering Servant, the Christ who took our flesh to save all flesh but had a special love for the downtrodden and destitute, the marginalized and manipulated.

A third challenge, then: on the one hand, to lift the law a bit closer to its ideal—not domination but service; on the other, to lift the blindfold from Lady Justice, to let her see that all too many of her children are less than equal before her eyes.

Justice . . . wisdom . . . service. Good friends, yours is indeed a proud profession. But today's question is not what this profession asks of its practitioners in the abstract. Today's problem—a problem suggested cynically by today's dark "lawyer jokes"—is the image you project. In your total lives, are you men and women of biblical justice, men and women who have covenanted with God to deal with others as God has dealt with you? Are you wise with the foolishness of a Christ who loved unto crucifixion even those he condemned as "whitewashed tombs," "full of hypocrisy and iniquity," "brood of vipers," those whom he asked "how are you to escape being sentenced to hell?" (Mt 23:27, 28, 33)? Whose good servants are you? God's of course. But under God, servants of only the law-abiding? Primarily of such as can pay for the privilege? Or servants too, not solely but singularly, of those who can only beg you to make their lives a bit more human?

Your presence here, good friends, increases immeasurably the profound respect and high hopes I already entertain for you. For here you pledge allegiance to your sovereign patron, bend head and heart to him who is Just Judge, God's Wisdom, and Suffering Servant. You will leave this sacred spot with the Eucharistic Christ within you. Be what you receive! Be Christ to all whom you touch!

St. Bridget's Church
Richmond, Virginia
September 17, 1988

26

NO GREATER LOVE THAN THIS
Wedding Homily 1

- Song of Songs 2:8–14, 6–7
- 1 Corinthians 12:31—13:13
- John 15:9–16

This week the cover story in *Time* magazine headlines a catchy question: "Are Women Fed Up?"[1] The story focuses on a controversial survey which asserted that most wives are terribly dissatisfied: Husbands harass them emotionally and psychologically, are condescending and judgmental, do not listen; wives are the ones who usually initiate divorces, they have extramarital affairs, find deeper relationships with women friends.

The study has been roundly criticized, even by women, on various counts.[2] It is one-sided, subjective, biased; the author "goes in with a prejudice and comes out with a statistic."[3] Why, then, mention it here? Because despite the title, *Women and Love*, you emerge after 922 pages not knowing what that crucial four-letter word "love" means.[4] Not that a celibate Jesuit is competent to "tell it as it is." I shall simply suggest what Jennifer and Richard have discovered about love in God's own Book, in the readings they have chosen to initiate their life together. A word on each.

I

First, the selection from the Song of Songs hints all too swiftly at what the whole little book reveals: True love between man and maid is a wonderfully *human* thing. The Song does not provide a philosophical definition. It is a collection of lyric poems or fragments of poems about human love and courtship such as might well be sung at weddings. It is not particularly religious; it is movingly human, at times extraordinarily erotic. It tells of a man and a woman caught up utterly each in the other, wildly in love. The short extract you have just heard is her ecstatic cry when the man she loves comes in the spring to summon his bride:

> The voice of my beloved!
>   Behold, he comes,
> leaping upon the mountains,
>   bounding over the hills.
> My beloved is like a gazelle,
>   or a young stag.
> Behold, there he stands
>   behind our wall,
> gazing in at the windows,
>   looking through the lattice.
> My beloved speaks and says to me:
> "Arise, my love, my fair one,
>   and come away;
> for lo, the winter is past,
>   the rain is over and gone.
> The flowers appear on the earth,
>   the time of singing has come,
> and the voice of the turtledove
>   is heard in our land.
> The fig tree puts forth its figs,
>   and the vines are in blossom;
>   they give forth fragrance.
> Arise, my love, my fair one,
>   and come away.
> O my dove, in the clefts of the rock,
>   in the covert of the cliff,
> let me see your face,
>   let me hear your voice,
> for your voice is sweet
>   and your face is comely."
> (Cant 2:8–14)

The Song is the dream of all lovers, the very human love that is God's own creation, where a man and a woman are drawn in unique fashion to each other, so that they yearn, before all else, to share themselves totally—mind and heart, flesh and spirit—the way they share with no other in heaven or on earth. When you have this kind of love, you have what you have just heard: "Love is strong as death" (Cant 8:6). Such is the love that Richard and Jennifer declare is theirs, the love they declare to each other.

II

The problem with the Song of Songs is that the love it sings, though thoroughly human, is almost "out of this world." It is ecstatic, romantic, lyric. The passage which Jennifer and Richard have plucked from St. Paul gets them down to earth again, down to the routine that love for life must settle into. Listen again to Paul (cf. 1 Cor 13:4–7).

"Love is patient." Sounds so simple, but not after the honeymoon. Not an easy virtue when two live together 12 or 24 hours a day, week after week, month after month. Small things get on your nerves: socks on the floor; toothbrush in the shower; late for dinner; different schedules (what Art Buchwald called "latchkey husbands"); opposite opinions on Judge Bork[5] or John Paul II, on Rambo or Madonna.

"Love is not jealous." But lovers can be. Jealous of the other's success or salary. Jealous because he "checks out" the women at a party or is the center of attraction. Jealous because her legs are not only more shapely but faster.

"Love is not rude." But lovers can be rude and not realize it. A valentine in February? That's for kids. Anniversaries? A burden on my memory. I know a man who bought his wife a golf cart for Christmas because her car ate up too much gas. Even a kiss or a touch can turn routine.

"Love does not insist on its own way." But lovers can. Sunday is for spaghetti, come hell or high water; and the only eggs are brown eggs. Monday night is TV football; you knew that when you married me. Do things together? Of course. A friend of mine bought two season tickets to Rangers games, though his wife never gave a hoot about hockey.

"Love rejoices in the right." The problem is: What is right? Right is not created in a computer. Rarely do two wed who agree on what is right from A to Z. At times the search for the right is exactly that: a searing struggle to discover God's will—often complicated by competing values, different ways of looking at the same reality. It calls for communication, open and honest indeed, but loving and caring as well. The retort "That's the way *I* see it, and I don't care what anybody says" is a slap in love's face. If you love, you care terribly what the other says.

"Love endures all things." But the fact is, some love does not. Some love is destroyed by burdens too difficult to endure. Sickness that ravages her body can savage his spirit as well. Money, power, fame never cease to put asunder what God has joined together. And our freedom-loving culture is not conditioned to "endure all things."

III

Now if human weakness is not to weaken love, if St. Paul's dream of love is to come true for Jennifer and Richard, if the love that has begun is never to end, the Gospel they have chosen must pervade their persons, lift their lives: "This is my commandment, that you love one another as I have loved you" (Jn 15:12). But to love each other as the Lord Jesus loves them, they dare not rely simply on their native gifts: high intelligence, good will, bright smiles, powerful personalities. Splendid gifts indeed, but the love that is "patient and kind, not jealous or boastful, not arrogant or rude," the love that "does not insist on its own way, is not irritable or resentful, rejoices in the right," the love that "bears all things, believes all things, hopes all things, endures all things" (1 Cor 13:4–7), this is the love Paul preached to the Christians of Rome: ". . . God's love . . . poured into our hearts through the Holy Spirit who has been given to us" (Rom 5:5). You can love one another as Jesus loved only if God is housed in your heart.

Why is that? Look at the way Jesus loved. For love of us, the Son of God became like us, wore our flesh, walked our earth, died our death. Every thought and word, every footstep and gesture, was an act of love—for his Father and for us. The child he took in his arms and the robber to whom he promised paradise, these were you and I. The woman whose adultery he forgave was every man or woman who has ever sinned. He was born to die—for us; and the night before he died he gave us himself—his flesh for food, his blood as drink.

Love as Jesus loved? Obviously not easy, not a "piece of cake." It demands, Jennifer and Richard, that you focus, fix your eyes, not on yourself but on the other. That other has three faces. The first face is the other whose hands you will clasp moments from now, the other to whom you will give yourself "to have and to hold, from this day forward, for better for worse, for richer for poorer, in sickness and in health, until death do [you] part." The second face is the Other whose hands will join your hands together, the God who shaped woman and man to be wonderfully one, the God who brought you together in such wondrous wise, the God who Himself links you today for life, the God who makes your marriage a wedding not of two but of three, the God who in this sacrament of your love promises to be with you days without end, the God apart from whom your oneness cannot possibly endure. The third face is the other on whom you must henceforth focus together: the face of humanity. I mean the other less fortunate than you, the other crucified with or without Christ, the other whose hunger you must try to taste, whose anguish you must assuage, whose loneliness you must fill, whose despair you must destroy. Like Jesus, who "came that [we] may have life, and have it in overflowing fullness" (Jn 10:10), it is your task as committed Christians to bring the living dead to life. You dare not live for yourselves alone.

This is what it means to love as Jesus loved: to live for the other. And so to live even if, especially if, it involves a kind of crucifixion. Remember today's Gospel: "Greater love than this no one has: to lay down [your] life for [your] friends" (Jn 15:13). Out of such love is born the joy our Lord pledged to his disciples and to you: "that my joy may be in you, and that your joy may be full" (v. 11).

Good friends all: You are here because you love Jennifer and/ or Richard. But there is a "catch" to the invitation that summoned you here. You have not been invited to a spectacle; you are not simply spectators; it's not quite the same as watching the football Giants in the Meadowlands, cheering them on with all the passion in your power. You are inescapably involved in this couple's life together, intimate to it. Not just today, but as long as you and they shall live.

You see, Richard and Jennifer will live their love not on some fantasy island, far from the grime and grit of everyday existence. They will live their love in community, among men and women who share their ideals or despise them, men and women who love one another enough to die for them or hate one another enough to kill them, men and women who work and play, laugh and cry, dance for joy and quiver with pain—yes, men and women who wrestle with God, wrestle with one another, wrestle with their very own selves. In this context, if Jennifer and Richard are to live lives of love for others—love for each other, for the images of God around them, for God Himself—they need not only God's help but yours as well. Not only Waterford crystal or fondue forks . . . or even Burghardt kielbasa. They need the powerful example of your lives, of your own love for the other.

That is why, when Richard and Jennifer join hands as symbol of their love, I would ask the wedded among you to link your own hands and silently repeat—to each other, to the world around you, to the God within you—the awesome words that bind for ever: "I take you . . . to have and to hold . . . for better for worse, for richer for poorer, in sickness and in health, until death. . . ."

No gift more precious can you give to your Jennifer and your Richard.

Our Lady of the Lake Church
Sparta, New Jersey
October 17, 1987

27

YOU HAVE RAVISHED MY HEART
Wedding Homily 2

- Song of Songs 4:8–16
- 1 Corinthians 12:31—13:8a
- Matthew 22:35–40

It may sound strange coming from a Jesuit, but one of my favorite stories has to do with . . . love. The real-life situation was the tempestuous 60s, when cities were scorched from Watts to Washington, when campuses turned into battlefields, when the cries of the poor clogged our ears, when murderous hatred cut down two Kennedys and a King. In those years, some practitioners of my art, theology, floated a tempting theory. To estimate what is ethical, to live the life Christ commanded, you can toss the thousand and one principles of the past, the do's and don't's of the moral manuals. All you need is . . . love. Why? Because love has a built-in compass that homes it in unerringly on the core of a conflict, the bone and marrow of a moral issue. Love and you've got it made.

In response to the compass theory, an Anglican clergyman graced with wisdom and wit told a touching story—the story of an elephant, a loving elephant. This particular elephant noticed an ostrich leaving her nest to get a drink of water. The elephant rumbled over to the nest and, out of pure love, sat on the ostrich eggs to keep them warm. "Love," observed the clergyman, "love can be a fuddy-duddy, elephantine thing."[1]

On this awesome occasion, for this extraordinary expression of love we call marriage, Elizabeth and Edward have plucked three passages from Scripture that suggest an outlook on love far more profound, infinitely more exciting, than a warm ostrich egg. Let me titillate your thinking with a brief word on each.

I

We begin with the snippet from the Song of Songs. I wonder what your reaction was when you heard from a Catholic pulpit such sensuous poetry:

> You have ravished my heart, my sister, my bride,
>   you have ravished my heart with a glance of your eyes,
>   with one jewel of your necklace.
> How sweet is your love, my sister, my bride!
>   how much better is your love than wine,
>   and the fragrance of your oils than any spice!
> Your lips distill nectar, my bride;
>   honey and milk are under your tongue;
>   the scent of your garments is like the scent of Lebanon.
> A garden locked is my sister, my bride,
>   a garden locked, a fountain sealed.
>
> (Cant 4:9–12)

Embarrassed? Shocked? No reason to be. A book of the Bible sings ecstatically of something singularly human, so human that it goes back in time to the first man and woman shaped by God's hands, so human that it will still be here when the risen Son returns in glory to take the last of humankind to himself. That something singularly human is the love that is ceaselessly born between man and maid. I admit, the Song of Songs is not particularly religious; at times it is extraordinarily erotic. But isn't it quite like our surprising, unpredictable God to inspire a book that tells us in passionate phrases how grand and glorious a thing human love can be? And not because it is sublimated, swallowed up in love of God; the writer is not playing psychiatrist. On the sheerly human level, because man and woman are made such by a loving Lord, they are drawn each to the other; such is their nature, the way heaven fashioned them to be. That is why, when God brought the first woman to the first man, he cried aloud in ecstasy: "This one at last [not the birds of the air or the beasts of the field, but this one] is bone of my bone and flesh of my flesh. . . . Therefore a man leaves his father and his mother and cleaves to his wife, and they become one flesh" (Gen 2:23–24).

Read the Song of Songs right through, and discover that God is terribly proud of what He has shaped, proud of all of you who have ever fallen in love, proud of Edward and Elizabeth, delighted as only God can delight that they stand before Him today in a oneness that links not only their hands but their hearts, not merely their minds but their nerves and sinews, not simply their spirits but their flesh as well. God likes, God loves, how human Elizabeth and Edward are, because He loves what He has made; He sees in them living images of the man and woman He conceived before time in His understanding and His love. He looks on their touchingly human love and, somewhat as He looked ages ago on everything He had made, He sees that it is "very good" (cf. Gen 1:31).

II

At this point we move a giant step forward, from the Song of Solomon[2] to an epistle of Paul. Paul, too, has a thing about love, is almost obsessed by it; without love your life and mine has no meaning whatsoever. Listen to him. If I can speak (or even preach) like an angel—the way, say, the angel Gabriel announced to Mary that God wanted her to mother His Son—but there is no love in me, I'm a windbag, a New Year's Eve noisemaker. If I own the world's clearest crystal ball, can predict everything from the Super Bowl through the next snowstorm to the hour of our Lord's second coming; if my faith is powerful enough to move the Rockies from New Mexico to New England; if my intellect can grasp God Three-in-One and the billions of stars in outer space—with all this, if I "have not love, I am nothing" (1 Cor 13:2). Not even a little bit of something; I am . . . nothing. And suppose, like Francis of Assisi, I give every last item I own to Mother Teresa for her Indian outcasts, let a Christian-hating Khomeini burn me at the stake—if I "have not love, it profits me not one whit" (v. 3), not a tinker's dam. In God's eyes, no love, no Edward Bisese, no Elizabeth Kirwin, no Walter Burghardt. Just . . . nothing.

Strong language indeed, frightening. But that paragraph in Paul is only one side of the coin. The other side, Paul's next paragraph, is the scene you and I are privileged to share this evening. With Paul's help, Elizabeth and Edward spell out in limpid language what the Song of Songs painted in parti-colored pictures. They promise to be "patient and kind" (v. 4), even when nerves fray from socks in the bathroom to adverse approaches to American art. They will not be "jealous or boastful, arrogant or rude" (vv. 4–5), because they are so artistically sensitive to the image of God that is the other, aware that we all image an infinite God in infinitely different ways, knowing that difference need not divide, can blend into a superb symphony if only love conducts. They will refuse to "insist on [their] own way" (v. 5)—possible though the peril is, especially as the years stiffen not only our muscles but our minds—if only they do not forget that two-in-one demands indeed "I and thou" but forbids "mine and thine."

One word of warning. This kind of love, the love that "bears all things, believes all things, hopes all things, endures all things" (v. 7), is not a love Elizabeth and Edward manufacture in their own private lab: for ingredients, their buoyant personalities, high IQs, keen sensitivity, even delightful if weird senses of humor. The love Paul praises, the love he sings so lyrically, leaps light-years beyond those wondrous traits, is the love Paul proclaimed to the Christians of Rome: ". . . hope does not disappoint us, because God's love has been poured into our hearts through the Holy Spirit who has been given to us" (Rom 5:5). What offers precious promise for Paul's kind of love, for a love that will never end, is God's love. Not somewhere in outer space, but deep inside of you. The God who shaped you in His likeness, the God who brought you together against all the odds, this same God lives within you. And, wonder of wonders, this loving Father's only Son, who bloodied a cross to link you like this in love, will soon nestle in your palms, cradle on your tongues, home in your hearts. Such is the love that pervades you today; such is the love I pray for you through the years that beckon ahead.

III

So far, a song that strummed your thrillingly human love, and a letter that linked human love to divine love. One text remains: a twin command of Jesus that puts the finishing touches on your love. You see, the tenderly human love of husband for wife and wife for husband that Scripture carries back to Eden, and the love that a God within you lavishes on you so generously, these, strangely enough, are not enough. Not enough for Christian existence. Jesus made that clear beyond controversy. The "great commandment"? "You shall love the Lord your God with all your heart, and with all your soul, and with all your mind." The second commandment "like" the first? "You shall love your neighbor as yourself" (Mt 22:36–39).

What Jesus enjoins on Christians in general, this he enjoins on those who wed in Christ. Do you want your love to abide, to grow, to bear fruit? Then your love must go *up* and your love must go *out*.

It must go up. From your experience you realize that your love for each other calls for a response, a reaction to the gift, the wonder, the miracle that is the other. Not an offhand "Love ya"; not casual love-making. Rather a rich relationship where all you do, all you say, all you are is in some way directed to the other. Believe me, it is not otherwise with God. His presence within you, as real as the Real Presence in a consecrated loaf, demands a response. Not a mumbled Hail Mary, not a sleepy Sunday obligation. Rather an endless "What return shall I make to the Lord for all He has given me?" What return? Simply, your heart, your soul, your mind—all of it, without reservation, in good times and bad, in sickness and health, in poverty and wealth. And from this day forward, your love must go up together, as one, your clasped hands enfolded in the loving hands that were pinned to Calvary's wood . . . for you.

And your love must go out . . . together. As you exit these sacred doors, you re-enter a little world of massive contradiction, an acre of God's earth flowing with milk and honey, where hundreds go to bed hungry each night, hundreds huddle on D.C. grates to stay warm, thousands look in vain for work with dignity, uncounted children will never learn to read, black and white live an uneasy armistice, crack and coke deaden our hopeless, and death never takes a holiday. Though Christ's command rings clear, "You shall love your neighbor as yourself," I dare not tell you precisely how; that rests between you and the Lord to whom you must listen . . . together. This much at least I can promise you: Bring a smile to the lips, light a ray of hope in the eyes, of a crucified sister or brother, and your love for each other will take wing, will amaze even you.

Good friends all: a final word, uncommonly personal. Fifty years ago our good God graced me with one of His surprising, unexpected gifts. A very young Jesuit, not yet ordained, I was teaching at Regis High School in New York City. A colleague on the faculty, not long out of Holy Cross, walked the corridors and stalked the classrooms on two canes; for he had contracted polio, once and for all. After ten years at Regis, he taught for 15 at Loyola College in Baltimore, the last few years from a wheelchair. During those teaching years he picked up a doctorate in history and a doctorate in law. But even more importantly, he taught, masterfully, a whole generation of young men and women not only how to study but how to live. He kept up with all 25 years of them, followed their lives with affection and love. In turn, they heaped hills of correspondence upon him from the four quarters of the earth: every wedding, every baby, every service induction, you name it. His dear widow is blessed with them all.

It is 25 years since Harry Kirwin left us. He left thousands of us richer for his presence among us, for his love in our lives. For (1) his love wedded the tenderness and passion of the lover in the Song of Songs; (2) that very human love was patient and kind, not jealous or boastful, not arrogant or rude, did not insist on its own way, was not irritable or resentful, rejoiced only in the right, bore all things, believed all things, hoped all things, endured all things; and (3) that same love went up to God and out to others—wife and children of course, but out as well to God's every child, 4.0 or slow, hale or frail, joy-filled or in dark despair.

I dare to speak so intimately because Harry Kirwin has risen again for me in Liza;[3] I mean that sincerely. Seeing this remarkable rebirth, touching swiftly the other half of Harry's life in Margaret,[4] and sensing the profound love Eddie has for Liza, I predict with confidence a lifelong song of love that will please a wise Solomon, a practical Paul, and a Jesus gloriously alive in the two we so dearly cherish.

St. Gabriel's Church
Washington, D.C.
January 30, 1988

28
AS GOD'S CHOSEN ONES
Wedding Homily 3

- Genesis 1:26–28, 31a
- Colossians 3:12–17
- John 15:9–12

Good friends: Something quite remarkable has just happened in your hearing. You have heard *the Word of God*. The Word of God on the lips of men. Actually, three words: a word from God your Creator shaping man and woman out of love; a word from God-made-man locking love into a single sentence; a word from an apostle advising Christians how to live love from day to day. These words take on added meaning today, because they do not fall out of the blue, have not been let loose by lottery; they have been deliberately chosen by Denise and Chester. And so these texts tell us much about this woman and this man so dear to us: how they look at life; how they look at God, at each other, at you. Let me simply spell out what these words of God might be saying—to this loving couple indeed, but through them to us.

I

First, the reading from Genesis (Gen 1:26–28, 31a).[1] It offers three insights into God and the human person, into God and those who marry in God. (1) The God who had fashioned heaven and earth, the birds of the air and the beasts of the field and the fish of the sea, crowned creation by shaping two creatures in such a way that they, and they alone, were images of God's very self. (2) This Creator commanded them to be creative themselves, to fashion other selves from their own flesh and spirit. (3) God looked back upon everything that divine love had done . . . and it was "very good" (v. 31).

All that was indeed very good. But it is another marvel of God's creation, of God's caring, that the first chapter of Genesis is not imprisoned in the past. It is not sheer history. It moves today from a garden to a church, from Paradise to Richmond. Two products of God's prolific hand stand before us today, stand before God today. This new Adam, this new Eve, are themselves special; for each is like God. I mean, each entered this world possessing two of God's prerogatives: Each can know and each can love. Each mirrors the Christ who is *the* Image of the Father; for each carries Christ deep within. Each has been molded through three decades by a loving God in such wise that each can cry with St. Paul: "It is no longer I who live, but Christ who lives in me; and the life I now live in the flesh I live by faith in the Son of God, who loved me and gave himself for me" (Gal 2:20).

More than that. This evening God asks of them, as He asked of the primal pair, that they carry on His own creating. Not like bird or beast, by a God-given instinct to outlive themselves, to survive their own mortality. Rather like God Himself: to shape, consciously and lovingly, images not only of themselves ("chips off the old block") but of God.

We can get lost in God's command "Be fruitful and multiply, and fill the earth" (v. 28), confused by an earth already filled, where little ones die like September flies. We can get lost in numbers and miss the miracle that is a child. A child fashioned not solely by God, as were Adam and Eve, but from the flesh and spirit of a man and woman. A child so wonder-full that God's own Son became a child. Each child imaging the Christmas child. Each child Christ-come-again.

And the same God who looked back on the world's first week surely looks with a smile on what divine love has fashioned in Chester and Denise, on the love that has linked them in such singular oneness, on the gift they will express very shortly, the gift of each to the other. This God cannot but smile on what this love promises: other images of His own Christ. This too is "very good."

II

Second, the Gospel reading from John (Jn 15:9–12). We hear it so often that it makes no impact. When did you last plumb the depths of that text, take seriously the charge "This is my command-ment, that you love one another as I have loved you"? (v.12). Not "This is my suggestion, this I would like you to do if you can hack it, if it's no trouble." Very bluntly, "This is my commandment. This is what you must do if you claim to be a Christian." And not only "Love one another," but love one another as Jesus has loved you.

That commandment is laid on all of us, on each man or woman who claims to be Christian, claims to follow Christ. But it rests with uncommon weight on those who dare to marry in Christ. For here a man and a woman are promising each other a kind of total love they can give to no other—not to parents, not to siblings, not to their children. Here, if anywhere, we can expect the kind of love the Son of God took our flesh to reveal.

And what kind of love is that? "As I have loved you." Can Jesus be serious? Does he expect Denise and Chester to copy the love he lived for us? Does he ask them to play down their egos, at times submerge their extraordinary personalities, as he did, for the good of the family? He may. Is it possible that he might want them to live in obscurity, unknown and misunderstood, as he was, with relatives shouting they are "off their rocker," as his own relatives did? He might indeed. Might he ask them to live the Beatitudes, as he did, to be "poor in spirit" with those who are poor in degraded reality, to share the sorrow of "those who mourn," to be "merciful" even to those who do not merit mercy, to work for peace even with the Russian Bear (Mt 5:3–9)? Indeed he might. Will he ask them now and again, perhaps all their lives long, to walk the Way of the Cross with him? Not at all impossible. Could he ask either or both of them to lay down life itself for the other—not by a single act of martyr-dom but by a day-to-day crucifixion? Quite possible. But if he asks it, it will be because this is how he wants Denise and Chester to express their love not only for him but for each other—and to express it together, as one.

And if he does ask it, he promises them not simply a measure of sorrow, but a "joy no one will take from" them (Jn 16:22). In point of fact, there precisely is the paradox of Christian living: In dying is our rising, in crucifixion our resurrection, in self-giving self-fulfilment. It is the prayer of St. Francis of Assisi: "It is in giving that we receive; it is in loving that we are loved; it is in dying that we are born to eternal life."

Good friends, married love is not an endless "Love Boat."[2] The love that endures is a tough love. It's easy enough to rhapsodize with St. Paul: "Love is patient and kind, not jealous or boastful, not arrogant or rude. Love does not insist on its own way, is not irritable or resentful, does not rejoice at wrong, rejoices in the right. Love bears all things, believes all things, hopes all things, endures all things" (1 Cor 13:4–7). The problem lies in living it. Such love is not born of a high IQ or a Colgate smile, of a fat wallet or a thick skin. Such love is yours only if, as St. Paul told the Christians of Rome, "God's love has been poured into our hearts through the Holy Spirit who has been given to us" (Rom 5:5).

Discouraging? Quite the opposite. For in a few short moments you will witness something my college friends would call "wild." When Denise and Chester murmur "I do," those two monosyllables are the heart of a sacrament. And if you recall your catechism, a sacrament is a visible sign of invisible grace. What you will see and hear hides a divine promise: God's own "I do." God binds His love to them for life. "I am with you always" (Mt 28:20).

III

It is with God's love in their hearts and over their lives that Chester and Denise can live confidently the word of God they have plucked from Paul: "As God's chosen ones, put on compassion, kindness, patience, forgiving each other as the Lord has forgiven you. And above all these put on love. Let the peace of Christ rule in your hearts. Be thankful. Let the word of Christ dwell in you richly. And whatever you do, do everything in the name of the Lord Jesus" (Col 3:12–17). Rather than dwell abstractly on each of these gifts, let me concretize it with one of my favorite experiences, a touchingly true love story.[3]

Some years ago a dear friend of mine died. Perry had been married almost 60 years. The first anniversary of his marriage he was flat broke. So he went into a florist shop, asked the florist to trust him for a single rose. The florist did; Perry brought the rose to Bess—with a love letter. Each anniversary till he died, that lovely ritual was re-enacted: two roses, three, ten, 25, 40—always with a love letter. And one moving afternoon in a New York restaurant, with children and grandchildren all about, before the cake was cut, in came 50 roses—with a love letter. After 50 years Perry still greeted Bess with an affectionate kiss after each separation, no matter how short. Wherever they walked, he offered his arm, though she needed it not. Each meal he seated her at table, even when there was no one to see. And whenever this amateur bartender (from whom I learned so much!) mixed drinks for friends before dinner, no one ever drank before Perry called Bess from the kitchen—Bess who never drank—called her in for the first toast: "To the queen!"

This is not a commercial for cocktails. That love reflected St. Paul's charge to the Christians of Colossae—through good times and bad, through sickness and health, through hope and fear, through stress and peace—because above all else Perry and Bess had "put on love." Love of God, to whom they gave thanks in agony as well as ecstasy. And within that love, a ceaseless sense of wonder—each lost in wonder at the miracle of the other.

A final word, good friends. A word I wing to all of you. This evening you are not spectators at a spectacle, in awe and tears at a love story scripted in heaven or Hollywood. Your presence here is at once a reminder and a promise. A reminder that Denise and Chester need you—not to fill a church but to fill their lives, to gift them with your experience and your example, with your courage and your love. A promise that, a bit like God, you will always be there when they call, ready to share not so much fondue forks or Wedgwood ware as a gift still more precious: the healing in your hand or the eloquence in your eyes or the caring in your hearing. So then, when Chester and Denise link hands in a pledge of endless love, cover their hands with your own—and keep them covered till death do you part.

Cathedral of the Sacred Heart
Richmond, Virginia
June 4, 1988

29
IT TAKES THREE. . . .
Wedding Homily 4

- Song of Songs 2:8–10, 14; 8:6–7a
- Romans 12:1–2, 9–18
- Matthew 7:21, 24–29

It is always with some trepidation that I speak on marriage. For I come with four strikes against me: I'm a man, a celibate, a priest, and . . . a Jesuit. But I come with two factors in my favor: I have been a wedding-watcher for seven decades, and I love Katie and Roberto dearly. So, bear with me as my own "song of songs" swings through three movements: first, marriage as America 1988 sees it; second, marriage as Roberto and Katie enter it; third, marriage as God blesses it.

I

First, marriage as America 1988 sees it. It's a sobering picture. Not all negative, of course. Young men and women still fall fantastically in love, still vow life together till death, still struggle to make a "go" of marriage, still live wedded life courageously even unto crucifixion. Unnumbered couples celebrate 25, 50, 60 years of bittersweet love. I have seen married love deepen despite malignant melanoma.[1] I have seen married love survive a stillborn child and years of degrading poverty, survive cocaine and the curse of alcohol, survive neuroses and psychoses, survive abortion and adultery.

And still it is true, the American family today is in deep trouble. Our culture has a problem with the expression "for ever." Nothing lasts for ever: not Dior's designs or Billy Martin's baseball contract, not steel mills or family farms, not BMWs or the best of computers, not health or wealth, not good looks or Clairol hair, not even life. And, within recent decades, marriage. "Till death do us part" has given way to "as long as it works out."

Please understand me: I am not blanketing every divorce with an anathema. Judgment I leave to God. I am realist enough to recognize that, if marriage is made in heaven, marriages have to be lived on earth, and our earthbound existence leaves us woefully vulnerable to what Shakespeare called "the slings and arrows of outrageous fortune." In marriage as in priesthood, we realize what St. Paul put so powerfully to the Christians of Rome: All too often "I do not do the good I want, but the evil I do not want is what I do" (Rom 7:19). What I *am* saying, what all of us must admit, is this: There is something terribly wrong, dreadfully harmful, awfully frightening in our culture when 50 percent of marriages end in failure.

II

It is in this context that Katie and Roberto link their hands and their lives. It is in this atmosphere of paradox—lasting love and dashed hopes—that they give us fresh reason for hope. They give us fresh hope, on broad lines, by being who they are—living expressions of St. Paul's paean to love: "Love is patient and kind; love is not jealous or boastful; it is not arrogant or rude. Love does not insist on its own way; it is not irritable or resentful; it does not rejoice at wrong, but rejoices in the right. Love bears all things, believes all things, hopes all things, endures all things" (1 Cor 13:4–7).

But in a very special way this day, in this liturgy, Roberto and Katie raise our hopes. This they do in the readings you have just heard, the passages they have personally plucked from God's own Book. Each passage tells us how these two enter marriage, how they see it in the light of God's own revealing. A brief look at each.

Through the Old Testament Song of Songs Katie and Roberto tell us how splendidly *human* is the love of man and maid. This biblical book is not a child's primer on the birds and the bees, not calf or puppy love, not Victorian romance; at times it is downright erotic. But not to worry! It is God surprising us once again, God's way of spelling out the full humanness, the rich earthiness, of human loving. Lover and beloved rejoice in, thrill to, all that is the other: the sound of his voice, a glance from her eyes, their very bodies. There is nothing they hold back—nothing. As God imagined marriage before time was born, male and female are drawn to each other in ways beyond counting. Swiftly or slowly, two sense in each other what will make them whole, annihilate their isolation, destroy a damnable concentration on self. They long to share without reserve, to give till there is nothing left to give—bone and blood, flesh and spirit, mind and heart—where there is indeed "I and thou" but never "mine and thine." Such is the love before us today.

Through St. Paul's letter to the Christians of Rome Roberto and Katie tell us what it means to them for love to be "genuine" (Rom 12:9). One thing alone will they hate: whatever is evil; and even evil they will "overcome with good" (v. 21). A splendid ideal for two-in-one whose life together is given over to healing.[2] They promise to "rejoice with those who rejoice, weep with those who weep" (v. 15). A tough promise, especially in a society where crack is king and coke is killer, where children are choked and women are savaged, where death never takes a holiday. They will not lord it over others, will make friends with the lowly, with the unloved, the unlovable. As far as it rests with them, they will "live peaceably with all" (v. 18). Their hands and their hearts will be consecrated to the little ones of this world, those who beg mutely for a sign of love. What I am phrasing so abstractly Mother Teresa of Calcutta expressed, as always, with powerful simplicity:

> One day I was walking down the street and I saw a man sitting there looking most terrible, so I went to him and shook his hand (and my hand is always very warm), and he looked up and said, "Oh, what a long, long time since I felt the warmth of a human hand." He brightened up, he was so full of joy that there was somebody that loved him, there was somebody who cared.[3]

Through Jesus' Sermon on the Mount Katie and Roberto tell us that they will build their house of love not on sand but on rock. Not on shifting sand: not on the foundations the world can offer— wealth, power, fame—helpful as these at times may prove. They will found their marriage on the Rock of ages: on the Lord God and His Christ.

III

This leads logically into my third point: how God blesses marriage. One thesis rings loud and clear from Christian theology and human experience: It takes three to make a marriage last. The hand that enfolds the clasped hands of Katie and Roberto is the hand of a loving Lord. This is not pious prattle. For at least two splendid reasons.

First, God it was who shaped male and female for each other, God who "blessed them" in the beginning and commanded them to "be fruitful and multiply," God who "looked on [what] He had made" and found it "very good" (Gen 1:28, 31). As in Eden then, so in St. Aloysius now, it is God who hovers over a man and a woman, God who blesses Roberto and Katie, God who smiles on them because what He sees He finds very good. Their yes to each other is more than a word; it is a gift. In the Catholic vision, Father Cullen, for all his remarkable personality and talents, is not the minister of this marriage, only the Church's official witness. The ministers of this marriage are Katie and Roberto. As ministers of a sacrament, they channel God, channel God's life, to each other.

Second, today is only an overture, a beginning. God will not leave them when they leave this church. Through God's gracious giving, their yes to each other is not simply a sacred sign; it contains a promise: In their life together God will always be there. Not in some hazy, ghostlike way, a bright cloud hovering over their home. He will never stop loving them, even if their love for Him should weaken. He will live in them as in a temple as long as they want Him to. Whenever they lift lips and heart to Him, He will be there to listen. It's not, I admit, an infallible preventive against all the diseases that can afflict life together, but it surely beats trying to go it alone. After all, as Jesus put it quite bluntly in another context, "With men and women it is impossible, but not with God; for all things are possible with God" (Mk 10:27). All things—even a half century of life and love.

One final word—to all of you who take delight in this day. Spectacular as this celebration is, it is not a sheer spectacle, and you are not solely spectators. You are intimately involved. Each of you has played some role—leading, supporting, bit player, whatever— in the story of Roberto and/or Katie that reaches new heights today. But whatever the Oscar or Emmy you deserve for your part, the play is not over. These two you love so lavishly will live wedded life not on a desert isle but on a paradoxical planet where men and women kill one another and die for one another, where the blood of Christ they drink in their Eucharist mingles with the blood they treat on beds of pain, where all too many grow fat while a billion fall asleep hungry, where the resurgence of rugged individualism and the seduction of self-love have ensnared all too many Christians, have made untold Catholics forget that we are members of Christ's body, in which no one of us can say of any other "I have no need of you" (1 Cor 12:21).

Very simply, these two need you. Not so much for Waterford crystal or Irish linen, welcome as these are. More importantly, they literally need *you*. They need your example. They need to see married love lived loyally, faithfully, courageously year after year, in fair weather and foul, in poverty and wealth, in laughter and tears, in delight and depression. They should find in you strong reason to hope for the kind of joy which Jesus promised "no one will take from you" (Jn 16:22).

So then, when Katie and Roberto join hands a few moments from now, I would ask the wedded among you to link your own hands, to murmur softly or in your heart: "I take you to have and to hold, for better for worse, for richer for poorer, in sickness and in health, until death do us part." No greater gift can you give to these two. No greater gift can they give to you.

St. Aloysius' Church
New Canaan, Conn.
August 6, 1988

30

FOR OTHERS . . . TILL DEATH
Wedding Homily 5

- Genesis 2:18–24
- Matthew 7:21, 24–29

As I move deeper into my twilight years, I find it ever so important to tell dear friends what I feel for them and what I hope for them. And so it is today. A short quarter hour from now, Barbara and Chris will begin a life that should never end, but a life they have never experienced. Nor have I experienced it. But after seven decades of wedding-watching, from proxy experiences ecstatic and saddening, from long meditation on what God has said and is saying to us, and in the light of my own love for this precious pair, I dare to lay before them my dream for their life together. My dream is simply phrased: I want their life to be *for others*. For others in three wondrous ways: (1) for each other, (2) for the others outside, (3) for the Other (capital O) who is God. A word on each.

I

First, I want Barbara and Chris to live for each other. Here the Genesis story is profoundly pertinent. Listen carefully, for you may have missed the mystery. After fashioning the first man, God declares: "It is not good for the man to be alone; I will make him a helper fit for him," someone corresponding to him, a counterpart (Gen 2:18). What does God do? God brings to Adam the beasts and birds just now created. Adam "names" them (v. 20). He recognizes them, sees them for what they are. And he sees that, however graceful and gentle, however lovely and lovable, none of these creatures is "fit for him"; none corresponds to him; none is his

196

counterpart. Yes, they are like him: They see and hear, touch and taste and smell. But they are not like enough to him.

Is the Lord frustrated? Not at all. God shapes a creature at once different from the man and strikingly similar. So similar, so kin to him, that Scripture in a burst of high imagination pictures God fashioning this other out of the man's very body. Note Adam's reaction; the effect is electric. When first the first man sets eyes on the first woman, he exclaims in ecstasy: "This one, at last, is bone of my bone and flesh of my flesh!" (v. 23). "This one"—three times he shouts it—here is man's joyous surprise as he welcomes his one equal on earth, his peer and companion. Here, the author adds, is an affinity, an attraction, so strong that it will loosen the strongest bonds in early life, the bonds that bind to parents and home: "That is why a man leaves his father and his mother and cleaves to his wife, and they become one flesh" (v. 24).[1]

This fascinating invention of divine imagining—two images of God similar in shape and spirit, yet not the same—what does this demand of you? It demands that while remaining two, you increasingly become one. At times submerging but never surrendering what makes you your own person, your precious self, you enrich that self with the other, enrich the other with your self. From your first kiss as husband and wife, through your different careers, to your supreme act of love, whatever you do is a yes to the other. Very simply, there is indeed "I and thou," but never "mine and thine."

II

Second, I want Chris and Barbara to live for the others outside. This is not just a nice, charitable, philanthropic thought I conjured up for this homily. It goes back to our Lord Jesus Christ. Not an invitation; a command: "Love your neighbor as [you love] yourself" (Mt 22:39).

A strange event captured the hearts of our world last month. Three California gray whales were trapped in Alaskan ice, unable to reach open water. For eight days scientists and oil-company personnel coaxed the exhausted leviathans toward an open lead in the ice pack; Eskimos sawed breathing holes in six-inch-thick ice; a Soviet ice-breaker reduced to rubble a towering ridge of ice, 400 yards wide and 30 feet high; experts discussed whether using dynamite would damage the whales' hearing. And now, more than a million dollars later, two whales are safely on their way to Baja California for the winter.[2]

Good friends, I have nothing against whales. I simply find such costly compassion misplaced. What of the men, women, and children who surround us? In our comfortable country over eleven million children live in poverty—about one in every four.[3] In our land where all are equal before the law, "more than 80% of the legal needs of the poor goes unattended."[4] In the midst of our medical miracles, AIDS patients discover doctors who will not treat them, and the profession cannot command such risk. In this capital city of our nation elderly folk rummage for food scraps in garbage cans, the homeless huddle for warmth on Georgetown's grates, our jails are overcrowded academies of crime, in the schools crack is king, and infant minds are stunted by malnutrition. Over and above those who suffer in body and mind, there is the silent majority that longs for love, for an ear that will listen, for a hand that will touch, for eyes that will not shrink from them in embarrassment.

Chris and Barbara are people of profound compassion. Each already feels deeply for the unfortunate. Today must mark a fresh phase in their compassion. Their hearts and their hands will continue to move out to others, but from here to eternity they will move out together—their hearts linked, their hands clasped. Not that Barbara turns nurse at Georgetown Hospital;[5] not that Chris invades her office to heal the employees. Rather that they see themselves as bonded to serve. Whatever one does in love, the other shares.

No homilist dares tell you precisely how you are to serve. So much depends on who you are and where you are, what the need is and what our Lord calls you to do. But serve you must; for the marriage of Christians dares not be a selfish union, simply two-in-one-flesh; it is two-for-all, two for community. Only thus can an America remarkably blessed become for the downtrodden not only "the home of the brave" but "the land of the free."

III

Third, I want Barbara and Chris to live for the Other (capital O) who is God. Dreadfully pious, not quite what you'd expect of a Jesuit? Perhaps, yet awfully real. It does not mean that you stroll around starry-eyed, hands folded in reverence, lips perpetually poised for prayer. It simply means that you are returning love for love.

You see, the reason why you two are here today is a 30-year miracle of love. Think what it took to get you here. A God who knew you from eternity called you into existence, poured into your first moment the breath of life. This same God had you grow, like the boy Jesus, "in wisdom and in years" (Lk 2:52) under parents who cherished you, responded to your every helpless cry, fed you, clothed you, took a fair amount of nonsense from you, and finally left you free to become your own man, your own woman. This same God gifted you not only with brown eyes but with high intelligence, not only with health but with humor. This same God so arranged His complex world that Scottsdale and the Big Apple mysteriously met and fell in love. This same God will shortly make you ministers of a sacrament—a sacred rite where each of you will give to the other not only yourself but God.

And the miracle will never cease. For this same God promises you today that, since it takes three to make a marriage, He will share your life, strengthen you when times are tough and enrich your laughter with His love. This same God will be there even if you forget Him; for without Him you cannot draw the next breath, cannot carry your love into tomorrow, cannot murmur "till death do us part."

Lavish love like this calls for love in response. Not some airy, flimsy, insubstantial feeling. Rather, the kind of love Christ had in view when he proclaimed the "great" commandment, the "first" commandment of all: "You shall love the Lord your God with all your heart, and with all your soul, and with all your mind" (Mt 22:36, 38). It shouldn't be too difficult. After all, you need not search for God in high heaven or in the bowels of the earth. He is closer to you than you are to yourself; for your God is within you. It will be still easier if you love God together, if you can talk to God together, talk about God together, entrust your two-in-oneness into His caring hands. Do that and your life together will merit the tribute a British author paid to Mother Teresa: "something beautiful for God."[6]

Good friends: A wedded life such as I have described Barbara and Chris cannot realize all by themselves. God's help they can count on. The question is: Can they count on you? Oh, not for Limoges porcelain or Irish linen, not for ice buckets or bassinets (but keep those coming!). Rather, can they count on you for the strength that comes from example—the example of tough, bitter-sweet wedded existence where, for one year or 50, you whose friendship they prize are living for each other, are living for others, are living for God?

To begin such powerful help, or to continue it, I have a bold suggestion. When Chris and Barbara join hands in their gift of self, why don't the wedded among you clasp your own hands and echo quietly: "I take you . . . to have and to hold . . . for better for worse . . . for richer for poorer . . . in sickness and in health . . . until death do us part"? I assure you, no greater gift can you give to your dear Barbara and Chris.

Holy Trinity Church
Washington, D.C.
November 26, 1988

31

THAT THEIR KISS STILL WORKS
Wedding Homily 6

- Song of Songs 2:8–10, 14, 16; 8:6–7
- 1 Corinthians 12:31—13:8
- Matthew 5:1–12

To preach at a wedding is at once a privilege.and a burden. For I am entering an area that is peculiarly personal, singularly sacred to one man and one woman. And yet, there is a message I want to convey not only to these two who are beginning their journey together, but to those of you who have traveled that road for one year or fifty. Three stages to my message: (1) a fact of life, (2) a truth of faith, (3) a story for the ages.

I

First, a fact of life. Very simply, marriage is a risk. You don't need a celibate Jesuit to tell you that; the evidence is all around you. Sociologists say that about 50% of marriages break up; the media confirm it in print and picture.

But once I've said that, let me add this: I am not playing a prophet of doom. Risk—which means exposing yourself to loss or injury, to disadvantage or even destruction—risk is part of human living. To be alive is to risk. To be single for life is a risk. To be a priest is indeed a risk. And so I am not surprised that it is risky for a man and a woman to murmur to each other: "I take you . . . to have and to hold . . . for better for worse, for richer for poorer, in sickness and in health, until death do us part." Not every marriage that opened with those risk-laden phrases has weathered the "worse," has overpowered poverty, has survived sickness of spirit or flesh.

In any and every risk, the critical question is this: Is the risk worth taking? Is there good reason to believe—not absolute certainty, only good reason to believe—that no matter what the years may bring, however devastating and unexpected, your love will survive it?

Your *love*. Ah, there's the rub, that elusive word "love." Not simply the chemistry that makes for one-night stands; not only the emotion, the feelings, that come and go. Over and above these, the deliberate, ceaseless gift of each to the other, the self-giving that does not disappear when darkness clouds your sky. This is the love I discern in Tom and Noreen, the kind of love that makes me want to shout for joy. For the love that envelops you two is the kind of love St. Paul described in down-to-earth phrases when he wrote to the Christians of Corinth: "Love is patient and kind; love is not jealous or boastful; it is not arrogant or rude. Love does not insist on its own way; it is not irritable or resentful; it does not rejoice at wrong, but rejoices in the right. Love bears all things, believes all things, hopes all things, endures all things" (1 Cor 13:4–7).

II

That powerful passage from Paul plunges me into my second point: a truth of faith. You see, the love the Apostle lyricizes is not a love you can buy at Woodies,[1] not a love Noreen and Tom can manufacture by themselves. This is the love Paul called "God's love . . . poured into our hearts through the Holy Spirit who has been given to us" (Rom 5:5).

You see, God did not forget about marriage once He had set it up, did not leave it to go its merry or merciless way. What you will witness shortly we call a sacrament—as much a sacrament as baptism and Eucharist. What is a sacrament? Very simply, a visible sign of God's grace. The words "I take you" which Noreen and Tom will murmur to each other are more than *their* promise to live in unique oneness for the rest of their lives. Through those words *God* guarantees that He will be with them in good times or bad, in poverty or wealth, in sickness or health, until death.

Not that God guarantees success. God promises that He will be there—to give strength and solace, courage and constancy, generosity and gentleness. But, for all God's powerful presence, we remain wonderfully and fearfully human, and God will always respect our freedom, will never force us, never compel us to be wise when we insist on being stupid, compassionate when we are bent on being selfish, pliant when we are determined to be pigheaded. And, for His own secret reasons, God still allows bad things to happen to good people—lets a Holocaust separate millions of Jewish lovers, famine destroy uncounted Sudanese families, alcoholism or schizophrenia rip a deep love to shreds, childlessness and even childishness lay a heavy hand on two-in-one.

What does this mean? On the one hand, God does not promise Tom and Noreen a rose garden, a perpetual paradise of pleasure, heaven on earth. On the other hand, God does say: "Put your hands in mine, trust me as my own Son did from Nazareth to Calvary, plan your life-together in prayerful oneness with me, and you have good reason to hope for days and years rich in laughter, a life that lends meaning to those less fortunate, a life that makes your acre of God's world a place of peace, of justice, of love."

III

My third point is a story for the ages. It is a true story. I first read it several months ago and it still haunts me. I read it again last week and knew instantly that I wanted to tell it to Tom and Noreen. The story stems from a surgeon—a doctor who weds to his scalpel an uncommon gift for what is uniquely human. He tells of a remarkable experience soon after a delicate operation:

> I stand by the bed where a young woman lies, her face postoperative, her mouth twisted in palsy, clownish. A tiny twig of the facial nerve, the one to the muscles of her mouth, has been severed. She will be thus from now on. The surgeon had followed with religious fervor the curve of her flesh; I promise you that. Nevertheless, to remove the tumor in her cheek, I had cut the little nerve.
>
> Her young husband is in the room. He stands on the opposite side of the bed, and together they seem to dwell in the evening lamplight, isolated from me, private. Who are they, I ask myself, he and this wry-mouth I have made, who gaze at and touch each other so generously, greedily? The young woman speaks.
>
> "Will my mouth always be like this?" she asks.
>
> "Yes," I say, "it will. It is because the nerve was cut."
>
> She nods, and is silent. But the young man smiles.
>
> "I like it," he says. "It is kind of cute."
>
> All at once I *know* who he is. I understand, and I lower my

gaze. One is not bold in an encounter with a god. Unmindful, he bends to kiss her crooked mouth, and I so close I can see how he twists his own lips to accommodate to hers, to show her that their kiss still works. I remember that the gods appeared in ancient Greece as mortals, and I hold my breath and let the wonder in.[2]

"To accommodate to hers." To accommodate to his. Scotch-tape that to your refrigerator. The story is symbolic; it tells us more than the words explicitly say. Here is the endless story of two-in-one, the sensitivity that makes for joy in the very heart of sorrow.

Good friends: I began this homily on a rather negative note—on marriage as a risk. Let me close on a more positive note—on marriage as a challenge. Today's celebration challenges Tom and Noreen—challenges them to live for each other, to live for the less fortunate others who surround them, to live for the Lord who alone can prosper their love. In the radiant dawn of their own self-giving, Noreen and Tom challenge all the wedded among you—invite you to join your own hands once again, to thank God for the pleasure and the pain you have shared, to murmur now more intensely than ever "I take you to have and to hold till death do us part." Today this couple you love invite you to love again as once you loved before, to prove that through all the bittersweet of the years your "kiss still works." As a wedding gift for Noreen and Tom, it sure beats even a rolling pin.

Holy Trinity Church
Washington, D.C.
December 10, 1988

NOTES

Prologue

1. George Dennis O'Brien (Boston: Beacon, 1986).
2. Ibid. 121.
3. Quoted in an editorial by James M. Wall, "Beyond Blandness in Preaching," *Christian Century* 105, no. 16 (May 11, 1988) 467–68, at 467.
4. See ibid. 467–68. Here I have been stimulated by Walls's re-creation of ideas in David S. Reynolds' new book, *Beneath the American Renaissance* (New York: Knopf, 1988), and by his own pertinent reflections thereon.
5. Karl Rahner, S.J., "Demythologization and the Sermon," in *The Renewal of Preaching: Theory and Practice* (Concilium 33; New York: Paulist, 1968) 20–38, at 21.
6. Ibid.
7. Ibid. 22.
8. A reference to the film *Roxanne*.
9. A reference to a highly popular early-80s film.
10. The number here given is as of July 15, 1988.
11. See, e.g., Gibson Winter, *The New Creation as Metropolis* (New York: Macmillan, 1966) chaps. 1 and 2, "The Call to Servanthood" and "The Servant Church in a Secularized World" (1–64); Karl Rahner, "Following the Crucified," *Theological Investigations* 18: *God and Revelation* (New York: Crossroad, 1983) 157–70.
12. To avoid the inconsistencies in certain printed versions of Dr. King's address, I have taken these excerpts from the live recording "I Have a Dream" produced by Twentieth Century Fox and distributed by ABC Records, TFS 3201 (n.d.), available through the courtesy of the

Audio-Visual Center in the Lauinger Library of Georgetown University, Washington, D.C.

13. From a review by David H.C. Read in *America* 147, no. 21 (Dec. 25, 1982) 417.

14. Frederick Buechner, *Telling the Truth: The Gospel as Tragedy, Comedy, and Fairy Tale* (San Francisco: Harper & Row, 1977) 49–50.

15. Karl Rahner, S.J., *The Eternal Year*, tr. John Shea, S.S. (Baltimore: Helicon, 1964) 57–63, at 58–59.

16. Ibid. 62.

17. *Tablet* (London) 242, no 7720 (July 2, 1988) 754–55 (a review of my *Preaching: The Art and the Craft* [New York/Mahwah: Paulist, 1987] by Vladimir Felzmann), at 754.

18. See *Catholic Mind* 66, no. 1223 (May 1968) 6–7; first printed in *Variety*, March 13, 1968, under the title "A Jesuit Valentine to Films," with this prefatory sentence: "After the speech, two members of the audience—one a priest, one a film-company publicist—were overheard making almost identical remarks: 'They should have him speak at the Academy Awards ceremonies; he'd make them understand that they were doing something important.' "

19. See "Chariots of Fire," in my collection *Still Proclaiming Your Wonders: Homilies for the Eighties* (New York/Ramsey: Paulist, 1984) 183–88.

20. See "Grazie, Signore!" in my collection *Grace on Crutches: Homilies for Fellow Travelers* (New York/Mahwah: Paulist, 1986) 191–96. The quotations derive from the fine review of the film by Richard A. Blake, "God's Grandeur," *America* 151, no. 10 (Oct. 13, 1984) 210.

21. See "A New Coke in Your Life?" in my collection *Lovely in Eyes Not His: Homilies for an Imaging of Christ* (New York/Mahwah: Paulist, 1988) 157–62.

22. From my homily "Zapping the Zelig," in my collection *Still Proclaiming Your Wonders* (n. 19 above) 189–94, at 189. See the reviews of the film by Pauline Kael, "The Current Cinema: Anybody Home?" *New Yorker*, Aug. 8, 1983, 84, 87, and Richard A. Blake, "Thalia," *America* 149, no. 4 (Aug. 6–13, 1983) 73.

23. Words and music by Wayne Kirkpatrick, Richard Mullins, Amy Grant, and Gary Chapman. Copyright 1985 River Oaks Music Company (BMI)/Meadowgreen Music Company (ASCAP)/Bug & Bear Music (ASCAP)/Fred & Ethel Music Company Inc. (ASCAP). (River Oaks Music Company/Meadowgreen Music Co. administered by Tree Publ. Co., Inc.).

24. *Time* 132, no. 4 (July 25, 1988) 69.

25. See ibid.

26. A reference to the Democratic National Convention of 1988, taking place as I struggled with this paragraph.

27. Quoted by Joel Porte, " 'I Am Not the Man You Take Me For,' " *Harvard Magazine* 81, no. 5 (May–June 1979) 50.

28. Yves Congar, O.P., "Sacramental Worship and Preaching," in *The Renewal of Preaching* (n. 5 above) 62.

Homily 1

1. Cf. Joseph A. Fitzmyer, S.J., *The Gospel according to Luke (I–IX)* (Garden City, N.Y.: Doubleday, 1981) 413.
2. Translation from Fitzmyer, ibid. 434, 442–43.
3. Cf. ibid. 444–45.
4. Reference to an ageless movie frequently repeated on TV around Christmas, *Miracle on 34th Street*.
5. "J.R." is a well-known character in the TV serial "Dallas."
6. Cf. Fitzmyer, *Luke I–IX* 363: "A Christian tradition, well antedating the Crusades, eventually localized the dwelling of Zechariah at 'Ain Karin, eight kms. W of Jerusalem. . . .'"
7. *Flannery O'Connor: The Habit of Being*, Letters edited by Sally Fitzgerald (New York: Farrar, Straus, Giroux, 1979) 453.
8. So Fitzmyer, *The Gospel according to Luke (X–XXIV)* (Garden City, N.Y.: Doubleday, 1985) 928–29.
9. St. Augustine, *On Holy Virginity* 3 (PL 40, 398); *Sermon 215*, no. 4 (PL 38, 1074).
10. *Time* 130, no. 23 (Dec. 7, 1987) 62–72.
11. Ibid. 62.
12. Cf. ibid. 3 (Table of Contents summary).
13. Ibid. 62, 63.
14. Ibid. 72.
15. "*Hinduism*, a mantric word thought to be a complete expression of Brahman and interpreted as having three sounds representing Brahma or creation, Vishnu or preservation, and Siva or destruction, or as consisting of the same three sounds, representing waking, dreams, and deep sleep, along with the following silence, which is fulfillment" (*The Random House Dictionary of the English Language* [New York: Random House, 1966] 1004). It is not my intention to disparage Om or to discourage its use by Christians. I am concerned about Christians who look elsewhere than to Christ for the substance of their spirituality.

Homily 2

1. See John L. McKenzie, *Second Isaiah* (Garden City, N.Y.: Doubleday, 1968) esp. 15–19.
2. See J. P. M. Walsh, *The Mighty from Their Thrones: Power in the Biblical Tradition* (Philadelphia: Fortress, 1987) 135–38.

3. A reference to a facet of a recent TV ministry scandal that involved excessive profits and a life style hardly imitative of the poor Christ.
4. From the beginning of the poem by Gerard Manley Hopkins, "S. Thomae Aquinatis Rhythmus ad SS. Sacramentum," in W. H. Gardner and N. H. MacKenzie, eds., *The Poems of Gerard Manley Hopkins* (4th ed.; London: Oxford University, 1970) 211.
5. Gerard Manley Hopkins, "As kingfishers catch fire," ibid. 90.
6. A popular TV soap opera.
7. See Bruce Ritter, *Sometimes God Has a Kid's Face* (New York: Covenant House, 1988).
8. Jay Cocks, "A Beat Box with Four Octaves," *Time* 132, no. 16 (Oct. 17, 1988) 79.

Homily 3

1. See Joseph A. Fitzmyer, S.J., *The Gospel according to Luke (I–IX)* (Garden City, N.Y.: Doubleday, 1981) 506–20.
2. Cf. ibid. 510: "The scenes . . . symbolize the seduction in the hostility, opposition, and rejection which confronted him constantly throughout his ministry. . . . The opposition was such that he was constantly tempted to use his power as Son to overcome it."
3. Ibid.
4. Mt. 4:3 has "stones" and "loaves."
5. It is not clear exactly what part of the Jerusalem temple is meant by the Greek *pterygion* ("pinnacle" or "winglet"); see Fitzmyer, ibid. 516–17.
6. Ibid. 512.
7. Cf. ibid.
8. Cf. Second Vatican Council, Decree on the Apostolate of the Laity, no. 5.
9. See my homily "To Make of It a New Creation," in *Still Proclaiming Your Wonders: Homilies for the Eighties* (New York/Ramsey: Paulist, 1984) 211–18, at 212–13.
10. See *Time* 128, no. 10 (Sept. 8, 1986) 57.
11. Cf. William Rasperry, "A Rising Tide of Materialism," *Washington Post,* Feb. 1, 1988, A15.
12. Joseph Nocera, "The Ga-Ga Years: Money Love, Market Lust, and the Seducing of America," *Esquire,* February 1988, 79–90, at 79–80.
13. Robert N. Bellah, "Religion & Power in America Today," *Commonweal* 109, no. 21 (Dec. 3, 1982) 650–55, at 652.
14. Cf. my homily "The Other, the Others, and You," in *Lovely in Eyes Not His: Homilies for an Imaging of Christ* (New York/Mahwah: Paulist, 1988) 154–55.

Homily 4

1. Hilary of Poitiers, *Commentary on Matthew* 2, 5 (PL 9, 927).
2. Ibid. 19, 5 (PL 9, 1025).
3. It is not a simple matter to provide an understandable exegesis of the thesis that in some genuine sense the flesh the Son of God took is the flesh of every human being born into this world. Sebastian Tromp sees eight ideas emerge from the vast reaches of patristic literature; cf. his *Corpus Christi quod est ecclesia* 1: *Introductio generalis* (2nd ed.; Rome: Gregorian University, 1946); I have summarized these eight facets of the all-inclusive incorporation of humanity into Christ in my essay "The Body of Christ: Patristic Insights," in the multiauthor volume *The Church as the Body of Christ* (Notre Dame: University of Notre Dame, 1963) 69–101, at 73–74.
4. I am not, of course, denying the essential role of Jesus' resurrection in our redemption. His dying was not a naked ending; it was a dying-unto-resurrection. It still remains true that the pivot on which our redemption turns is the cross.
5. Flannery O'Connor, "A Good Man Is Hard to Find," in *Flannery O'Connor: The Complete Stories* (New York: Farrar, Straus and Giroux, 1972) 116–33, at 131.
6. Ibid. 131, repeated at 132.
7. Gerard Manley Hopkins, "God's Grandeur," in W. H. Gardner and N. H. MacKenzie, eds., *The Poems of Gerard Manley Hopkins* (4th ed.; London: Oxford University, 1970) 66.
8. Eugene O'Neill, *Lazarus Laughed*, Act 1, Scene 1; in *The Plays of Eugene O'Neill* (New York: Random House, 1955) 280.
9. Second Vatican Council, Decree on the Apostolate of the Laity, no. 5.
10. Karl Rahner, *Schriften zur Theologie* 15: *Wissenschaft und christlicher Glaube* (Zurich: Benziger, 1983) 20.
11. See, for this expression, Karl Rahner's "dying in installments," in his "Following the Crucified," *Theological Investigations* 18: *God and Revelation* (New York: Crossroad, 1983) 157–70, at 169–70.
12. I am referring, respectively, to the titles of a well-known novel by Pearl Buck and a rather frightening film.
13. A reference to the title of a fairly recent TV serial.

Homily 5

1. For much of what follows about Jn 20:19–31, I am deeply indebted to Raymond E. Brown, S.S., *The Gospel according to John (xiii–xxi)* (Garden City, N.Y.: Doubleday, 1970) 1018–61.

Homily 6

1. A reference to a traditional May hymn to our Lady that begins "Bring flowers of the rarest. . . ."
2. Translation from Joseph A. Fitzmyer, S.J., *The Gospel according to Luke (I–IX)* (Garden City, N.Y.: Doubleday, 1981) 434, 442–43.
3. See. e.g., Raymond E. Brown, S.S., *The Gospel according to John (xiii–xxi)* (Garden City, N.Y.: Doubleday, 1970) 925–26.
4. Here I am largely indebted to an insightful article by Elizabeth A. Johnson, C.S.J., "Mary and the Female Face of God," *Theological Studies* 50 (1989) 500–526, which I recommend enthusiastically not only to preachers but to all who seek a more profound understanding of our God as imaged by women as well as men.
5. See *Osservatore romano,* Sept. 21, 1978.

Homily 7

1. For further details and the sources of my quotations, see Monica Furlong, *Merton: A Biography* (San Francisco: Harper & Row, 1980) esp. 202–340 passim; John Eudes Bamberger, "In Search of Thomas Merton," *America* 147, no. 9 (Oct. 2, 1982) 165–69; and my *Seasons That Laugh or Weep: Musings on the Human Journey* (New York/Ramsey: Paulist, 1983) 78–82.
2. For greater detail, but still in homiletic form, see "St. Augustine: Sanctity and Conversion," in my *Saints and Sanctity* (Englewood Cliffs, N.J.: Prentice-Hall, 1965) 37–47.
3. St. Augustine, *Confessions* 2, 1; tr. F. J. Sheed, *The Confessions of St. Augustine* (New York: Sheed & Ward, 1943) 27.
4. *Confessions* 3, 1; tr. Sheed 41.
5. *Confessions* 6, 15; tr. Sheed 126.
6. *Confessions* 8, 7; tr. Sheed 170.
7. *Confessions* 8, 8; tr. Sheed 171.
8. *Confessions* 8, 12; tr. Sheed 178–79.
9. A phrase from the poem *The Hound of Heaven* by Francis Thompson.
10. *Confessions* 10, 36; tr. Sheed 249.
11. Reference to the famous film *The Phantom of the Opera,* recently staged in brilliant fashion as a musical by Andrew Lloyd Webber.
12. *The Long Loneliness: The Autobiography of Dorothy Day* (New York: Harper & Brothers, 1952) 149–50.
13. Quoted in William D. Miller, *Dorothy Day: A Biography* (San Francisco: Harper & Row, 1982) 341; emphasis mine.
14. Ibid. 343–44.
15. *The Long Loneliness* 286; emphasis mine.

Homily 8

1. To understand a number of references in this homily, it is imperative to realize that it was preached at an annual gathering of Jesuits and former Jesuits of the New York Province of the Society of Jesus.
2. Joseph A. Fitzmyer, S.J., "The Letter to the Romans," *The Jerome Biblical Commentary*, ed. Raymond E. Brown, S.S., Joseph A. Fitzmyer, S.J., and Roland E. Murphy, O.Carm. (Englewood Cliffs, N.J.: Prentice-Hall, 1968) 53:126.
3. Ibid.
4. John Paul II, Address to the Third Assembly of Latin American Bishops, Puebla, January 28, 1979. An English translation is available in *Origins* 8, no. 34 (Feb. 8, 1979) 530–38. I have not used this translation for the passage quoted, because it translates the Spanish *indispensable* as "essential" (536), apparently unaware that this forces an interpretation that would settle an ongoing problem in exegesis of magisterial teaching: Is the search for justice "essential" or "integral" to the gospel? It is sufficient to say "indispensable": To struggle for justice is a facet of evangelization which the Church may not refuse.
5. See Robert N. Bellah, "Religion & Power in America Today," *Commonweal* 109, no. 21 (Dec. 3, 1982) 650–55. I have developed this theme at greater length in several homilies, e.g. "The Other, the Others, and You," *Lovely in Eyes Not His: Homilies for an Imaging of Christ* (New York/Mahwah: Paulist, 1988) 149–56, at 154–55.
6. See *Time* 128, no. 10 (Sept. 8, 1986) 57.

Homily 9

1. Donald P. McNeill, Douglas A. Morrison, and Henri J. M. Nouwen, *Compassion: A Reflection on the Christian Life* (Garden City, N.Y.: Doubleday, 1982) 4. My first point owes much to this uncommonly sensitive and moving book; see especially pp. 3–9.
2. Peregrine Worsthorne, "A Universe of Hospital Patients: Further Remarks on the British Condition," *Harpers* 251 (November 1975) 38, as quoted in *Compassion* (n. 1 above) 5.
3. For the three authors and their book, see n. 1 above.
4. Quoted in *Compassion* 6.
5. Ibid. 27.
6. From excerpts in *Catholic Health World* 4, no. 13 (July 1, 1988) 1 and 12, with corrections from a text graciously supplied by the editor of that journal.

Homily 10

1. Parents on a popular TV serial, "Leave It to Beaver."
2. I have developed the experiences and significance of Job at length in a homily titled "In God We Trust," published in my collection *Tell the Next Generation: Homilies and Near Homilies* (New York/Ramsey: Paulist, 1980) 39–43.
3. Yves Congar, O.P., *Challenge to the Church: The Case of Archbishop Lefebvre* (Huntington, Ind.: Our Sunday Visitor, 1976) 42.
4. The translation is that of Gerard Manley Hopkins, "S. Thomae Aquinatis Rhythmus ad SS. Sacramentum," in W. H. Gardner and N. H. MacKenzie, eds., *The Poems of Gerard Manley Hopkins* (4th ed.; London: Oxford University, 1970) 211.

Homily 11

1. A reference to a popular TV serial.
2. See Margot Hornblower, "Not in My Backyard, You Don't," *Time* 131, no. 26 (June 27, 1988) 44–45.
3. Ibid. 44.
4. Ibid.
5. Ibid.
6. Ibid.

Homily 12

1. Domino's and Sutton Place Gourmet are local (Washington, D.C.) references to a pizza service and a caterer respectively.
2. In this homily I am borrowing generously, often verbatim, from my essay "Godhead Here in Hiding: Eucharist and University," published first in *Georgetown* magazine, spring 1987, 2–19, then reprinted as a separate brochure, *Godhead Here in Hiding*, by Georgetown University, spring 1987, 20 pp.
3. Cf. David B. Barrett, "World Church Membership," *Britannica Data Manual, 1987* 338; the actual number given is 900,545,840.
4. Gregory Dix, *The Shape of the Liturgy* (Westminster, Eng.: Dacre, 1945) 744.
5. Second Vatican Council, Constitution on the Sacred Liturgy, no. 7.
6. Gerard Manley Hopkins, "S. Thomae Aquinatis Rhythmus ad SS. Sacramentum," in W. H. Gardner and N. H. Mackenzie, eds., *The Poems of Gerard Manley Hopkins* (4th ed.; London: Oxford University, 1970) 211.
7. Second Vatican Council, Decree on the Apostolate of the Laity, no. 5.

8. The last two references are to current films.
9. John Donne, *Holy Sonnets*, no. 15.

Homily 13

1. Walter Kerr, *The Decline of Pleasure* (New York: Simon and Schuster, 1962) 48. Despite its title, this is a remarkably perceptive, insightful book on contemplation for today's world.
2. Quoted by Kerr, ibid. 67.
3. Ibid. 245.
4. New York: Covenant House, 1988.
5. Ibid. 90–92.

Homily 14

1. Alpha Sigma Nu, National Jesuit Honor Society, with 29 chapters.
2. A reference to a contemporary TV serial.
3. The bishop is St. Irenaeus of Lyons.
4. From Gerard Manley Hopkins, "God's Grandeur," in W. H. Gardner and N. H. MacKenzie, eds., *The Poems of Gerard Manley Hopkins* (4th ed.; London: Oxford University, 1970) 66.
5. *Time* 132, no. 18 (Oct. 31, 1988) 60–65.
6. I should confess that in this homily I am not using the words "mind," "soul," and "heart" precisely as Deuteronomy and Mark intended; but I do not believe that my approach is unfaithful to Scripture. See the footnote to Deut 6:5 in *The Oxford Annotated Bible with the Apocrypha: Revised Standard Version,* ed. Herbert G. May and Bruce M. Metzger (New York: Oxford University, 1965) 223: "*Heart* (mind, will), *soul* (self, vital being), *might* express the idea of loving God . . . with the full measure of one's devotion."

Homily 15

1. On the October 1987 "crash," see "Panic Grips the Globe," *Time* 130, no. 18 (Nov. 2, 1987) 22–33.
2. In this homily I am combining (often verbatim) material from two homilies previously preached on this Sunday: cf. "Well Done, Faithful Servant!" in my *Grace on Crutches: Homilies for Fellow Travelers* (New York/Mahwah: Paulist, 1986) 146–51, where the stress is on fidelity or faithfulness, and "Only If You Risk," in my *Sir, We Would Like To See Jesus: Homilies from a Hilltop* (New York/Ramsey: Paulist, 1982) 137–42, where the stress is on risk.

3. See Joachim Jeremias, *The Parables of Jesus* (rev. ed.; New York: Scribner's, 1963) 58–63. I do not take into account the Lukan version of the parable (Lk 19:12–27).
4. See ibid. 61–62.

Homily 16

1. New York/Ramsey: Paulist, 1984, 149–54. The title of the homily is "With Great Power and Glory."
2. See my booklet *Towards Reconciliation* (Washington, D.C.: United States Catholic Conference, 1974) esp. 1–6.
3. I am not denying the conviction of hundreds of theologians across the Christian centuries who have argued that the Son of God would have become man even if sin had not entered the world through our first parents. See the informative volume by Juniper B. Carol, O.F.M., *Why Jesus Christ?* (Manassas, Va.: Trinity Communications, 1986).
4. Quoted by John Shea, "Hell: Some Like It Hot," *U.S. Catholic* 53, no. 11 (November 1988) 9–12, at 12.
5. From Shea, ibid. 11–12.
6. Ibid. 12.

Homily 17

1. For this approach to the Solemnity of the Body and Blood of Christ, I was primarily inspired by the biblical/liturgical meditation of Patrick J. Ryan, "Blood Relationship," *America* 158, no. 21 (May 28, 1988) 567.
2. So I learn from the article by William Dameshek, "Blood," *World Book Encyclopedia* 2 (1975 ed.) 324–28, at 325.
3. See, e.g., Ceslas Spicq and Pierre Grelot, in Xavier Léon-Dufour, *Dictionary of Biblical Theology* (2nd ed.; New York: Seabury, 1973) 52–53, at 52.
4. I have no room here for the "ordinances" (cf. Exod 21–23), the numerous laws formulated to deal with various cases, in contrast to the unconditional law of the Israelite theocracy, e.g. the Decalogue.
5. For further information on Old Testament sacrifice, see Charles Hauret, "Sacrifice," *Dictionary of Biblical Theology* (n. 3 above) 512–15, at 512–14.
6. It is not clear from the New Testament accounts whether Judas received the body and blood of Christ with the others.
7. I have this story from the sermon of a Protestant preacher, who heard it from a woman doctor from Mafraq, over coffee in the Beirut Inter-

continental Hotel. I have shortened the story somewhat, without omitting essentials.

Homily 18

1. Gerard Manley Hopkins, "The Blessed Virgin Compared to the Air We Breathe," in *The Poems of Gerard Manley Hopkins,* ed. W. H. Gardner and N. H. MacKenzie (4th ed.; London: Oxford University, 1970) 93–97, at 95.
2. Second Vatican Council, Dogmatic Constitution on the Church, no. 63.
3. Pope Pius XII, in defining our Lady's assumption into heaven (Nov. 1, 1950), left open the theologically debated question whether she died or not. Surely with full awareness of the issue, he simply used the phrase "when the course of her earthly life was finished."
4. A difficult passage, but so interpreted by, e.g., Raymond E. Brown, S.S., *The Gospel according to John (xiii–xxi)* (Garden City, N.Y.: Doubleday, 1970) 925–26.
5. There is indeed no mention in Scripture of an appearance of the risen Jesus to his mother; but I agree with St. Ignatius Loyola that anyone with intelligence will realize that surely he must have appeared to her.

Homily 19

1. The full name of the child baptized is Hope Chang Woolsey La Farge, daughter of Edward Theodore and E. F. Maida Williams La Farge.
2. I am not implying here that humanness or personhood begins at birth and not before; I am simply suggesting that when the infant "comes into view," he or she joins the human community more obviously.
3. Damocles was a "flatterer in the court of Dionysius I of Syracuse. To rebuke his constant praises of the happiness of kings, Dionysius seated him at a royal banquet with a sword hung over his head by a single hair" (*Webster's New International Dictionary of the English Language* [new ed. unabridged; Springfield, Mass.: Merriam, 1958] 665).
4. Clearly, this sentence supposes that our specific imaging of Christ (as distinguished from our imaging of God in general) begins with baptism. A very early Christian conviction, however, insisted that the first man was created in the image of Christ-to-come. So, e.g., St. Irenaeus, second-century bishop of Lyons.
5. Gerard Manley Hopkins, "As kingfishers catch fire . . . ," Poem 57 in

W. H. Gardner and N. H. MacKenzie, eds., *The Poems of Gerard Manley Hopkins* (4th ed.; London: Oxford University, 1970) 90.

Homily 20

1. This homily was delivered at a memorial liturgy for Edward Bennett Williams 39 days after his death on August 13, 1988.
2. During the 1988 baseball season, especially the first half, the Baltimore Orioles, owned by Mr. Williams, were less than impressive.
3. A reference to the well-known columnist and humorist Art Buchwald.
4. The references are to the College of the Holy Cross, where Mr. Williams studied as an undergraduate, and Georgetown University, from whose Law Center he received his degree in law.
5. *Confessions* 10, 27.
6. Jack Kent Cooke and Richard Nixon respectively.
7. Antony, about Caesar, in William Shakespeare, *Julius Caesar*, Act 5, Scene 5, line 68.

Homily 21

1. This is a simplification, of course; not all the rebellious, e.g., were bent on dechristianizing France. Cf. A. Latreille, "French Revolution," *New Catholic Encyclopedia* 6 (1967) 186–93, esp. 190.
2. Karl Rahner, "The Faith of the Priest Today," *Woodstock Letters* 93 (1964) 5.
3. An allusion to the unexpected problems faced by Senator Joseph Biden for frequent use of other people's striking remarks without explicit attribution; it ended in his withdrawal from the presidential race (September 1987).
4. John Courtney Murray, S.J., *The Problem of God Yesterday and Today* (New Haven: Yale University, 1964) 86, 101–3.
5. *Profiles of Outstanding Alumnae,* published by the Academy of the Sacred Heart, 4521 St. Charles Avenue, New Orleans, La., 70115, no date.
6. Ibid., Preface.
7. Second Vatican Council, Decree on the Apostolate of the Laity, no. 5.
8. See Marie Josephine Carr, *Valiant Woman of Pioneer Missouri* (brochure apparently privately printed, no date) 23–24.
9. Letter from M. J. Bultó to the RSCJ communities in America, Rome, May 1968.
10. Cf. John W. Glaser, "Unmet Health Needs of America's Children,"

typescript issued by St. Joseph Health System, Orange, Calif., 1985, 11 pp., at 4.

Homily 22

1. The occasion was the liturgical commemoration, by the Religious of the Sacred Heart in the District of Columbia area, of Rose Philippine Duchesne's canonization, which had taken place in Rome on July 3, 1988.
2. See the booklet by Marion Bascom, *Rose Philippine Duchesne, Pioneer Missionary of the New World* (Purchase, N.Y.: Manhattanville College, n.d.) 9.
3. Ibid. 11.
4. Ibid. 19.
5. Ibid. 22.
6. Ibid. 27.
7. Ibid. 31.
8. John Courtney Murray, S.J., "The Magnificence of a Heart That Can Dare Great Things," in the booklet *Philippine Duchesne, RSCJ: A Collection,* ed. Catherine Collins, RSCJ, Melanie A. Guste, RSCJ, and Anna Thompson (Washington, D.C.: Center for Educational Design and Communication, 1988) 49–53, at 52.
9. From Bascom, *Rose Philippine Duchesne* 32.
10. For details see the recent work by V. V. Harrison, *Changing Habits* (New York: Doubleday, 1988).
11. Madeleine Sophie Cooney, RSCJ, "Meditation on Philippine Duchesne," in *Philippine Duchesne, RSCJ: A Collection* (n. 8 above) 63–66.
12. Ibid. 66.

Homily 23

1. Joseph T. Durkin, S.J., *Georgetown University: First in the Nation's Capital* (Garden City, N.Y.: Doubleday, 1964) 7.
2. From Gerard Manley Hopkins, "God's Grandeur," in W. H. Gardner and N. H. MacKenzie, *The Poems of Gerard Manley Hopkins* (4th ed.; London: Oxford University, 1970) 66.
3. The last two items are references to a recent film and a contemporary musical.
4. From the translation of Aquinas' *Adoro te* by Gerard Manley Hopkins, "S. Thomae Aquinatis Rhythmus ad SS. Sacramentum," in Gardner and MacKenzie (n. 2 above) 211.
5. A veiled allusion to the expression "Hoya saxa" that has long symbol-

ized Georgetown and whose precise meaning is debated, for its origins are clouded by the mists of history.

6. This paragraph and another in the first section borrow liberally from my baccalaureate sermon in 1987 at Colgate University; see "The Other, the Others, and You," in my *Lovely in Eyes Not His: Homilies for an Imaging of Christ* (New York/Mahwah: Paulist, 1988) 149–56, at 154–55.

7. From a commencement address by Mother Teresa at Gonzaga College High School, Washington, D.C.; see Gonzaga's *News from Nineteen Eye Street,* June 1988, 7.

8. Second Vatican Council, Pastoral Constitution on the Church in the Modern World, no. 78.

9. *Time* 132, no. 7 (Aug. 15, 1988) 37–42. It was occasioned by heated controversy over the Martin Scorsese film of Nikos Kazantzakis' *The Last Temptation of Christ.*

10. Ibid. 42, quoting Dean Robert Moye of California's Fuller Theological Seminary.

Homily 24

1. John Paul II, encyclical *Laborem exercens* ("On Human Work"), Sept. 14, 1981 (tr. from *On Human Work* [Washington, D.C.: United States Catholic Conference, 1981] 3).

2. Studs Terkel, "Here Am I, a Worker," *New York Times,* March 19, 1973.

3. In the official Latin, "Labor omnia vincit."

4. This is the title of chapter 4 in *Economic Justice for All: Pastoral Letter on Catholic Social Teaching and the U.S. Economy* (Washington, D.C.: National Conference of Catholic Bishops, 1986) 145–62.

Homily 25

1. The Red Mass is celebrated in many Catholic dioceses at the opening of the judicial year, often as a votive Mass in honor of the Holy Spirit. It has a venerable history that traces back to 13th-century France, England, and Italy. On the origin of the name, scholars are not at peace. In one theory, the priest-celebrant was vested in red, and so the judges of the High Court in Edward I's reign (1272–1307), all of them doctors of the law, conformed to ecclesiastical tradition and also wore red robes. Others hold for an origin with more profound content: The liturgical red signifies a willingness to defend the truth inspired by the Holy Spirit, even if it demands one's own blood.

2. For details, see my homily "As God Has Done unto You," in my

collection *Tell the Next Generation: Homilies and Near Homilies* (New York/Ramsey: Paulist, 1980) 121–26, at 122–23.
3. Two popular TV serials.
4. The facts and (estimated) figures in this paragraph are drawn from "The Sad Fate of Legal Aid," *Time* 131, no. 25 (June 20, 1988) 59.

Homily 26

1. "Back Off, Buddy," *Time* 130, no. 15 (Oct. 12, 1987) 68–73.
2. See ibid. 69.
3. Ibid.
4. Ibid., specifically the remarks of Dr. Thomas Szasz, psychiatrist-author who teaches at the State University of New York at Syracuse.
5. A reference to a highly emotional debate across the U.S. on the nomination of Robert Bork for a place on the Supreme Court.

Homily 27

1. I have made use of this same story in another wedding homily, "Love Never Ends?", published in my *Grace on Crutches: Homilies for Fellow Travelers* (New York/Mahwah: Paulist, 1986) 175–78, at 175.
2. In point of fact, the addition of Solomon's name to the title of the book rests on no support save the tradition that he was the composer of many proverbs and songs. See 1 Kgs 4:32: "He also uttered 3000 proverbs, and his songs were a thousand and five."
3. Harry Kirwin was Elizabeth's (Liza's) father; he died in 1963.
4. Margaret (Gould Thompson Kirwin), still among the living as I preached this homily, was Harry's wife and mother of their three children: Elizabeth Ann Seton, Catherine Siena, and Thomas More.

Homily 28

1. I have presumed to borrow this first point, with minor modifications, from an earlier wedding homily, "As I Have Loved You," in my collection *Still Proclaiming Your Wonders: Homilies for the Eighties* (New York/Ramsey: Paulist, 1984) 206–10, at 206–7.
2. A reference to a contemporary TV serial, where the cruise ship is shaped of romance and, despite all obstacles, love triumphs at the end of all the commercials.
3. I have used this story before; see the homily "Humor, Wonder, and the Other," in my collection *Grace on Crutches: Homilies for Fellow Travelers* (New York/Mahwah: Paulist, 1986) 164–69, at 168.

Homily 29

1. See the moving memoir by Richard Meryman, *Hope: A Loss Survived* (Boston: Little, Brown, 1980).
2. Roberto is a medical doctor, Katie a nurse.
3. From a commencement address by Mother Teresa at Gonzaga College High School, Washington, D.C.; see Gonzaga's *News from Nineteen Eye Street,* June 1988, 7.

Homily 30

1. The ideas developed in these two paragraphs I have expressed in much the same language in two other wedding homilies, with somewhat different ends in view. See my collections *Still Proclaiming Your Wonders: Homilies for the Eighties* (New York/Ramsey: Paulist, 1984) 201–5, at 201–2, and *Grace on Crutches: Homilies for Fellow Travelers* (New York/Mahwah: Paulist, 1986) 160–64, at 160–61.
2. *Time* 132, no. 19 (Nov. 7, 1988) 130.
3. Figures provided by the Campaign for Human Development, an organization established in 1970 by the U.S. Catholic bishops to provide financial support to self-help projects organized and managed by low-income groups; see *America* 159, no. 15 (Nov. 19, 1988) cover ii.
4. See "The Sad Fate of Legal Aid," *Time* 131, no. 25 (June 20, 1988) 59.
5. At the time of the wedding Chris was a resident at Georgetown Hospital.
6. See Malcolm Muggeridge, *Something Beautiful for God: Mother Teresa of Calcutta* (New York: Harper & Row, 1971).

Homily 31

1. A convenient name for Woodward & Lothrop, a prominent chain of department stores in the District of Columbia, Maryland, and Virginia.
2. Richard Selzer, *Mortal Lessons: Notes on the Art of Surgery* (New York: Simon and Schuster, 1976) 45–46.